The Hatherleigh Guide

to

Treating
Substance Abuse

Part II

The Hatherleigh Guides series

The Hatherleigh Guide

to

Treating
Substance Abuse

Part II

■ Hatherleigh Press • New York

Gary Holmes, PhD, CRC
Emporia State University (Emporia, KS)

John Homlish, PhD
The Menninger Clinic (Topeka, KS)

Sharon E. Robinson Kurpius, PhD
Arizona State University (Tempe, AZ)

Marilyn J. Lahiff, RN, CRRN, CIRS, CCM
Private practice (Englewood, FL)

Chow S. Lam, PhD
Illinois Institute of Chicago (Chicago, IL)

Paul Leung, PhD, CRC
University of Illinois at Urbana-Champaign (Champaign, IL)

Carl Malmquist, MD
University of Minnesota (Minneapolis, MN)

Robert J. McAllister, PhD
Taylor Manor Hospital (Ellicott City, MD)

Richard A. McCormick, PhD
Cleveland VA Medical Center-Brecksville Division (Cleveland, OH)

Thomas Miller, PhD, ABPP
University of Kentucky College of Medicine (Lexington, KY)

Jane E. Myers, PhD, CRC, NCC, NCGC, LPC
University of North Carolina-Greensboro (Greensboro, NC)

Don A. Olson, PhD
Rehabilitation Institute of Chicago (Chicago, IL)

William Pollack, PhD
McLean Hospital (Belmont, MA)

Keith M. Robinson, MD
University of Pennsylvania (Philadelphia, PA)

Susan R. Sabelli, CRC, LRC
Assumption College (Worcester, MA)

Gerald R. Schneck, PhD, CRC-SAC, NCC
Mankato State University (Mankato, MN)

George Silberschatz, PhD
University of California-San Fransisco (San Fransisco, CA)

David W. Smart, PhD
Brigham Young University (Provo, UT)

Julie F. Smart, PhD, CRC, NCC
Utah State University (Logan, UT)

Joseph Stano, PhD, CRC, LRC, NCC
Springfield College (Springfield, MA)

Anthony Storr, FRCP
Green College (Oxford, England)

Hans Strupp, PhD
Vanderbilt University (Nashville, TN)

Retta C. Trautman, CCMHC, LPCC
Private practice (Toledo, OH)

Patricia Vohs, RN, CRRN, CRC, CIRS, CCM
Private practice (Warminster, PA)

William J. Weikel, PhD, CCMHC, NCC
Morehead State University (Morehead, KY)

Nona Leigh Wilson, PhD
South Dakota State University (Brookings, SD)

The Hatherleigh Guide to Treating Substance Abuse, Part II

Project Editor: Joya Lonsdale
Assistant Editor: Stacy Powell
Indexer: Angela Washington-Blair, PhD
Cover Designer: Gary Szczecina
Cover photo: Christopher Flach, PhD

© 1996 Hatherleigh Press
A Division of The Hatherleigh Company, Ltd.
420 East 51st Street, New York, NY 10022

Compiled under the auspices of the editorial boards of *Directions in Mental Health Counseling, Directions in Clinical Psychology,* and *Directions in Rehabilitation Counseling.*

Library of Congress Cataloging-in-Publication Data

The Hatherleigh guide to treating substance abuse, part II —1st ed.
     ISBN 1-886330-49-2

First Edition: November 1996

10 9 8 7 6 5 4 3 2 1

About the photograph and the photographer

Hallway, San Francisco, 1996
At the end of a long hallway of recovery, this door offers an exit to clients who abuse substances.

Christopher Flach, PhD, is a psychologist in private practice in southern California. An avid photographer for more than 20 years, his favorite subjects include people and nature. He has studied photography with Ansel Adams, and his work has been on display in public galleries and in private collections.

Table of Contents

Illustrations

Introduction

Substance abuse is a complex phenomenon that does not comply with a single system of classification. It exists among all groups regardless of race, age, gender, or socioeconomic status. Within each demographic category exist high-risk situations that affect the onset and severity of substance abuse. Special factors such as a preexisting disability can put a person at risk for substance abuse; those with mental illness or orthopedic, neurologic, or psychological deficits are particularly vulnerable. The elderly and youth are equally at risk based on factors related to personal, social, and societal demands and expectations that individuals feel unable to meet. Substance abuse can also make the individual more susceptible to human immunodeficiency virus/acquired immunodeficiency syndrome (HIV/AIDS), stroke, traumatic brain injury, or mental illness. Availability and receptivity within treatment depend on the awareness of and responsiveness to individual needs.

Substance abuse inhibits a patient's ability to function independently in society; it often destabilizes functioning in daily living, socializing, working, and studying. Substance abuse places the individual as well as the family at risk for additional, often more challenging, problems.

Prevention should be directed to special populations considered at risk. Treatment, in its many variations, offers opportunities for individuals to confront the ravages of their abuse patterns and begin or resume productive lives, including the return to employment.

Within the treatment system, increasing evidence suggests that individuals who suffer from a multiplicity of disabling conditions — from severe mental illness to limited educational achievements — require specialized assistance in evaluation and treatment planning. These coexisting conditions place added pressure on an already challenged staff operating with reduced budgets and increased outcome expectations. In addition, the influence of managed care and welfare reform make treatment effectiveness and consumer outcomes even more critical than in the past.

Historically, substance abuse treatment providers have viewed substance abuse as its own disability, with frequent stereotypes about the substance abuser's profile and treatment needs. What is increasingly apparent when looking at the epidemiology of individuals in treatment is that stereotypes often have harmed the treatment process and that successful outcomes require more than the cessation of abuse. A common belief has been that the individual will be able to resume functioning in a legal and competitive market when he or she merely stops abusing substances. Once issues related to abuse are addressed, however, new problems related to working and maintaining sobriety and drug-free living generate a host of new challenges.

Improved services in substance abuse prevention and treatment can best be achieved by a more realistic understanding of individuals at risk and individuals currently receiving services. When special populations are recognized, outreach efforts are improved and opportunities for meaningful intervention with successful outcomes are increased.

Building on the general theoretical framework set by *The Hatherleigh Guide to Treating Substance Abuse, Part I*, this second volume in the two-volume set tackles the needs of special populations within the broad spectrum of substance-abusing individuals. By identifying these at-risk populations and developing insight into their unique needs, treatment programs may be strengthened to address the challenges faced by the individual consumer and by those who interact with the individual in the home, community, hospital, clinic, school, or workplace.

The Hatherleigh Guide to Treating Substance Abuse, Part II challenges substance abuse professionals in treatment programs, health facilities, schools, community-based rehabilitation programs, and the workplace to evaluate for substance abuse with regard to at-risk populations whose abuse might well be overlooked in the face of other presenting problems. It provides a framework for understanding these problems and the interrelationship of substance abuse within groups having special needs. The authors provide well-developed, achievable treatment strategies, new research findings, and case studies that demonstrate excellent models for clinical practice. The reader also is given additional references to pursue.

This book discusses substance abuse as a workplace problem and employment as a rehabilitation outcome. The business community, grappling with problems experienced by current employees, often is reluctant to hire new employees with a substance abuse history. Similarly, the rehabilitation community needs to recognize the prevalence of substance abuse in persons with other disabilities and the potential negative impact the abuse has had on employment performance. Only when these communities come together to recognize issues of mutual concern can the goal of economic independence along with the control of substance abuse be realized.

Chapter 1 by John Thomas deals with the problems of substance abuse in the workplace. Contrary to common belief, most individuals with a substance abuse problem are employed. Substance abuse costs business and industry tens of billions of dollars in absenteeism, accidents, high turnover, and poor morale. Thomas discusses the benefits of employee assistance programs (EAPs) for screening, assessment, intervention, and referral.

Chapter 2 by Cardoso, Chan, Thomas, Roldan, and Ingraham addresses the critical issue of substance abuse as it coexists with other disabilities, such as those resulting from traumatic brain injuries and spinal cord injuries. Cardoso and colleagues highlight research findings that substance abuse not only contributes to an increased incidence of disability but that it also undermines treatment. They suggest that substance abuse cannot be characterized as a singular disability but one that has varying causes and consequences. They encourage rehabilitation professionals to increase their understanding of substance abuse so as to better serve the needs of their clients.

In Chapter 3, Mindy Fullilove and Isabelle Dieudonné introduce the critical concerns of substance abuse and pregnancy. The challenge to the woman, who is extremely fragile as she struggles with the interrelated problems of her own illness as well as its impact on her unborn child, is clearly detailed. The effects on the fetus from abusing various substances are discussed and strategies for treatment are provided.

A special population of substance abusers, adolescents, is examined in great depth in Chapters 5–7. Robert DuPont, in Chapter 5, addresses the failure of standard preventive measures, drug testing, and counseling to help the adolescent substance abuser. Treating addiction in adolescents, he contends, often requires participation in solid addiction programs such as the 12-step programs of Alcoholics Anonymous. Addiction should be regarded as a familial problem rather than the exclusive failure and responsibility of the substance abusing adolescent.

In Chapter 6, Thomas Collingwood examines physical fitness as an effective prevention and treatment method for adolescents who are at risk for substance abuse. Within the context of a highly structured, well planned, clinically sensitive health and fitness program, the adolescent at risk can gain self-confidence and develop skills in goal setting, decision making, planning, and problem solving.

Tomás José Silber and Daniel Silber, in Chapter 7, raise ethical issues in treating adolescents who abuse substances. They discuss the importance of balancing the autonomy of adolescents with the paternal desire to protect them. In some cases, protecting the adolescent may delay or diminish possibilities for successful outcomes. The adolescent, as with the adult consumer, should determine the course of his or her treatment according to developmental capacity.

In Chapter 8, Jayne Reinhardt and George Fulop examine the effects of substance abuse on another vulnerable population: the elderly. With the "graying" of America and the prevalence of alcoholism in elderly clients, all mental health professionals should familiarize themselves with the special treatment needs of the elderly alcoholic. Underdetection, caused by factors such as isolation, denial, or misdiagnosis, is a critical concern. Treatment programs for the elderly must go beyond sobriety and address daily concerns such as loneliness, loss of independence, and declining health.

Michael Shernoff, in Chapter 9, examines the effects of substance abuse on patients living with HIV/AIDS. Drug treatment and HIV prevention are separate but strongly connected service systems; screening is critical in both treatment environments. Coordinated service delivery between HIV/ AIDS programs and substance abuse treatment programs is essential to effectively treat this life-threatening comorbidity.

Chapters 4, 10, and 11 focus on the special population of individuals with severe mental illness, comorbid with substance abuse and alcoholism. The need for making a differential diagnosis and for establishing treatment that addresses all conditions (substance abuse, alcoholism, and mental illness) are examined.

In Chapter 4, Jack Cornelius, Ihsan Salloum, Dennis Daley, and Michael Thase address a highly underresearched and prevalent condition: comorbid major depression and alcoholism. Depressed alcoholics have many symptoms in common with nonalcoholic major depressed patients and nondepressed alcoholics; however, some symptoms are more severe in this dual-diagnosis population such as suicidality. The high level of suicide potential for this group supports the need for a better clinical understanding and for defined treatment strategies that address both conditions.

In Chapter 10, Norman Miller examines the comorbidity of addictive and other psychiatric disorders. Rates of addictive disorders appear to be increasing among psychiatric patients. Only recently has clinical practice attempted to integrate the treatment of both disorders in the same patient and in the same setting. Miller presents various treatment models that are now being implemented.

The authors of Chapter 11, Douglas Ziedonis and William Fisher, present substance abuse as the most common comorbid disorder with the diagnosis of schizophrenia. They present the Motivation-Based Dual Diagnosis Treatment Model, which integrates the strengths of all treatment philosophies, meets the individual's level of readiness to identify an abuse problem, encourages forward movement, and empowers and enhances the patient's self-efficacy.

Strong forces of change confront the entire health care system—forces that will have an impact on administrators, clinicians, researchers, and consumers alike. Within this uncertain climate, the clinician must remain focused on the primary concern of patient care. Clinicians must recognize the multiple challenges that patients are experiencing as well as the new categories of patients who are coming to the attention of the health care community. This is especially the case in substance abuse prevention, intervention, and treatment programs. There appears to be an escalation in the challenges faced by substance abuse consumers and, consequently, the complex needs they bring to the health professional.

The Hatherleigh Guide to Treating Substance Abuse, Part II is at the forefront of confronting these complex issues by providing research information and strategies for substance abuse prevention, detection, intervention, and rehabilitation. The strategies presented in this book offer the consumer the possibility of change as well as the opportunity to become empowered and achieve higher levels of self-efficacy and productivity in an increasingly competitive and demanding society.

Eileen Wolkstein, PhD
New York, New York

Dr. Wolkstein is Adjunct Assistant Profession/Research Scientist, Rehabilitation Counseling Program, New York University, New York, NY. She is also Director of Training and Dissemination, NIDRR Funded Research and Training Center in conjunction with Drugs and Disabilities, Wright State University School of Medicine, Dayton, OH.

1

Substance Abuse in the Workplace: The Role of Employee Assistance Programs

John C. Thomas, PhD, CEAP, CSAC, NCC, NCAC II

Dr. Thomas is an Employee Assistance Consultant with E. I. DuPont de Nemours & Company in Waynesboro and Front Royal, VA.

KEY POINTS

- Alcoholism in employees costs American businesses $100 billion dollars per year.

- A worker's substance abuse can generate interpersonal problems among co-workers and hamper morale within the work group.

- The workplace is an opportune setting for addressing substance abuse. A contractual relationship exists between the employer and the employee, which allows the employer to intervene if job performance deteriorates.

- Employers can use two strategies to manage employees with addiction problems: identification (drug testing) and assistance

(such as implementing an *employee assistance program* [EAP].)

- The economic benefits of EAPs to companies are significant. EAPs increase productivity and decrease health care costs, lost work time, and absenteeism.

- EAPs aim to help troubled employees and their dependents deal with a wide range of personal problems.

- EAPs present excellent career opportunities for mental health and chemical dependency professionals. Professionals considering an EAP career should ask themselves a series of questions outlined in this chapter.

INTRODUCTION

In 1989, America watched the coastline of Alaska fill with thousands of gallons of oil in the worst oil spill of the nation's history. An Exxon oil tanker had run aground, dumping 11 million gallons of crude oil into Alaska's Prince William Sound, destroying wildlife and businesses. In a subsequent lawsuit (Exxon Valdez, District Court, Alaska, Docket #A89-0095-CV, June 13, 1994), Exxon was charged with negligence because the company was aware that the captain of the ship had a long-standing drinking problem. A federal jury in Alaska found that Exxon acted recklessly in placing a man with a history of alcohol abuse in a safety-sensitive position. This ruling, the first in a four-part trial, meant that the estimated 10,000 plaintiffs who had brought the suit could seek punitive damages.

Unfortunately, substance abuse in the workplace is not solely the problem of Exxon. Research continues to dispel the image of the unemployed substance user (Lehman, Holcom, & Simpson, 1990). In a survey of chief executive officers of Fortune 1000 companies, Chernoff (1989) found that 88% of those who responded viewed substance abuse as a significant problem in society, and 22% viewed it as a problem in their own workplace, almost triple the percentage of 5 years before. A 1990 Gallup poll (Bureau of National Affairs, 1990) discovered that 22% of the 1,007 workers surveyed said that illegal drug use is "somewhat widespread" where they work. Forty-one percent (41%) believed that co-workers' drug use seriously affects their ability to do their own jobs. Eight percent (8%) had been offered drugs at work, and 7% had been approached to purchase drugs at work.

Problems within the workplace are not limited to substance abuse. In a survey of employee and employer attitudes, Starch (1995) found that 92% of employees and 93% of managers agreed that personal problems cause trouble at work. Although employers do not really have to deal directly with these particular problems, they do have to deal with the employees who struggle with such issues.

Employees do not check their personal problems at the door when they enter the workplace. Instead, it becomes the business of the company when these problems become apparent through deficiencies in the quality and quantity of job performance, theft, sabotage, and insurance claims (Myers, 1984). Efforts to address the problems of substance abuse in the workplace have been spearheaded on two fronts: business and legislation. The latter generally addresses illicit drug use, ignoring the problems caused by alcohol and other drugs in the workplace. Business has sought to deal with the problems of substance abuse through *work-based intervention programs.* The *employee assistance program* (EAP) is one model that has been developed in the spirit of this form of intervention.

The EAPs provide unique opportunities and challenges for counselors to offer prevention and treatment services to employees with alcohol and other drug problems. The philosophy, training, and skills of substance abuse counseling are well suited to the delivery of quality EAP services. In addition, this background presents rehabilitation counselors with opportunities to assist companies and managers in intervening in workplace substance abuse issues. This chapter provides an overview of substance abuse in the workplace, outlines how counselors can become part of this growing field, and discusses in detail the role of EAPs in helping employers address problems in the workplace related to their employees' alcohol and drug abuse.

THE SCOPE OF THE PROBLEM

Substance abuse problems are found in people, not cans, bottles, pills, paper, syringes, or capsules. According to the U.S. Department of Health, Education, and Welfare, as early as the 1970s, substance abuse constituted the single major problem affecting job performance (Moree & Jenigan, 1979). In fact, substance abuse in the workplace has concerned management and labor leaders in the United States since the mid-1800s

(Trice & Schonbrunn, 1981). It is the leading employee behavioral problem faced by supervisors (Moree & Jernigan, 1977).

Contrary to popular belief, most persons addicted to alcohol or other drugs are employed (National Institute on Drug Abuse, 1990). The workplace represents a unique setting in that a contractual relationship exists between the employer and the employee, which allows the employer to intervene if job performance deteriorates (Roman, 1976).

Prevalence of Substance Abuse in the Workplace:

Substance abuse generally has been viewed as either a health or a law enforcement problem and has not been widely seen as a labor problem. Alcohol and other drug use affects Americans of all ages, incomes, and professions. Some experts believe that a conservative estimate of the number of employees with alcohol- or drug-related problems is between 4% and 20% (Doweiko, 1993). If 20% is the correct estimate, then 50 million Americans—of 250 million people—are addicted to either drugs or alcohol (Avis, 1993). In one well-conducted study by the Institute of Medicine (1990), 13 million Americans were diagnosed as alcoholics, and 14.4 million used illegal drugs.

In May 1996, the Substance Abuse and Mental Health Services Administration (SAMHSA) reported the most recent findings of the National Household Survey on Drug Abuse (Hoffmann, Brittingham, & Larison, 1996). This report summarized the key results of several years of Household Surveys and reached several conclusions:

- From 1985 to 1993, the percentage of full-time, part-time, and unemployed workers who reported current and past drug use declined significantly. From 1985 to 1993, the prevalence of heavy alcohol consumption remained relatively steady among full- and part-time workers, whereas the unemployed experienced significant gains in heavy alcohol use.

- Part-time workers, aged 18–49, reported a higher rate of illicit drug use than full-time workers; the reported rates of heavy alcohol consumption were about the same for both groups.

- Between 1991 and 1993, the highest rates of current and past illicit drug use were reported by construction workers, food preparers, and waiters and waitresses. Heavy alcohol use followed a similar pattern, with auto mechanics, vehicle repairers, light-truck drivers, and laborers also reporting high consumption rates. The lowest rates of illicit drug use were among police, detectives, administrative support personnel, teachers, and child care workers; the lowest levels of heavy alcohol use were found in data clerks, personnel specialists, and secretaries.

- Unmarried employees (i.e., divorced, separated, or never married) had twice the rate of illicit drug and heavy alcohol use as that of married workers.

- Workers who reported having three or more jobs in the previous 5 years were about twice as likely to be current or past illicit drug users as those who had two or fewer jobs. An estimated 5.5 million full-time employed Americans, aged 18–49, reported having used illicit drugs in the previous month; 16.6% of all employed workers, both full- or part-time, had used drugs in the past year.

- The percentage of full-time workers reporting participation in a mandatory employer drug test in the past 12 months was 12.7% as compared to 7.3% reporting current drug use. Some occupations with the highest rates of reported illicit drug use were among those with the lowest rates of participation in mandatory drug testing programs.

- The percentage of illicit drug users who reported skipping work in the previous 30 days (15.9%) was more than double that of employees reporting no current illicit drug use (7.5%). The rate for those reporting heavy alcohol use (13.1%) was slightly less than double those with no heavy alcohol use (7.7%).

- Reports of absences from work during the previous month because of illness or injury were significantly higher among those reporting current illicit drug use and heavy alcohol consumption (12.0% and 10.2%, respectively) compared to 8.3% of those not so identified.

- Since 1985, the rates of illicit drug use and heavy alcohol consumption for full-time employees have been about the same as for the total population, with rates for the unemployed population soaring consistently higher.

Alcohol use and abuse are generally accepted in our society; not surprisingly, alcohol is America's number one drug of choice (Ray & Ksir, 1990). No employer is immune to the potential hazards of alcohol abuse among workers. The National Institute on Alcohol Abuse and Alcoholism ([NIAAA], 1991) reported that 71% of the adult population drinks and that 1 in 15 adults will develop alcoholism.

LEGAL REQUIREMENTS OF EMPLOYERS

A company must comply with particular regulations, depending on the type of work that company performs (e.g., contracts with the federal government). The Drug-Free Workplace Act of 1988 requires federal contracts of at least $25,000 with public and private business and federal grantees to maintain a drug-free workplace. Although a full-service EAP is not mandated, the law requires that an employer: (a) provide a drug awareness program to all employees and (b) notify the federal contractor of any employee directly involved in any drug conviction.

Another law, issued by the Department of Transportation in November 1988, is relevant to employers whose employees operate commercial vehicles in interstate commerce. "Commercial" vehicles weigh 26,000 pounds or more or are designed to transport hazardous materials or 15 or more persons. This law particularly pertains to airline, railroad, U.S. Coast Guard, and pipeline and gas facility personnel.

The Americans with Disabilities Act (ADA) of 1990 prevents employers from discriminating against qualified applicants and employees on the basis of a disability. It protects persons who have physical or mental impairment that substantially limits one or more major life activities, who have a record of such an impairment, or who are regarded as currently having such an impairment. Although it protects persons addicted to alcohol who, despite being in recovery, may still be actively consuming alcohol, the ADA does *not* protect active illicit drug users. Thus, this law distinguishes between alcoholics and drug addicts. Such a distinction raises many prime concerns for employers, such as which type of rehabilitation program should be offered. For instance, assistance to alcoholics is considered a "reasonable accommodation" for the disability; however, the incentive to provide similar assistance to recovering illicit drug users is nonexistent under the ADA. Denenberg (1991) notes the changes brought about by the ADA law in collective bargaining agreements with respect to substance abuse. She reports that a 1970 U.S. Bureau of Labor Statistics survey found only 6% of collective bargaining agreements contained clauses specifically dealing with alcohol use, and even fewer clauses covered drug use, compared with 57% of the major agreements by the end of the 1980s. Many of these provisions also covered opportunities for treatment and recovery.

THE IMPLICATIONS OF SUBSTANCE ABUSE

Although the percentage of employees who use substances is small, such usage has a pervasive economic and social influence (Erfurt & Fook, 1989; Miller, 1989). The problem can be measured in terms of dollars, but it is also saliently evidenced in the lives of people.

Persons affected by an employee's use of substances can be generalized into five groups: the user, family members, co-workers, the employer, and the consumer. Evidence shows that the deleterious effects of alcoholism are not isolated to the drinker (Steinglass, Bennett, Wolin, & Reiss, 1987). For every alcoholic person, an average of 2.2 family members, friends, or work associates are affected by the alcoholism (West, 1984). In this section, the impact on each group is examined; it is important to keep in mind, however, that the consequences of substance abuse do not fit neatly into any set of categories.

The User:

Substance abuse problems produce a multitude of possible effects on users. The possible consequences on the user's health are well documented. The effects of alcohol and drugs on the body (e.g., the immune, endocrine, reproductive, gastrointestinal, musculoskeletal, and central nervous systems) can cause exceptional damage, whether within a short period or over the course of many years of use. Users tend to neglect their nutrition, are sleep deprived, and are more vulnerable to illness. Drugs and alcohol impair performance by increasing reaction times and decreasing visual sensitivity (Linnoila, 1978). Beyond the physical consequences are financial, job, emotional, and interpersonal difficulties.

Family Members:

In 1973, Hecht estimated that 20% of all requests for help concerning childhood problems at guidance clinics and social service agencies stemmed from a family drinking problem. More recent research on children of alcoholics clearly documents the negative consequences of parental alcohol abuse on children's drinking (Ackerman, 1983), among other emotional and behavioral problems (Russell, Henderson, & Blum, 1985). Specifically, adult children of alcoholics (ACOAs) have decreased levels of self-esteem (Berkowitz & Perkins, 1988), lower levels of psychological well-being (Svanum & McAdoo, 1991), diminished cognitive functioning (Plescia-Pikus, Long-Sutter,& Wilson, 1988), poorer sociability (Calder & Kostiniuk, 1989), difficulties with the law (McKenna & Pickens, 1981), and increased difficulties with alcohol (Goodwin, 1983). Black, Bucky, and Wilder-Padilla (1986) found ACOAs more likely than adult children of nonalcoholics (non-ACOAs) to have an alcoholic spouse, lower self-esteem, dependency problems, experienced separation and divorce, and poor communication skills. The researchers also found that ACOAs have more reported depression, trust problems, and intimacy problems. According to Mathews and Halbrook (1990), the work site becomes a place where ACOAs reenact unresolved family of origin issues. Other-directedness, a common characteristic of ACOAs, causes them to develop varying dependent attitudes and behaviors. In essence, they are people pleasers who seek to avoid conflict and defer to other workers' needs and manipulation.

These issues will influence job performance and the use of EAP services. Ackerman (1983) estimated that 55% of the adults entering EAPs were ACOAs. Of the EAP cases for the New England Telephone Company, 31% involved ACOAs (Masi & Spencer, 1977).

A 1982 Kemper Insurance Company study revealed that half of this company's EAP problems were reducible to certain employee traits, including conflict with authority figures, fear of losing control of intense feelings, difficulty identifying and appropriately expressing feelings, and having unrealistic expectations of and chronic disappointment in others (Meacham, 1987).

Co-workers:

When someone in a company is impaired, both the employee's work group and the organization are affected. In addition to experiencing interpersonal problems and lowered morale, co-workers often cover for the impaired worker (as a family member would for an impaired relative). Work groups take on the same characteristics that addicted families assume, such as enabling and scapegoating. In examining the effects of substance use on co-workers, researchers found that co-workers believed that impaired workers produced work of a deficient quality, communicated poorly, and were associated with an increased probability of injuries and equipment damage. These co-workers viewed the efforts of managers in dealing with the substance abuse problem more negatively and reported negative job satisfaction to a greater degree than did employees who had no known exposure to a substance abuser in the workplace (Lehman, Farabee, & Simpson, 1992).

The deleterious effects of substance abuse in the workplace are not limited to drugs alone; alcohol has also been implicated in similar behavioral problems in employees. In a study comparing heavy drinkers with light drinkers, heavy drinkers were seen by others as having lower technical achievement, lower self-direction, fewer interpersonal relationships, and increased conflict avoidance (Blum, Roman, & Martin, 1992).

The Employer:

The implications of substance abuse for employers are measured in terms of dollars. In fact, companies pay twice — through their own losses and through taxes for government-funded antidrug programs. Mounting evidence indicates that employee substance use and abuse have a negative impact on the workforce. Employee substance use has been linked with excessive absenteeism (Bross, Pace, & Cronin, 1992), decreased job performance (Blum, Roman, & Martin, 1993), employee turnover (Zwerling, Ryan, & Orav, 1990), and workplace accidents and fatalities (Bernstein & Mahoney, 1989; Bross et al., 1992).

In the most recent findings on the impact of substance abuse on employers, Harwood, Napolitano, Kristiansen, and Collins (1984) reported that workers who abuse alcohol or drugs are late for work 3 times more often than nonabusers; they have 2.5 times as many absences of 8 days or more; they use 3 times the normal amount of sick benefits; and they are 5 times more likely to file workers' compensation claims because they are involved in accidents 3.6 times more often than others.

It has been estimated that alcoholism alone directly causes 50 million lost workdays per year, equaling more than $20 billion per year. The National Council on Alcoholism estimates the annual loss to American business is approximately $71 billion. According to the U.S. Department of Health and Human Services (1987), 47% of employees involved in industrial accidents, 40% of employees involved in fatal industrial accidents, and 50% of victims of fatal industrial fires were under the influence of alcohol. In 1992, the Alcohol, Drug Abuse, and Mental Health Administration reported that the annual cost of alcoholism to American business is nearly $100 billion (U.S. Department of Labor, Small Business Administration, and the Office of National Drug Control Policy, 1992), up from $85.8 billion in 1988 (Lee, 1993). The impact on businesses is measured in terms of lost productivity, employee turnover, absenteeism, increased health care costs, accidents and injuries, and losses stemming from impaired judgment and creativity. More hidden are the diverted supervisory and managerial time, cut profits, and diminished ability to compete.

Several studies have documented these effects of an impaired worker on an employer. Employees of the Georgia Power Company who were referred to an EAP or entered treatment for drug abuse had 1.5 times as many absences, filed more than twice the number of workers' compensation claims, and used more than twice as many medical benefits as did a matched set of controls (Sheridan & Winkler, 1989). In another study (Crouch, Webb, Buller, & Rollins, 1989), higher absences and accident rates were found among employees who tested positive for drug use compared with a control group. A national sample of U.S. Postal Service employees was surveyed to examine the relationship between preemployment drug-tested applicants and absenteeism, attrition, and safety. After 1.3 years from the start of employment, employees who tested positive during preemployment had an absenteeism rate 59.3% greater than that of employees who tested negative and a 47% greater rate of being terminated. No statistically significant findings were noted for safety. In two studies of job applicants (Normand, Salyards, & Mahoney, 1990; Zwerling et al., 1990), persons who tested positive for marijuana use during preemployment showed increased risks for job separation, accidents and injuries, disciplinary actions, and absenteeism when compared with persons who tested negative. Employees who tested positive for cocaine use showed higher rates of absenteeism and injuries when compared with employees who tested negative (Trice & Beyer, 1984).

The Consumer:

A hidden victim of substance abuse in the workplace is the consumer. Whether one is a passenger on a airplane or purchaser of a lawn mower, there is an inherent expectation of receiving quality, safe, and efficient products and services. Substance abuse by employees, however, results in more defective products, poorer service, generally higher costs because of the financial impact of substance abuse on the employer, and even risks of harm to the consumer.

CHARACTERISTICS OF A SUBSTANCE-ABUSING EMPLOYEE

Everyone seems to have some notion of what constitutes a person addicted to alcohol or other drugs and maintains a stereotypical image of what that person is like. In the early or middle stage of abuse, persons with substance abuse problems are less obvious and more difficult to recognize. The owner of a 150-employee business revealed that he knew almost everyone in the company and was fully confident that his company was drug free. What he did not know was that during the past 8 months, the author had worked with 20 of his employees who were minimally heavy abusers, if not fully and actively addicted to alcohol and other drugs.

Does the troubled employee display shocking or bizarre behavioral patterns? Generally not. The usual work problems of these employees — low productivity, interpersonal problems, decreased work quality, absenteeism, waste, accidents, and injuries — have plagued management for generations. From the employer's viewpoint, the problem substance abuser is an employee at any level in the organization whose work is becoming unsatisfactory because of excessive or inappropriate use of substances. Almost all employees will experience some problems throughout their work career that will, in one way or another, affect job performance. In addition to recognizing the degree to which job performance is affected, it is imperative to discern whether or not a repeated pattern has emerged.

The following is a list of indicators of a troubled employee:

- *Spotty attendance.* The employee has multiple instances of unauthorized leave; excessive sick leave; frequent Monday and Friday or after-payday absences; excessive tardiness; leaving work early; peculiar and increasingly improbable excuses for absences; a higher absence rate than that of other employees; and frequent, incidental absences with or without a medical explanation.

- *On-the-job absenteeism.* The employee exhibits continued absence from his or her post, long breaks, physical illness on the job, and frequent trips to the rest room or water fountain.

- *High accident rates and claims.* The worker has a history of accidents on and off the job and frequent trips to the nurse's office.

- *Difficulty in concentration.* Jobs take more time than usual.

- *Confusion.* The employee has difficulty in recalling instructions, details, and past mistakes and in handling complex tasks.

- *Sporadic work patterns.* The worker has alternate periods of high and low productivity.

- *Personal signs of abuse.* The employee arrives at or returns to work in an obviously abnormal condition, such as smelling of alcohol or demonstrating difficulty walking.

- *Lower job efficiency.* Common occurrences are missed deadlines, mistakes, wasting of materials, poor decisions, unmet goals, decreased quantity of work, lowered quality of work, and customer complaints.

- *Poor employee relationships on the job.* The employee may exhibit an overreaction to real or imagined criticism, an inability to accept responsibility for obvious mistakes, mood swings, and poor morale. The employee may borrow money from co-workers, cause staff dissent, and harbor unreasonable resentments. In short, the troubled employee's performance problems are typically more common and severe than those of the "normal" employee.

Whenever an employee begins to exhibit signs of declining performance or marked, continuing changes in work patterns, something significant has occurred to alter this person's lifestyle. Employees establish patterns of work behavior within the first 2 years of employment and tend to maintain these patterns throughout the remainder of their association with a company, barring any crisis or life change. When these problems become severe, as in the case of substance abuse and dependence, employees will make promises to return to normal levels of performance; however, if the problem goes untreated, the employee will be unable to do so (Wrich, 1982).

Studies reveal that before the inevitable behavioral changes on the job, problem drinkers (as a group) were friendly and well liked within the company and were generally considered to be average or above-average workers, many with potential for advancement. They often showed considerable technical competence or job know-how and usually had long records of company service. Their generally satisfactory past work record, often representing substantial investment in training and experience, tended to prolong or delay decisive action by management (Lehman et al., 1992).

Steele (1988) mentions two perspectives in determining the causes of employee substance use. The first perspective is based on the assumption that drug and alcohol problems are "transported" into the workplace. This view represents substance use as an external problem with respect to the job setting. The second perspective assumes that internal factors in the workplace produce conditions that lead to substance use (Delaney & Ames, 1995; Trice & Sonnenstuhl, 1990); employees may consume alcohol or other drugs as a way to relieve workplace stress and other factors. Both views are valid; external and internal factors influence employee substance use. Employers would be wise to determine which employees may be at risk for substance use and abuse and identify the workplace characteristics associated with increased use (Martin, 1990).

OPTIONS FOR EMPLOYERS

Next to the family, the workplace is probably the most important setting for shaping and constraining alcohol- and other drug-related problems and behavior (Beattie, Longnbaugh, & Fava, 1992).

Employers can use two strategies to deal with employees with substance abuse problems: *identification* or *assistance*. Employers who use identification methods rely on drug-testing programs to screen all job applicants and employees based on reasonable cause or a random method. Depending on the company's philosophy and policy, applicants who test positive are generally denied employment, and employees who test positive also may be terminated unless some form of assistance is offered. In general, employers who use identification alone deal with substance abuse problems by eliminating the users from employment. Employers who do retain employees who test positive are unable to determine the level of behavioral impairment through drug testing.

Employers may offer some form of assistance, such as an EAP. The goal of the assistance approach is to identify problems early and to rehabilitate impaired workers. Often, early intervention does not occur because the supervisor and work group may compensate for the worker's inadequacies, thereby "enabling" the continued substance abuse. Typically, a variety of factors contribute to protect the impaired employee from the consequences of his or her behavior: fear of causing the employee to lose his or her job; being reprimanded oneself by other supervisors, co-workers, or the impaired employee; and personal loyalty to the employee. Earlier intervention could translate into greater morale and monetary savings for the company. It is because of this benefit that EAPs have been called the best prospect of turning around the problem of substance abuse in the United States (Walsh, Burmaster, Gray, & Daniels, 1990).

THE FACETS OF EAPs

Work-based intervention programs originated in the occupational alcoholism programs of the 1940s. By 1974, the NIAAA had adopted the term *employee assistance program* to describe job performance-based intervention programs in the workplace. Throughout the 1970s and 1980s, people from a variety of backgrounds (recovering alcoholics, substance abuse counselors, mental health counselors, social workers, nurses, and human resource workers) made the transition into the EAP field. In the early to mid-1980s, efforts were undertaken by the Association of Labor-Management Administrators and Consultants on Alcoholism and the major EAP occupational association, now known as the Employee Assistance Professional Association (EAPA), to define the boundaries of EAP practice, reaffirm the EAP commitment to the constructive confrontation strategy, maintain focus on the troubled employee, and promote working in an EAP as a unique career. In 1988, Roman and Blum reaffirmed the "core technology" of EAP work, outlining those tasks exclusively practiced by EAP workers, thus setting EAP work apart from other occupations.

The EAPs have adopted a broader approach to employee concerns. As part of a company's personnel or medical department or as external providers, EAPs currently seek to help troubled employees — as well as their dependents — deal with a wide range of personal problems. These programs, often referred to as "broad brush," expanded to provide comprehensive services based on the recognition that employee job performance could be affected by personal problems that did not involve alcohol (Wrich, 1982). In their effort to promote employee job performance, EAPs have evolved to provide a host of new services aimed not only at treatment but also prevention. The term *megabrush* has been coined to describe the inclusion of these services in an EAP (Erfurt, Foote, & Heirich, 1992). The significance of EAPs is pointed out by Backer (1989, p. 9): "EAPs are often seen as one of the latest steps in America's 100-year-long search for methods to improve worker performance as a way to meet organizational goals."

Data on the growth of EAPs in major private-sector corporations were initially generated through the Executive Caravan field surveys conducted by the Opinion Research Corporation (Roman, 1979). In 1972, it was estimated that approximately 300 EAP programs existed (NIAAA, 1972). By 1974, that number had grown to 621 programs in operation or development (Keller, 1974). By 1978, about 3,000 people were working in this growing field (Roman, 1988), and by the late 1980s, nearly 80% of the Fortune 500 companies had introduced EAPs (Pope, 1990). A report from the Bureau of Labor Statistics stated that 6.5% of establishments offered EAP services in 1988; a follow-up survey of those same work sites found that, in 1990, 11.8% had an EAP (Hayghe, 1991). In 1991, it was estimated that 45% of full-time employees worked for an employer who provided an EAP (Roman & Blum, 1992). A 1993 study conducted by the Research Triangle Institute (RTI) found that 33% of all nonpublic work sites had assistance programs, serving more than 55% of all U.S. employers with 50 or more employees (Hartwell et al., 1994). The RTI also noted that an additional 9% of the work sites that did not offer an EAP planned to implement one within the next year. According to the Federal Employee Assistance Administration (1993), comprehensive EAPs serve the 85 major federal departments and agencies, as well as the U.S. Congress. With the exception of the nuclear power industry and the transportation industry, in which federal mandates have required EAPs, the development and installation of EAPs in the private sector has been almost exclusively voluntary.

Types of EAPs:

Although EAPs have grown rapidly since their inception, they have taken on various forms and exist with differing levels of investment in EAP services. Roman (1988) recognizes four types of EAPs. The first type, most often found in large companies with substantial resources, is the *internal/in-house program*. It is staffed by employees of the organization and provides services on the site.

Internal EAPs may be more expensive than external EAPs

(Sipkoff, 1995); however, they offer the advantage of having someone within the company who knows the organizational dynamics and culture and is generally more accessible than the external counterparts. Because of a major shift toward behavioral managed care companies to control mental health and chemical dependency costs, many companies are outsourcing their internal EAPs to *external vendors,* who contract for desired EAP components.

This second type of EAP generally uses two variations in contracting services. The first variation is *fixed fee-for-services* or *capitated program,* based on the number of employees and remains unchanged regardless of utilization. The second variation of external contracting is *fee-for-service,* in which employers pay only when employees use the services or when the employer desires specific services of the EAP. The advantage of the fee-for-service EAP lies in the reduction, or even the elimination, of up-front costs, which often results in lower costs for services. In essence, the lower the utilization of services, the less expensive the program is to the company. It is somewhat surprising, then, that of 252 companies surveyed by William M. Mercer, Inc. (1995), 90% (227) of the respondents who used an external EAP vendor chose a fixed fee-for-service program, compared to the remaining 10% who used a fee-for-service structure.

An important point to consider when examining external EAP programs is who the service provider will be. Often mental health providers in private practice or even treatment facilities will offer EAP services as a means of soliciting clients or patients. When such a service is used, the employer should consider requiring the provider to do only assessment and referral services. This can avoid clients being referred back to the assessment provider or facility, and will allow the client the opportunity to be matched with the best provider, facility, or service to adequately and appropriately resolve the problem.

The third type of EAP involves *labor organizations.* In these programs, peer- or co-worker-based EAPs give education and training, assist troubled employees, and provide other related EAP services. These programs are built on and around peer referral rather than supervisory referrals. To be successful, employees who staff these programs — often recovering alcoholics and addicts — need considerable training to provide appropriate and adequate services. Bamberger and Sonnenstuhl (1995) found in a study of peer referral programs that utilization rates and chemical dependency utilization rates are contingent on the degree to which the site EAP committees and its peer counselors are embedded in the multiple networks that exist at each work site. They also found that peer counselors must be seen as trustworthy, understanding, and credible.

The fourth type of EAP mentioned by Roman targets members of *professional organizations*. This model, primarily used among groups of physicians and lawyers, may withdraw licensure or take other disciplinary measures to pressure its constituency to seek help. An additional type of EAP is called a *consortium*, in which small business employers join together to share the services and expense for the EAP. The consortium approach helps to lower the cost per employee and ensures the EAP provider an adequate amount of business.

Denzin (1995) states that "private managed EAPs appear to be the wave of the future" (p. 364). He notes that some 2,000 companies now compete with one another in the arenas of employee assistance and managed health care. The rise in EAPs throughout the United States has initiated a credentialing process through the EAPA and, in some states, licensure, helping to ensure quality care.

Rationale Behind Workplace Intervention Programs:

A basic assumption behind workplace intervention programs is that an employee's substance-abusing behavior, if it becomes a chronic problem, will have a negative impact on job performance. Workplace intervention programs, such as EAPs, are instituted by management or labor; they may work conjointly to provide mental health services to distressed employees in the hope of preventing deterioration in job performance (i.e., early identification) or restoring an affected performance. EAPs also figure prominently in the implementation of organizational change, as well as sustaining organizational functioning in companies that are not undergoing a rapid transformation. Typically offered as an employee benefit at no cost to the employee, an EAP's services include identification, assessment, referral, short-term counseling (in some models), follow-up assistance, consultation, and various types of training for employees and family members.

Another aspect of job-based intervention is the need to assess work environments and their potential impact on substance-abusing behavior and problems. Factors in the workplace such as availability, weak social controls, permissiveness, lack of accountability, or job stress may encourage the use and abuse of substances. These aspects may hamper an EAP's effectiveness in dealing with employee problems. For instance, newly recovering employees must reenter the environment that may have contributed either directly or indirectly to their problem.

The Economic Benefits of EAPs:

The Saratoga Institute HR Financial Report (Fitzenz, 1994) states that the cost of replacing an exempt employee is $8,566 and a nonexempt employee, $1,261. The costs of added health care, lost productivity, and safety infractions require that changes be made to reduce expenditures and increase profits.

Mental health services have progressed from a two-party system (i.e., client and provider) to a three-party system (i.e., client, provider, and insurance carrier) to a four-party system (i.e., client, provider, insurance carrier, and EAP or health maintenance program). EAPs have emerged to ensure that employees and dependents receive the most appropriate and highest quality mental health service at a reasonable fee (Penzer, 1987). EAPs are rapidly becoming a front-line defense against the rising costs of treatment. In a literature review, Holder, Lennox, and Blose (1993) found that businesses experienced significant economic savings by treating alcoholism in their employees. EAPs provide a vehicle for the provision and management of such treatment.

Holder (1987) reviewed studies on cost reductions in treating alcoholics by examining health care costs for alcoholics before, during, and after treatment. He found significant increases in health care costs up to and during treatment, with an extended decline in the posttreatment period. A more recent examination (Blose & Holder, 1991) concluded that costs for alcoholics declined over a 7-year posttreatment period to a level slightly higher than that for nonalcoholics. Trends in these costs suggested that the health care costs of alcoholics and nonalcoholics would eventually even out.

According to the U.S. Department of Labor (1990), for every dollar employers invested in an EAP, they saved $5.00–$16.00. The average annual cost per person for EAP services in 1995 was $24.70 (William M. Mercer, Inc., 1995). A national study by the RTI (Hartwell et al., 1996) reported that the average EAP cost per person was $21.83 for an internal program and $18.09 for an external program. They also found that, in external EAPs, costs varied by region, with the South having the lowest costs ($15.78) and the Northeast ($19.33) and West ($21.17) having the highest average costs. Because of limited sample sizes for internal EAPs, median cost estimates were not possible by region.

Savings in health care costs and productivity measures for employers who invest in EAPs have held true over the years across all types of industries. For example, in the 1980s the Northrop Corporation reported a 43% increase in the productivity of each of its first 100 employees to enter an alcohol treatment program. After 3 years of sobriety, Northrop retained an average savings for each employee of nearly $20,000 (Campbell & Graham, 1989). The HARTline company in Tampa, Florida, comparing pre-EAP 1984 figures with those of 1986 and 1987, years in which EAP programs were installed, found major downward shifts in accidents and cost. Their results showed that accidents declined by almost 50%, workers' compensation claims dropped from 60 to 49, completed arbitration cases fell from 12 to 4, and liability expenses dropped from over $1 million in 1984 to $29,951 in 1986 (Pope, 1990). The City of Los Angeles Department of Water and Power reported a savings of $350,000 over a 4-year period in reduced sickness-related absenteeism for employees with alcohol problems after implementing an EAP (Yankrick, 1992). Oldsmobile's Lansing, Michigan plant initiated an EAP and found that lost "man" hours declined by 49%, use of health care benefits declined by 29%, leaves of absence declined by 56%, grievances declined 78%, disciplinary problems were reduced 63%, and accidents decreased by 82% (Asis O. P. Norton Information Resource Center, 1990). The University of Michigan Faculty and Staff Assistance Program conducted a 5-year follow-up study to examine sick-leave usage and retention data. The combined retention and sick-leave cost savings were estimated to be $65,341, a very conservative estimate because of the limited data over the 5-year period (Bruhnsen, 1994).

In one of the better studies examining the economic benefits of an EAP, McDonnell Douglas Helicopter Company found that per capita mental health/chemical dependency costs were reduced by 34%, the admission rate for psychiatric treatment was reduced by 50%, admissions for chemical dependency by 29%, and the average length of stay for psychiatric conditions was lowered by 47% (The ALMACAN, 1989). Pope (1990) quotes the director of McDonnell Douglas's EAP, who states, "For 1988, we realized a return of $5.1 million. It's an indication that we're serving both the workers and the company" (p. 81). Companies who established EAPs saw a 33% decline in utilization of sick benefits, a 65% decline in work-related accidents, and a 30% decline in workers compensation claims (Bernstein, 1992). Every and Leong (1994) discussed the cost-effectiveness of an internal EAP at a nuclear power plant. They reported that early intervention through the EAP saves money by decreasing health care costs, lost work time, and absenteeism, and by increasing productivity. The authors also found savings through decreased grievances, decreased need for disciplinary action, and reduced litigation.

EAPs continue to demonstrate their value and cost effectiveness to business and industry. Given their success, it would be logical for most companies to offer EAP services. Surprisingly, the majority of companies that do not offer EAPs (33%) cite the high cost of these programs as the most common reason. Thirteen percent (13%) report lack of value to the organization, 17% say that they simply have not considered offering an EAP, and 15% report lack of employee interest. Twenty-two percent (22%) of the respondents who do not currently offer an EAP are either planning to implement one in the next year or are considering doing so (William M. Mercer, Inc., 1995).

Integration of an EAP into an Organization:

An EAP is established either as part of a company's organizational framework (an internal program) or an adjunct to the organization (an external program). Internal programs are found primarily in large businesses. Services are usually available at the work site although one of the company's various properties also may be available. External models are community-based programs contracted to provide EAP services on an as-needed or per capita basis (i.e., annual payment per employee).

Some research suggests that external programs have greater utilization than internal programs. A study conducted by Straussner (1985) found that external programs receive more self-referrals and are used by middle and upper management to a greater degree. Drawbacks of external programs include the loss of EAP visibility within the workplace, less knowledge of a particular organization's dynamics, and loss of informal contacts throughout the organization.

Basic EAP Services or Components:

With the proliferation of the need for these services, both private- and public-sector providers — who often are ill-trained in EAPs — have risen to the occasion by offering some form of EAP. This has created numerous kinds of existing programs and services.

William M. Mercer, Inc. (1995) conducted a study of 252 EAPs, finding that the majority of EAPs (89%) provided referral and counseling or short-term therapy. The remaining 11% confined themselves to assessment and referral services. Of those that did provide counseling, 5% offered only telephone counseling, compared with 70% that offered both in-person and telephone sessions. The EAPs studied offered varying numbers of counseling sessions; 77% provided up to 10 sessions, whereas 23% offered unlimited counseling sessions.

The following aspects are essential for a full-service EAP:

- *Policy statement.* A clearly worded policy statement should indicate the company's rationale for implementing the program (e.g., to assist employees with personal problems and to address job performance problems). The statement also should define what kind of problems are covered by the EAP, how an employee can seek help, and a commitment to confidentiality. It should outline the responsibilities of the employer, employee, union (if applicable), and program staff.

- *Procedures for case finding.* Procedures should entail developing specific methods to handle referrals from any source, defining the program's parameters, protecting information, and maintaining client contact and follow-up with supervisors.

- *Accountability.* Procedures for program management

should be consistent with management and labor interests, define staff roles, support sound business practices, and facilitate program evaluation.

- *Identification of treatment resources.* EAP providers should investigate qualified and effective treatment providers of inpatient, partial, and outpatient services; clearly define each program's or provider's areas of expertise to appropriately match provider and client; and include potential sources within the community (e.g., 12-step meetings, food bank, churches that provide benevolence funds).

- *Intake, assessment, screening, and referral.* EAPs should provide personalized clinical assessment sessions for employees and family members to determine the nature of the presenting problem(s) and formulate recommendations for treatment. Some programs provide a short-term counseling model to avoid using insurance dollars.

- *Program marketing.* Various methods to promote the EAP should be used, including mailing a letter to the home, brochures, posters, and business cards.

- *Supervisor training.* Supervisor training should be offered. This is a specialized training initiative to orient supervisors to company policy and the benefits of the EAP, help them recognize the signs and symptoms of a troubled or impaired employee, and present a process of intervening with a troubled employee.

- *Employee orientation training.* An orientation training should be provided to all employees. This training presents the EAP as a company benefit and service, emphasizing the broad-brush nature of the program and how to gain access to services.

- *Record keeping.* Case records should be maintained by appropriate means, and program utilization data should be provided to the employer in an aggregate form.

- *Evaluation.* Program process and outcome studies should be conducted to ensure that quality services are being provided.

ARE EAPs FOR YOU?

EAPs continue to grow in popularity in all types of U.S. work sites (Hartwell et al., 1996). They offer excellent career opportunities for a variety of mental health and chemical dependency professionals (Hershenson & Power, 1987). One study (William M. Mercer, Inc., 1995) found that 78% of the EAPs were staffed by either a psychologist or other therapist. Social workers comprised 59% and nurses, 13%. Other EAP personnel included substance abuse counselors (3%) and Certified Employee Assistance Professionals (CEAP; 3%).

Salary ranges are competitive and in some cases better than in other mental health arenas. Open Minds (1992) reported that on average an EAP director's base annual salary was $87,910. The Employee Assistance Professional Association's CEAP update (1996) stated that in 1995 the average salary for a CEAP was $48,757 compared to $47,063 for noncertified professionals.

Two professional associations support EAPs. The Employee Assistance Professional Association (EAPA), formerly called the Association of Labor-Management Administrators and Consultants on Alcoholism (ALMACA), and the Employee Assistance Society of North America (EASNA), have developed certification procedures for EAP professionals and offer a wide variety of information. For information on how to contact these professional associations, see Table 1.1.

Table 1.1
PROFESSIONAL ORGANIZATIONS THAT SUPPORT
EMPLOYEE ASSISTANCE PROGRAMS (EAPs)

Employee Assistance Professional Association (EAPA)
2101 Wilson Blvd.
Suite 500
Arlington, VA 22201
(703) 522-6272

Employee Assistance Society of North America (EASNA)
2728 Phillips
Berkley, MI 48072
(810) 545-3888

In deciding whether or not you should offer EAP services or become involved in the EAP field, consider the following questions:

1. What is my expertise in working with mental illness?

Because the scope of EAPs is broad, a diverse background in dealing with various mental health issues is necessary for accurate screening, assessment, diagnosis, and referral to appropriate treatment providers. An EAP practitioner must be an excellent diagnostician, skilled in biopsychosocial assessment procedures. In general, only one or two sessions are typically required to render a diagnosis.

2. Am I knowledgeable and skilled?

Training and experience in chemical dependency are essential for an EAP practitioner. Because of the stigma associated with substance abuse problems, specialized skills are necessary in the assessment process to detect these issues accurately. Knowledge and experience with 12-step programs (e.g., Alcoholics Anonymous, Narcotics Anonymous, Cocaine Anonymous, Al-Anon, Narc-Anon, Co-Dependents Anonymous) are necessary to lower client resistance to participating in these support groups. Many companies with internal EAPs require that a counselor have a minimum of 2 years' experience in substance abuse treatment before being hired.

3. Can I make appropriate referrals?

Skill in care determination and case management functions has become increasingly crucial because treatment options and choices are scrutinized thoroughly at various levels. An EAP practitioner needs to be aware of community resources and be in a position to make the best referral possible. Matching a client's problems and personality with the appropriate treatment provider is a critical element of a successful EAP.

4. Am I skilled in and comfortable with public speaking?

Essential components of any EAP are the training programs offered to supervisors and employees. Such programs generally represent the first contact many workers have with an EAP and the counselor providing the assessment services. The ability to conduct interesting presentations to a wide range of employee groups will promote confidence in these services.

5. Can I motivate clients to enter treatment?

Traditionally, EAP practitioners have relied on employees' jobs as leverage in motivating them into treatment. This has been effective, but practitioners are realizing the increasing need to be well versed in motivational techniques other than just confrontation. These factors may involve the degree of client distress, a spouse or significant other, children, and co-workers, just to name a few.

A recently developed approach to motivating clients during assessment has been referred to as "motivational interviewing" (Miller & Rollnick, 1991). Instead of viewing motivation as a personality trait, motivation is seen as a dynamic state of readiness, and techniques designed to enhance the client's state of motivation are used.

6. What do I think about modifying the standards of confidentiality and anonymity to meet company policy or legal mandates?

Because of safety-sensitive jobs, some companies require notification of employee substance abuse, even for self-referred employees. This may necessitate informing particular personnel about employee substance use. Although employers do not need to be informed of a diagnosis, the particular abused substance, or other personal client information, client anonymity is breached when notification is made that a certain employee who is in a safety-sensitive position requires treatment or is unfit because of a substance abuse problem. As in most clinical situations, informed consent is critical before any evaluation is conducted.

7. Am I knowledgeable in substance abuse legislation and its impact on company policy and procedures?

Consulting with company personnel on matters dealing with disability and the requirements of certain businesses is a critical aspect for EAP counselors. Counselors must possess a knowledge of organizational dynamics, substance abuse, relevant legislation, and appropriate intervention techniques.

8. What do I know about organizational dynamics and behavior?

The problem presented by employees in the EAP practitioner's office often is symptomatic of a larger problem within the organization. EAP counselors may need to provide ongoing organizational consultation on the dynamics of the workplace to get to the root of the problem.

9. What is my own relationship with substances?

We are affected by the dynamics associated with our family of origin, personal experiences, and current behavioral patterns. Understanding our current thoughts and values concerning alcohol and other drugs is critical in providing objective services. One company's EAP counselor was addicted to alcohol and abused cocaine. He would minimize clients' use of substances and regard employees as in control of their drinking provided they could work or play a sport. Such help obviously falls short of competence and borders on unethical.

DEVELOPING THE SKILLS FOR EAP SERVICES

If a counselor decides to offer EAP services, the following questions should be considered:

1. What types of services am I competent to offer?

The EAPs offer a wide variety of services. Although not all employers desire a full-service EAP, you may be consulted about these services at a later date.

2. What types of programs am I willing to provide and what services do I not need to provide?

An employer may ask you to provide EAP services to protect the company or individual against liability charges or to meet legislative mandates. Therefore, you must decide what they consider ethical and effective in providing EAP services. One company contacted the author about providing an EAP service to its 600 employees. In discussing the company's needs, I concluded that the company simply wanted assessment and referral services; it did not want supervisory training or employee orientation sessions, and its policy called for any substance abuser to be terminated from the company. Moreover, the insurance carrier did not cover substance abuse or mental health treatment. Based on my belief about what constitutes an effective EAP, I turned down the opportunity to contract with this employer.

3. How do I plan to market these services?

It is critical to know an employer's frame of reference when marketing an EAP. In general, employers are not interested in the humane reasons for implementing an EAP. Their focus tends to fall on controlling costs and increasing profits.

USING THE EAP STRATEGY

1. How can a substance abuse counselor assist employers in dealing with substance abuse problems in the workplace?

Management's responsibility is to provide a safe, secure, and healthy work environment for its employees. Counselors should assist management in reviewing all relevant policies and procedures. Policies should document that the company does not tolerate drug or alcohol use on the job and present the rationale behind the policy (e.g., safety, health, liability, productivity). What constitutes an infraction of this policy and the consequences of such an act should be clearly defined. Procedurally, the policy should state the company's desire to rehabilitate employees and outline steps that management, supervisors, personnel, and the EAP will perform to ensure the proper handling of these cases.

One company with which the author has consulted offered employees 30 days with pay to obtain appropriate treatment through an EAP. Although employees were not required to participate in treatment, they were expected to remain drug free while on the job. Following treatment or a 30-day leave (or both), employees were granted a "back-to-work conference" with treatment providers and the supervisor to discuss the consequences of continued substance abuse in light of the company's expectations. This employer required identified abusers to participate in a 1-year monitoring program, necessitating drug screening on a random basis.

The company's insurance package should be reviewed to determine whether alcohol and other drug abuse treatment services are covered. Providing an EAP without the ability to refer an employee to appropriate treatment with insurance coverage is self-defeating.

An ongoing alcohol and drug awareness program should be developed to teach employees the company's policy and the consequences of any infraction. Employees should understand the signs and symptoms of alcohol and drug abuse, the addiction process, and how treatment can be obtained via the EAP. It is critical to emphasize that the EAP is an opportunity to address *any* concerns the employees have concerning their substance-abusing behavior or the problem of co-workers or family members.

2. What training is necessary for counselors to assist supervisors and managers in dealing with impaired or troubled employees?

Supervisors play a significant role in dealing with troubled employees and maintaining a drug-free workplace. In a national sample of EAPs (Schneider, Colan, & Googins, 1990), over 92% agreed that EAPs must offer training for supervisors to have a quality EAP. Over 87% of these respondents reported having conducted supervisory training within the past year. The objective behind any EAP is the early identification of employee problems to maintain job performance. The key to early identification is the supervisor's ability to observe changes in employee behavior and performance. Deterioration must be documented and meet the agreed-on standards of employers and employees.

Managers and supervisors use the performance of employees as a basis for constructive confrontation. Special supervisory training is offered by EAPs to instruct managers in recognizing the signs and symptoms of troubled employees, how EAPs are linked to performance and disciplinary processes, the effects of employees' problems on job performance, and constructive confrontational techniques.

Because the propensity for supervisors to use EAPs largely depends on how familiar they are with the EAP and how accessible it appears (Milne, Blum, & Roman, 1992), appropriate and adequate training of managers is essential.

Over the years, EAP practitioners have developed a 5-step plan to train managers in working with impaired employees. These steps include observation, documentation, confrontation, referral, and reintegration. In training supervisors, EAP practitioners teach methods of observation (i.e., the signs and symptoms of troubled employees) to provide a basis for documentation. It is a supervisor's job to take corrective action when a worker's performance begins to deteriorate. Therefore, supervisors must know how to identify troubled employees and what to do thereafter. Supervisors are encouraged not to diagnose or treat these employees, but to stress job performance as the basis of confrontation.

Constructive confrontation is taught to help supervisors handle troubled workers, as well as empower them to acknowledge the existence of a problem and accept a referral to the EAP. These techniques emphasize job performance as the focus of the confrontation. The success of constructive confrontation in returning employees with alcohol problems to effective performance has been confirmed (Trice & Beyer, 1984). Data from two national samples of more than 600 managers in a large corporation indicated that supervisors of problem drinkers took more action than did supervisors of employees with other problems. Also, employees and supervisors credited the improvements in work performance of prob-lem-drinking employees, which were greater than those of other problem employees, to constructive confrontational in-terventions.

Although EAPs strongly encourage and teach supervisory referrals, it seems to occur too infrequently. Blum and Roman (1992) report that 15% of those who work for organizations with EAPs have contacted the provider about an employee they supervise. In a major work addressing the role of the supervisor, Beyer and Trice (1978) found that only 10% of EAP cases were by supervisor referral. In 40% of the situations involving performance problems, supervisors counseled em-ployees themselves; in 14% of the cases, they took no action; and in 13% of the cases, the supervisors' actions proved to be detrimental. Ultimately, only 32% of the reported cases re-sulted in some kind of counseling or treatment.

Bayer and Gerstein (1988, 1990) researched the circum-stances under which supervisors identify, confront, and refer employees to EAPs. Their model, referred to as the Bystander Equity Model of Supervisory Helping Behavior, attempts to explain supervisors' willingness to become involved in a help-ing relationship with problem employees. They propose a series of hypotheses covering the conditions under which a supervisor would act "prosocially" (i.e., by assisting the em-ployee in making a referral to the EAP). According to this model, many situational, individual, and environmental fac-tors interact to determine whether supervisors will recognize, confront, and refer impaired workers to the EAP.

Bayer and Gerstein advocated that supervisors would be more likely to identify, confront, and refer employees when one or more of the following conditions existed:

- The characteristics of an employee's problem or work site behavior are severe or atypical.

- The two persons have a greater degree of similarity in terms of race, gender, and common beliefs.

- Inequity in the supervisor-employee relationship increases as the subordinate's performance deteriorates.

- The organizational or personal costs of referral to the supervisor are low.

- A negative relationship exists between the personal or organizational costs and the severity of the subordinate's problem.

The investigations of Bayer and Gerstein indicated that supervisors identified troubled employees through attendance, conduct, irritability, anger, contentiousness, poor productivity or job performance, apathy, alienation, and discontent. When these problems were designated as severe, supervisors were more willing to refer or offer assistance. Supervisory characteristics, such as tenure, span of control, and previous EAP training, resulted in differences in identification and referral. Finally, Bayer and Gerstein concluded that the characteristics of the situation surrounding the employee and supervisor were related to employee recognition and supervisory action.

Reichman, Young, and Gracin (1988) suggest that identifying employee alcohol problems based on job performance identified only a small percentage of employees with substance abuse problems, and these were the more severe cases. They encourage company health promotion or wellness programs and EAPs to work conjointly to identify problems earlier.

Regardless of the extent of referrals from managers, EAPs report positive feedback from their supervisor training programs and believe them to be essential in carrying out the mission of the EAP (Googins, Schneider, & Colan, 1990). Not only does supervisor training help in monitoring employee job performance, but it assists supervisors in improving their managerial skills. Googins and colleagues (1990) advocate for

EAPs to link themselves with the management training field, specifically, with other corporate training initiatives. This union would enable the EAP to become fully integrated into the corporate culture and organization.

3. How are referrals made to an EAP?

To provide mental health rehabilitation services to employees, EAPs operate essentially through two different avenues of access: *self-referrals* and *supervisory/management referrals*. The latter category often is divided into informal (e.g., suggesting that the employee seek help) and formal (e.g., a condition of employment) referrals. Some EAPs distinguish between peer and union referrals from the aforementioned routes of access.

In the early years of occupational alcoholism and EAPs, referrals were primarily supervisory in nature. Encouraging employees to refer themselves is a more recent development. Self-referred clients are generally quite positive and highly motivated, whereas clients referred by a third party are less motivated and more guarded (Hansen, Stevie, & Warner, 1972; Ritchie, 1986). Moreover, self-referrals may be a key to lowering health care costs (Bernstein, 1992). Thomas and Johnson (1992, 1993) found that employer-referred (i.e., supervisory) clients were more likely to have grown up in homes where alcohol was abused (72.5%) when compared with self-referrals (31.7%). Employer-referred clients had fewer years of education and showed less preference for organized religion when compared with clients who sought EAP services on their own. Another study (Solomon, 1983) indicated that employer referrals tend to be men, perhaps because supervisors reported feeling more comfortable referring men than women for drinking-related problems.

Braun and Novak (1986) found that employees in middle and upper management, persons in professional occupations, employees 50 years of age or older, men, and victims of intense stress were less likely to use the services of an EAP. Clients who used EAPs perceived the services as confidential, free, and convenient, as well as an alternative to job loss. Other characteristics of EAP users were that they were more open to change, were more often peer referred, believed their supervisors supported the EAP, and desired help.

In a study on EAP utilization and outcome measures, Blum and Roman (1992) surveyed 439 EAP sites. On average, about 30% of the cases stemmed from employee substance abuse problems. Many of the cases recorded by the EAPs as "marriage and family problems," the largest single caseload category, involved substance abuse problems of spouses or other dependents. An average of 6% of employees used the EAPs during a 12-month period. A national survey in 1991 (Blum & Roman, 1992) found that more than 8% of covered employees had used the EAP program in the past for a personal problem and 6% had used the EAP for a family member's problem. Additionally, 48% of the employees surveyed knew of someone who had used the EAP.

4. What organizational risk factors are involved in substance abuse problems?

Eleven job-based risk factors for substance abuse problems have been identified (Kinney & Leaton, 1978):

1. Absence of clear goals (and absence of supervision)

2. Freedom to set work hours (isolation and low visibility)

3. Low structural visibility (e.g., away from the business site)

4. Overinvestment in the job

5. Occupational obsolescence

6. New work status

7. On-the-job drinking "requirement" (e.g., entertaining prospective customers/clients)

8. Reduction of social controls

9. Severe role stress

10. Competitive pressure

11. Presence of illegal drug users

Trice and Sonnenstuhl (1988) examined the research on drinking-related behavior and risk factors associated with the workplace. They noted four perspectives: (a) *the workplace culture perspective* examines certain workplace groups and organizations that set norms encouraging heavy drinking; (b) *the social control perspective* associates the lack of employee supervision or low job visibility with excessive drinking; (c) *the alienation perspective* holds that a direct causal link exists between unfulfilling work and drinking, by which the drinker seeks to relieve the sense of powerlessness resulting from work; and (d) *the stress perspective,* which rationalizes that employees who develop heavy drinking behavior are doing so to cope with excessive workplace stress.

SPECIFIC ISSUES FOR COUNSELORS ASSOCIATED WITH EAPs

1. Who really is the client?

An important question emerges when an EAP's services are used: who, in fact, is the client? An initial response to such a question may reveal that the employee being assessed or whose case is being managed is considered the client. Yet the contractual nature of the services and the organizational focus of the EAP cloud the issue. From a system perspective, an employee may be viewed as the identified patient of a particular work group, department, or organization; the company, then, is the actual system and target of intervention. This type of thinking helps counselors conceptualize the broader issues in the workplace or particular work group, and it further clarifies the their role in regard to the employee and the organization. A helpful distinction can be made by viewing the company as the customer and those seeking services as the client.

2. Is confidentiality granted to employees who seek EAP services?

The "Standards for Employee Alcoholism and/or Assistance Programs" (1983) call for "confidentiality only" requirements for clients who are referred by their supervisors and "confidentiality and anonymity" requirements for clients who refer themselves to counseling (Lewis & Lewis, 1986). Confidentiality typically is highly valued and protected in EAPs, especially in internal models. Employees who work in safety-sensitive positions, as well as those who fall under a legal mandate, may be granted limited confidentiality if impairment on the job could cause harm. Otherwise, a release must be signed by the employee, allowing the practitioner to discuss relevant and pertinent data with treatment providers and management. In such cases, supervisors or managers receive only information concerning the employee's cooperation, progress, and prognosis. The diagnosis and other personal information are not disclosed unless specifically ordered by the client.

3. How does a counselor assess a client who has been referred by management to the EAP?

The EAPs constitute a uniquely different setting from most

private and public mental health services in that many clients are there because they have been "strongly encouraged" or even required to participate. Although these clients could be considered voluntary (based on their choice to use the services rather than lose their jobs or suffer some other form of disciplinary action), most of them resist and resent their presence in the practitioner's office. Working with "involuntary clients" involves a set of skills beyond that of working with clients who seek services on their own.

In conducting an assessment, it is important to begin on the same level as the client. After a counselor presents a customary ethical opening, relating information about the nature of EAP services and confidentiality, the fact that the employee is there under duress could be discussed. For example, I may say, "I understand that it seems very unfair for you to have to be here. I do not like to feel that I am forced to do something that I would rather not do or that I have no value in. Nevertheless, you choose to be here, for good reasons, and it seems wise that we make the best of it."

The employee's perception of the job situation and whether a problem exists can offer a wealth of information on how to proceed with the assessment. The employee should realize that a counselor understands the reason for the referral and plays a role in the job-jeopardy process. To evaluate performance, a job history from the employee regarding current position, job, and previous jobs should be attained. Furthermore, counselors should question the employee concerning past performance appraisals, raises, and bonuses.

Directness, openness, reflection of understanding, and clarity are critical in building a rapport with resistant employees. To lower defensiveness in an employee who is obviously guarded, the author often uses paradox as a way of gathering necessary information to formulate a provisional diagnosis. For instance, I might say, "There are probably some things that you have determined you are not going to discuss with me or allow me to know. I understand your right to privacy and would also ask you not to share anything that you believe to be private."

4. How can clients addicted to alcohol or other drugs be adequately screened and assessed by counselors?

Sonnesnstuhl (1990) described three stages of help-seeking by employees who come to an EAP: containment, triggers to action, and lingering concerns. *Containment* refers to the breaking down of an employee's ability to manage the problem alone. *Triggers to action* are the factors that encouraged the employee to seek professional help. They involve: (a) *cultural factors* (e.g., the occurrence of an interpersonal crisis, perceived interference with social or personal relations, sanctioning, perceived interference with vocational or physical activity), (b) *supervisory factors* (e.g., confrontations, informal suggestions), and (c) *co-worker factors* (e.g., recommendations from peers, confrontations, shared experiences with EAPs). An employee must finally overcome *lingering concerns* about the cost of treatment, its impact on the personnel record, confidentiality, and the ability to obtain services without affecting work time. Supervisors, human resources personnel, and other employees can assist the impaired worker in resolving these issues. Sonnesnstuhl (1990) stated that an employee's progress through these stages varies according to the degree of stigma the individual attaches to a specific problem, with family problems generally being more acceptable and substance abuse problems being highly stigmatized.

The use of standardized inventories as a means of screening substance abuse problems is an important part of an EAP practitioner's assessment. Although screening asymptomatic persons is less well established, standard screening devices should be used with all clients. The Children of Alcoholics Screening Test (CAST) (Jones, 1983) and the Michigan Alcoholism Screening Test (MAST) (Selzer, 1971) have been documented as beneficial to EAP practitioners (Thomas & Johnson, 1992, 1993).

The CAST is a 30-item, self-administered yes/no inventory that typically requires 10 minutes to complete; it measures the respondent's feelings, attitudes, perceptions, and experiences that were shared by clinically diagnosed children of alcoholics during therapy. Scores on the CAST are derived by accumulating the number of affirmative responses. The total score ranges from 0 (no experience with parental alcohol misuse) to 30 (multiple experiences with parental alcohol abuse). Scores of 6 or more generally indicate that the respondent is a child of an alcoholic. The CAST points to possible sources of problems and how secondary alcoholism or other drug addiction can pose problems in subsequent generations. Recent studies support the use of the CAST as a reliable and valid instrument for research and clinical practice (Lease & Yanico, 1995; Sheridan, 1995).

In screening for current alcohol problems, the MAST is a widely used, research-directed detection device. It has been used in clinical and nonclinical settings to provide a simple, quick, economical, and reliable means of identifying the effects of drinking on a person's functions. The MAST is a collection of 25 face-valid items that ask about drinking habits and drinking-related problems throughout the respondent's lifetime. It is, in essence, a list of common signs and symptoms of generic alcoholism to which a respondent answers "yes" or "no." The inventory takes approximately 10 minutes to complete, whether self-administered or conducted by an interviewer. It determines the respondent's self-appraisal of his or her drinking habits, including the involvement of helping agencies, as well as the social, vocational, medical, legal, and familial problems frequently associated with excessive drinking. Thus, its primary focus is on the alcohol-related behavior associated with alcoholism; it does not address the quantity of consumption or psychological constructs.

SUMMARY

Substance abuse is a widespread problem in the workplace. As one means of combating this concern, employers have implemented EAPs to intervene before substance abuse among employees affects job performance or to assist already-troubled employees. EAPs offer both opportunities and challenges to persons practicing in the rehabilitation and substance abuse fields. Counselors trained in providing clinical occupational services can assist management in promoting productivity, meeting legal requirements, reducing health care costs, and handling impaired workers appropriately. These counselors must be prepared to provide expert consultation on the issues of substance abuse, work group behavior, and relevant legislation.

REFERENCES

Ackerman, R. J. (1983). *Children of alcoholics: A guidebook for educators, therapists, and parents*. Holmes Beach, FL: Learning Publications.

The ALMACAN (1989). McDonnell Douglas Corporation's EAP produces hard data. *The ALMACAN*, 18-26.

Avis, H. (1993). *Drugs and life*. Madison, WI: Brown & Benchmark.

Backer, T. E. (1989). *Strategic planning for the workplace drug abuse programs*. (DHHS Publication No. ADM 87-1538). Rockville, MD: U.S. Department of Health and Human Services.

Bamberger, P., & Sonnenstuhl, W. J. (1995). Peer referral networks and utilization of a union-based EAP. *The Journal of Drug Issues, 25*(2), 291-312.

Bayer G., & Gerstein, L. (1988). An adaptation of models of prosocial behavior to supervisor intentions with troubled employees. *Journal of Applied Social Psychology, 18,* 23–27.

Bayer, G., & Gerstein, L. (1990). EAP referrals and troubled employees: An analogue study of supervisors' decisions. *Journal of Vocational Behavior, 34,* 304–319.

Beattie, M. C., Longnbaugh, R., & Fava, J. (1992). Assessment of alcohol-related workplace activities: Development and testing of your workplace. *Journal of Studies on Alcohol, 53,* 469-475.

Berkowitz, A., & Parkins, H. W. (1988). Personality characteristics of children of alcoholics. *Journal of Consulting and Clinical Psychology, 56,* 206-209.

Bernstein, J. (1992). Getting the most out of EAPs. *Journal of Health Care Benefits,* Jan/Feb, 61-65.

Bernstein, M., & Mahoney, J. J. (1989). Management perspectives on alcoholism: The employer's stake in alcoholism treatment. *Occupational Medicine, 4(2),* 223-232.

Beyer, J. M., & Trice, H. M. (1978). *Implementing change: Alcoholism policies in work organizations.* New York: Free Press.

Black, C. Bucky, S. F., & Wilder-Padilla, S. (1986). The interpersonal and emotional consequences of being an adult child of an alcoholic. *International Journal of Addictions, 21,* 213-231.

Blose, J. D., & Holder, H. D. (1991). The utilization of medical care by treated alcoholics: Longitudinal patterns by age, gender, and type of care. *Journal of Substance Abuse Treatment, 3,* 13-27.

Blum, T. C., & Roman, P. M. (1992). Identify alcoholic problems in the workplace: A description of EAP clients. *Alcohol Health and Research World, 16(2),* 120-128.

Blum, T. C., & Roman, P. M., & Martin, J. K. (1992). Alcohol consumption and work performance. *Journal of Studies on Alcoholism, 53,* 61-70.

Blum, T. C., & Roman, P. M., & Martin, J. K. (1993). Alcohol consumption and work performance. *Journal of Studies on Alcohol, 54,* 61-70.

Braun, A. L., & Novak, D. E. (1986). A study of EAP non-utilization. *EAP Digest,* Nov/Dec, 52-55.

Bross, M. H., Pace, S. K., & Cronin, J. K. (1992). Chemical dependence: Analysis of work absenteeism and associated medical illnesses. *Journal of Occupational Medicine, 34,* 16-19.

Bruhnsen, K. (1994). Michigan study shows EAP clients use less sick leave, stay longer. *EAPA Exchange, 11*, 27.

Bureau of National Affairs, Inc. (1990). Workers support drug testing. *Bulletin to Management*, January 4, 1990.

Calder, P., & Kostiniuk, A. (1989). Personality profiles of children of alcoholics. *Professional Psychology: Research and Practice, 20*, 417-418.

Campbell, D., & Graham, M. (1989). *Drugs and alcohol in the workplace: A guide for managers*. New York: Facts of File.

CEAP Update. (1996). *CEAP Salaries higher than non-CEAPs*. Arlington, VA: Employee Assistance Professional Association.

Chernoff, G. J. (1989). Drug problem 'significant' to the nation's top executives. *The U.S. Journal*. Washington, DC: Alcohol and Drug Problems Association.

Crouch, D. J., Webb, D. O., Buller, P. F., & Rollins D.E. (1989). A critical evaluation of the Utah Power and Light Company's Substance Abuse Management Program: Absenteeism, accidents, and costs. In S. W. Gust & J. M. Walsh (Eds.), *Drugs in the workplace: Research and evaluation data* (NIDA Research Monograph No. 91.). Rockville, MD: National Institute on Drug Abuse.

Delaney, W. P., & Ames, G. (1995). Work team attitudes, drinking norms, and workplace drinking. *The Journal of Drug Issues, 25*(2), 275-290.

Denenberg, T. S. (1991). The arbitration of employee substance abuse rehabilitation issues. *The Arbitration Journal, 46*, 17-33.

Denzin, N. (1995). Living and dying in an employee assistance program. *The Journal of Drug Issues, 25*(2), 363-378.

Doweiko, H. F. (1993). *Concepts of chemical dependency*. Belmont, CA: Wadsworth.

Erfurt, J., & Foote, A. (1989). *Impact of intensive worksite followup on EAP effectiveness*. Presented at the National Institute on Drug Abuse (NIDA) Conference on Drugs in the Workplace: Research and Evaluation Data, Bethesda, MD.

Erfurt, J. C., Foote, A., & Heirich, M. (1992). Integrating employee assistance and wellness: Current and future core technologies of a megabrush program. *Journal of Employee Assistance Research, 1*, 1–31.

Every, D. K., & Leong, D. M. (1994). Exploring EAP cost-effectiveness: Profile of a nuclear power plant internal EAP. *Employee Assistance Quarterly, 10*(1), 1-12.

Federal Employee Assistance Administration, Fiscal Year 1993, U.S. Office of Personnel Management, Employee Health Services Branch, Washington, DC.

Fitzenz, J. (Ed.). (1994). Saratoga Institute/SHRM/Financial SHRM Report: Tenth Anniversary.

Goodwin, D. W. (1983). Alcoholism. In R. E. Tarter (Ed.), *The child at psychiatric risk* (pp. 195-213). New York: Oxford University Press.

Googins, B., Schneider, R., & Colan, N. (1990). Re-examining the role of supervisory training. In S. W. Gust, J. M. Walsh, L. B. Thomas, & D. J. Crouch (Eds.), *Drugs in the workplace: Research and evaluation data* (Vol. II, pp. 209-221). Rockville, MD: U.S. Department of Health and Human Services.

Hansen, J. C., Stevie, R. R., & Warner, R. W., Jr. (1972). *Counseling: Theory and practice.* Boston: Allyn & Bacon.

Hartwell, T. D., French, M. T., Potter, F. J., Steele, P. D., Zarkin, G. A., & Rodman, N. F. (1994). Prevalence, cost, and characteristics of employee assistance programs (EAPs) in the U.S. Research Triangle Park, NC: Research Triangle Institute.

Hartwell, T. D., Steele, P. D., French, M. T., Potter, F. J., Rodman, N. F., & Zarkin, G. A. (1996). Aiding troubled employees: The prevalence, cost, and characteristics of employee assistance programs in the United States. *American Journal of Public Health, 86*(6), 804-808.

Harwood, H. J., Napolitano, D. M., Kristiansen, P., & Collins, J. J. (1984). *Economic costs to society of alcohol and drug abuse and mental illness: 1980.* Research Triangle Park, NC: Research Triangle Institute.

Hayghe, H. (1991, April 26-28). Anti-drug programs in the workplace: Are they here to stay? *Monthly Labor Review.* U.S. Department of Labor, Bureau of Labor Statistics.

Hecht, M. (1973). Children of alcoholics are children at risk. *American Journal of Nursing, 73,* 1764–1767.

Hershenson, D. B., & Power, P. W. (1987). *Mental health counseling: Theory and practice.* New York: Pergamon Press.

Hoffman, J. P., Brittingham, A., & Larison, C. (1996). *Drug use among U.S. workers: Prevalence and trends by occupation and industry categories.* Rockville, MD: Substance Abuse and Mental Health Services Administration.

Holder, H. D. (1987). Alcoholism treatment and potential health care cost saving. *Medical Care, 25*(1), 52-71.

Holder, H. D., Lennox, R. D., & Blose, J. O. (1993). The economic benefits of alcoholism treatment: A summary of twenty years of research. *Journal of Employee Assistance Research, 1,* 63–82.

Institute of Medicine. (1990). *Treating drug problems: A study of the evolution, effectiveness, and financing of public and private drug treatment systems.* Washington, DC: National Academy Press.

Jones, J. W. (1983). *The children of alcoholics screening test.* Chicago: Camelot Unlimited.

Keller, M. (1974). Problem drinkers on the job. In M. Keller (Ed.), *Alcohol and health: Second special report to Congress* (pp. 169-181). Washington, DC: U.S. Department of Health, Education, and Welfare.

Kinney, J., & Leaton, G. (1978). *Loosening the grip: A handbook of alcohol information.* St. Louis: Mosby.

Lease, S. H., & Yanico, B. J. (1995). Evidence of validity for the Children of Alcoholics Screening Test. *Measurement and Evaluation in Counseling and Development, 27*(4), 200-210.

Lee, P. R. (1993). Preface. In E. Gordis (Ed.), *Alcohol and health: Eighth special report to Congress* (p. xi). Washington, DC: U.S. Department of Health, Education, and Welfare.

Lehman, W. E. K., Farabee, D. J., & Simpson, D. D. (1992). *Co-worker substance use and its relationship with employee attitudes and morale.* Fort Worth, TX: Texas Christian University, Institute of Behavioral Research.

Lehman, W. E. K., Holcom, M. L., & Simpson, D. D. (1990). *Employee health and performance in the workplace: A survey of municipal employees of a large southwest city.* Fort Worth, TX: Texas Christian University, Institute of Behavioral Research.

Lewis, J. A., & Lewis, M. D. (1986). *Counseling programs for employees in the workplace.* Monterrey, CA: Brooks/Cole.

Linnoila, M. (1978). Psychomotor effects of drugs and alcohol on healthy volunteers and psychiatric patients. In G. Olive (Ed.), *Advances in pharmacology and therapeutics: Drug action modification comparative pharmacology* (Vol. 8). New York: Pergamon Press.

Martin, J. K. (1990). Jobs, occupations, and patterns of alcohol consumption: A review of literature. In R. M. Roman (Ed.), *Alcohol problem intervention in the workplace: Employee assistance programs and strategic alternatives.* New York: Quorum Books.

Masi, F. A., & Spencer, G. E. (1977). *Alcoholism and employee assistance programs in industry: A new frontier for social work.* Washington, DC: National Conference of Catholic Charities.

Mathews, B. & Halbrook, M. (1990). Adult children of alcoholics: Implications for career development. *Journal of Career Development, 16*(4), 261-268.

McKenna, T., & Pickens, R. (1981). Alcoholic children of alcoholics. *Journal of Studies on Alcohol, 32,* 364-372.

Meacham, A. (1987). Adult children at work. *Changes,* Jan/Feb, 24–25.

Miller, L. (1989). *Estimates of the costs of alcohol and drug abuse to society.* Presented at the National Institute on Drug Abuse (NIDA) Conference on Drugs in the Workplace: Research and Evaluation Data, Bethesda, MD.

Miller, W., & Rollnick, S. (1991). *Motivational interviewing: Preparing people to change addictive behavior.* New York: Guilford Press.

Milne, S. H., Blum, T. C., & Roman, P. M. (1992). *Factors influencing the implementation of an employee assistance program as a human resources innovation.* Paper presented at the Southern Management Association Annual Meeting, New Orleans.

Moree, G. B., & Jenigan R. J. (1977). *Treat alcoholic workers and stop the dollars drain.* Minneapolis: CompCare.

Myers, D. M. (1984). *Establishing and building employee assistance programs.* Westport, CT: Quorum Books.

National Institute on Alcohol Abuse and Alcoholism. (1972). *Alcohol and alcoholism: Problems, programs, and progress.* Washington, DC: U.S. Government Printing Office.

National Institute on Alcohol Abuse and Alcoholism. (1991). *Alcohol research: Promise for the decade.* Rockville, MD: Author.

National Institute on Drug Abuse. (1990). *National household survey on drug abuse.* Rockville, MD: Author.

Normand, J., Salyards, S. D., & Mahoney, J. J. (1990). An evaluation of preemployment drug testing. *Journal of Applied Psychology, 75*, 629–639.

Open Minds. (1992). *Industry statistics: Behavioral health industry compensation varies widely by occupation, 5*(6).

Penzer, W. N. (1987). Toward sustaining quality mental health services. *EAP Digest*, March/April, 35–40.

Plescia-Pikus, M., Long-Sutter, E., & Wilson, J. P. (1988). Achievement, well-being, intelligence, and stress reaction in adult children of alcoholics. *Psychological Reports, 62*, 603-609.

Pope, T. (1990). An eye on EAPs. *Security Management, 34*, 81-83.

Ray, O. & Ksir, C. (1990). *Drugs, society, and human behavior.* Boston: Times Mirror/Mosby.

Reichman, W., Young, D. W., & Gracin, L. (1988). Identification of alcoholics in the workplace. In M. Galanter (Ed.), *Recent developments in alcoholism* (Vol. 6, pp. 177-179). New York: Plenum.

Ritchie, M. H. (1986). Counseling and the involuntary client. *Journal of Counseling and Development, 64,* 516–518.

Roman, P. M. (1976). *The promise and problems of employee assistance programs in higher education.* Paper presented at the Conference on Employee Assistance Programs in Higher Education, Columbia, MO.

Roman, P. M. (1979). The emphasis on alcoholism in employee assistance programs: New perspectives on an unfinished debate. *Labor Management Journal on Alcoholism, 9,* 186-191.

Roman, P. M. (1988). Growth and transformation in workplace alcoholism programming. In M. Galanter (Ed.), *Recent developments in alcoholism* (Vol. 6, pp. 131-158). New York: Plenum.

Roman, P. M., & Blum, T. C. (1988). The core technology of employee assistance programs: A reaffirmation. *The ALMACAN, 18,* 17-22.

Roman, P. M., & Blum, T. C. (1992). Drugs, the workplace, and employee-oriented programming. In D. R. Gerstein & H. J. Harwoods (Eds.), *Treating drug problems* (Vol. II, pp. 197-244). Washington, DC: National Academy Press.

Russell, M., Henderson, C., & Blum, S. (1985). *Children of alcoholics: A review of the literature.* Buffalo, NY: State Division of Alcoholism and Alcohol Abuse, Research Institute of Alcoholism.

Schneider, R., Colan, N. & Googins, B. (1990). Supervisor training in employee assistance programs: Current practices and future directions. *Employee Assistance Quarterly, 6*(2), 41-55.

Selzer, M. (1971). Michigan Alcoholism Screening Test (MAST): The quest for a new diagnostic instrument. *American Journal of Psychiatry, 127,* 1653.

Sheridan, J. R., & Winkler, H. (1989). An evaluation of drug testing in the workplace. In S. W. Gust, & J. M. Walsh (Eds.), *Drugs in the workplace: Research and evaluation data* (NIDA Research Monograph No. 91). Rockville, MD: National Institute on Drug Abuse.

Sheridan, M. J. (1995). A psychometric assessment of the children of alcoholics screening test (CAST). *Journal of Studies on Alcohol, 56*(2), 156-160.

Sipkoff, M. Z. (1995). External EAPs less expensive than internal EAPs. *Open Minds fax reports*. Gettysburg, PA: Open Minds.

Solomon, S. (1983). Women in the workplace: An overview of NIAAA's occupational alcoholism demonstration project. *Alcohol Health and Research World, 7,* 305–310.

Sonnesnstuhl, W. J. (1990). The process of assisting alcoholics in the workplace differs from other troubled employees. *Exchange, 20,* 18–24.

Standards for employee alcoholism and/or assistance programs. (1983). *EAP Digest*, May/June, 42–43.

Starch, R. (1995). *The impact of behavioral health care on productivity: A look at employer and employee attitudes.* Los Angeles: Managed Health Network, Inc.

Steele, P. (1988). Substance abuse and the workplace, with special attention to employee assistance programs: An overview. *The Journal of Applied Behavioral Science, 24,* 315-325.

Steinglass, P., Bennett, L. A., Wolin, S. J., & Reiss, D. (1987). *The alcoholic family.* New York: Basic Books.

Straussner, L. A. (1985). The nature and growth of contractual EAPs. *The ALMACAN, 15,* 20–23.

Svanum, S., & McAdoo, W. G. (1991). Parental alcoholism: Examination of male and female alcoholics in treatment. *Journal of Studies on Alcohol, 52,* 127-132.

Thomas, J. C., & Johnson, N. P. (1992). Family alcohol problems of employee assistance program populations. *Employee Assistance Quarterly, 8(2),* 1–13.

Thomas, J. C., & Johnson, N. P. (1993). The interface of parental and personal alcohol problems in employee assistance program populations. *Employee Assistance Quarterly, 8(3),* 43–63.

Trice, H. M., & Beyer, J. M. (1984). Work-related outcomes of the constructive confrontation strategy in a job-based alcoholism program. *Journal of Studies on Alcohol, 45,* 393-404.

Trice, H. M., & Schonbrunn, M. (1981). A history of job-based alcoholism programs: 1900-1955. *Journal of Drug Issues, 11*, 171-198.

Trice, H. M., & Sonnenstuhl, W. (1988). Drinking behavior and risk factors related to the workplace: Implications for research and prevention. *Journal of Applied Behavior Science, 24*(4), 327-346.

Trice, H. M., & Sonnenstuhl, W. (1990). On the construction of drinking norms in work organizations. *Journal of Studies on Alcohol, 51*(3), 201-220.

U.S. Department of Health and Human Services. (1987). *Sixth special report to the U.S. Congress on alcohol and health.* Rockville, MD: Author.

U.S. Department of Labor. (1990). *What works: Workplaces without drugs.* Rockville, MD: Author.

U.S. Department of Labor, Small Business Administration, and the Office of National Drug Control Policy. (1992). *Working partners: Confronting substance abuse in small business.* Rockville, MD: Author.

Walsh J., Burmaster, D., Gray M., & Daniels, M. (1990). Alcohol and drug abuse in the workplace. *Proceedings of a National Conference on Preventing Alcohol and Drug Abuse in Black Communities, 5*(2-4), 126-132.

West, L. J. (Ed.). (1984). *Alcoholism and related problems: Issues for the American public.* Englewood Cliffs, NJ: Prentice-Hall.

William M. Mercer, Inc. (1995). William M. Mercer's fax facts survey results: EAPs. Philadelphia: Author.

Wrich, J. T. (1982). *Guidelines for developing an employee assistance program.* Center City, MN: Hazelden.

Yankrick, R. (1992). Taking inventory. *The EAP Association Exchange, 22*(7), 22-29.

Zwerling, C., Ryan, J., & Orav, E. J. (1990). The efficacy of preemployment drug screening for marijuana and cocaine in predicting employment outcome. *Journal of the American Medical Association, 264*, 2639-2643.

2

Substance Abuse and Disability

Elizabeth de Silva Cardoso, MEd, Fong Chan, PhD, Kenneth R. Thomas, EdD, Gwen Roldan, PhD, and Kirby Ingraham, MSW.

For a list of authors' affiliations, see page 91

KEY POINTS

- Alcohol and drug abuse is prevalent in persons with traumatic brain injuries and spinal cord injuries.

- Substance abuse both contributes to an increased incidence of disability and undermines rehabilitation gain.

- Alcohol and drug abuse problems in persons with other disabilities frequently go unrecognized. Rehabilitation professionals often are not trained adequately to work with substance abuse issues.

- The most commonly abused substances by rehabilitation clients are hallucinogens, opioids and opiates, cocaine, sedatives, amphetamines, and volatile solvents-inhalants.

- The DSM-IV criteria used to assess substance use are presented.

- Substance abuse assessment and treatment programs discussed in this chapter include the disease model, relapse prevention model, and biopsychosocial model.

- Professionals should be aware of the clinical signs of substance abuse, the kinds of medical examinations that can be used, psychometric instruments that may help identify substance abuse problems early in the rehabilitation process, and current trends in assessment and treatment.

- The substance abuse treatment field is beginning to focus on person-centered individualized treatment as well as the 12-step approach developed by Alcoholics Anonymous.

INTRODUCTION

The prevalence of alcohol and drug abuse among persons with other disabilities (e.g., traumatic brain injuries and spinal cord injuries) is becoming a salient issue in rehabilitation (Brismar, Engstrom, & Rydberg, 1983; Ingraham, Kaplan, & Chan, 1992; Lowenfels & Miller, 1984; National Institute on Disability and Rehabilitation Research, 1990; O'Donnel, Cooper, Cessner, Shehan, & Ashely, 1981-1982). Increased awareness of alcohol and drug abuse problems in rehabilitation stems from research showing that substance abuse not only contributes to an increased incidence of disability, it also undermines rehabilitation gain. The role of alcohol and other drugs in traumatic brain injury, for instance, is well documented, with an incidence of intoxication at injury of approximately 50% (Chan et al., 1995). According to Yarkony (1993), approximately 250,000 patients in the United States have a spinal cord injury. The majority of those injuries occur in men (82%), and the average age of onset is approximately 28 years old. In many cases, substances are used when persons sustain spinal cord injuries (Yarkony, 1993). Heinemann (1986) cited studies reporting intoxication at the time of spinal cord injury to be as high as 68% and suggested that impaired judgment because of substance use is related to an increase in risk-taking behavior and injury. However, other studies reported a more conservative range of 17% to 49% (Heinemann, Doll, & Schnoll, 1989).

Alcohol and drug abuse also limits rehabilitation outcome by contributing to functional limitations (Greer, 1986, 1989; National Institute on Disability and Rehabilitation Research, 1990). Indirect and direct self-destructive behaviors associated with alcohol and drug abuse, such as refusal of essential treatment and other forms of self-neglect, may continue after the onset of disability and adversely affect the potential for rehabilitation (Ingraham et al., 1992). A follow-up study by Burke, Wesolowski, and Gruth (1988) found that alcohol and other drug abuse is directly related to some community adjustment failures in patients with traumatic brain injuries.

It is logical to assume that alcohol and drug abuse will have an adverse effect on vocational rehabilitation outcomes because clients with substance abuse problems have a higher frequency of vocational adjustment difficulties. Alcohol abuse also is known to significantly compromise work performance. The National Institute on Alcohol Abuse and Alcoholism (1982) reported that workers with alcohol problems show much higher rates of absenteeism, accidents, time off for illness, and workers compensation claims than workers without alcohol problems. Similarly, a recent Texas Employment Commission (1990) report indicated that drug abusers were: "late for work 3 times more often than nonabusers; absent 2.5 times more often; one-third less productive; 3.6 times more likely to be involved in an accident; and 10 times more likely to be involved in job-related death."

Ingraham and associates (1992) examined the extent of alcohol abuse among persons with other disabilities by administering the *Michigan Alcoholism Screening Test* to 134 rehabilitation clients. They found that clients with chronic mental illness and clients with limitations resulting from physical trauma had an appreciably higher rate of alcohol abuse than other identified client groups (e.g., clients with congenital and developmental disabilities). Subsequently, they asked 40 rehabilitation counselors to estimate probable abuse rates for these client groups and found that the counselors slightly overestimated the alcohol abuse problems among clients with congenital and developmental disabilities and significantly underestimated the prevalence of alcohol abuse among clients with physically induced trauma or chronic mental illness.

Ingraham and co-workers (1992) concluded that rehabilitation counselors lack sophistication concerning the dual problems of alcohol abuse and disability, concurring with Heinemann (1986), who stated that rehabilitation professionals' lack of awareness may be because of unfamiliarity with and inadequate training in issues of alcohol abuse and disability. Heinemann (1986) argued that rehabilitation professionals must be trained to recognize substance abuse problems and to intervene in a timely and effective manner. Heinemann (1986) concluded that "early identification of persons with spinal cord injuries who abuse or are addicted to substances should minimize the incidence of secondary complications of spinal cord injuries, decrease the cost of rehabilitation, and improve rehabilitation outcome."

Unfortunately, according to a recent report (National Institute on Disability and Rehabilitation Research, 1990), alcohol and drug abuse problems experienced by persons with other disabilities frequently go unrecognized; moreover, rehabilitation professionals often are not trained adequately to work with alcohol and drug abuse issues. Accordingly, this "primer" clarifies the terms used to designate different levels of use, sets out the criteria used to assess use levels, and lists the most abused substances before discussing the conceptual models for, assessment of, and treatments applied to substance abuse disorders. Lastly, factors and difficulties in assessing and treating brain and spinal cord injury clients are explicated.

SUBSTANCE-RELATED DISORDERS: TERMS AND LEVELS OF USE

In the fourth edition of the *Diagnostic and Statistical Manual of Mental Disorders* (DSM-IV) (American Psychiatric Association [APA], 1994), alcohol and other drug use disorders are defined under the umbrella term *substance-related disorders*. Specifically, substance-related disorders include disorders related to the actual abuse of alcohol and drugs, to the side effects of medication, and to deliberate exposure to toxic substances. The DSM-IV classifications provide the best means for conceptualizing and defining substance abuse problems. Substances discussed are grouped into 11 classes: alcohol; amphetamine or similarly acting sympathomimetic agents; caffeine; cannabis; cocaine; hallucinogens; inhalants; nicotine; opioids; phencyclidine (PCP; "angel dust") or similarly acting arylcyclohexylamines; and sedatives, hypnotic drugs, or anxiolytic agents (APA, 1994). Alcohol shares similar features with the sedatives, hypnotic, and anxiolytic agents, and cocaine shares features with amphetamines or similarly acting sympathomimetic agents. The term *polysubstance dependence and other or unknown substance-related disorders* is used to include most disorders related to medications or toxins.

The current literature addressing the use of alcohol and other drugs contains rampant inconsistencies in the use and definitions of terms such as *substance, chemical, drug, abuse, dependence, addiction, problem drinker,* and *alcoholism.* Professionals in the field do not always distinguish between these different terms and often use them interchangeably. Though levels of substance abuse occur along a continuum, it is useful to name and define them separately.

In the substance abuse field, three levels of substance involvement are commonly identified: *use, abuse,* and *dependence.* Substance use can be experimental or casual, with the person demonstrating successful control over the occasional use. Substance abuse is the maladaptive use of a substance (i.e., excessive use, compulsion to use, and continuation of use) in spite of negative consequences to self, others, or property. Substance dependence is the compulsive use of substances, with increased amounts of the substance required to achieve the desired effect despite negative consequences to one's life (Harrington, 1994).

In the DSM-IV (APA, 1994), substance-related disorders also are divided into two groups: *substance use disorders* (substance dependence [Table 2.1] and substance abuse [Table 2.2]) and *substance-induced disorders* (substance intoxication [Table 2.3] and substance withdrawal [Table 2.4]).

The criteria set for substance dependence, abuse, intoxication, and withdrawal are applicable across the 11 classes of substances. For example, when substituting the term *alcohol* for the term *substance,* the diagnostic criteria for the generic substance-related disorder will become the criteria for diagnosing alcohol-related disorders. Correspondingly, alcohol-related disorders can be divided into two groups: *alcohol use*

Table 2.1
DSM-IV CRITERIA FOR SUBSTANCE DEPENDENCE

A maladaptive pattern of substance use leading to clinically significant impairment or distress as manifested by three (or more) of the following occurring at any time in the same 12-month period:

1. *Tolerance,* as defined by either of the following:

    (a) a need for markedly increased amounts of the substance to achieve intoxication or desired effect *or*

    (b) a markedly diminished effect with continued use of the same amount of the substance

2. *Withdrawal,* as manifested by either of the following:

    (a) the characteristic withdrawal syndrome for the substance *or*

    (b) the same or closely related substance is taken to relieve or avoid withdrawal symptoms

3. The substance often is taken in larger amounts or over a longer period than was intended

4. There is a persistent desire or unsuccessful efforts to cut down or control the use of the substance

5. A great deal of time is spent in activities necessary to obtain the substance (e.g., visiting multiple doctors or driving long distances), use the substance (e.g., chain-smoking), or recover from its effects

6. Important social, occupational, or recreational activities are given up or reduced because of substance use

7. The substance use is continued despite knowledge of having a persistent or recurrent physical or psychological problem that is likely to have been caused or exacerbated by the substance (e.g., current cocaine use despite recognition of cocaine-induced depression or continued drinking despite recognition that an ulcer was made worse by alcohol consumption)

Specific if:

With Physiological Dependence: evidence of tolerance or
        withdrawal
Without Physiological Dependence: no evidence of tolerance or
        withdrawal

Course specifiers:

Early Full Remission
Early Partial Remission
Sustained Full Remission
Sustained Partial Remission
On Agonist Therapy
In a Controlled Environment

Source: American Psychiatric Association. (1994). *Diagnostic and
statistical manual of mental disorders* (4th ed.). Washington, DC: Author.
Reprinted with permission from the American Psychiatric Association.

---

disorders (alcohol dependence and alcohol abuse) and *alcohol-
induced disorders* (alcohol intoxication and alcohol withdrawal).

MOST COMMONLY ABUSED SUBSTANCES

Stude (1993) indicated that other than alcohol, substances
most commonly abused by rehabilitation clients are: hallucinogens, opioids and opiates, cocaine, sedatives, amphetamines,
and volatile solvents-inhalants.

Hallucinogens:

According to Stude, lysergic acid diethylamide (LSD) and
PCP are the most commonly used hallucinogens; they produce
perceptual and cognitive changes, including delusions, hallucinations, and psychoses. LSD is usually taken orally and
produces an effect in 30 to 40 minutes. It can cause visual
alterations in shapes and colors and physical symptoms such

Table 2.2
DSM-IV Criteria for Substance Abuse

A. A maladaptive pattern of substance use leading to clinically significant impairment or distress as manifested by one (or more) of the following occurring within a 12-month period:

   1. Recurrent substance use resulting in a failure to fulfill major role obligations at work, school, or home (e.g., repeated absences or poor work performance related to substance use; substance-related absences, suspensions, or expulsions from school, neglect of children or household)

   2. Recurrent substance use in situations in which it is physically hazardous (e.g., operating machines when impaired by substance use)

   3. Recurrent substance-related legal problems (e.g., arrests for substance-related disorderly conduct) *or*

   4. Continued substance use despite having persistent or recurrent social or interpersonal problems caused or exacerbated by the effects of the substance (e.g., arguments with spouse about consequences of intoxication or physical fights)

B. The symptoms have never met the criteria for substance dependence for this class of substance.

Source: American Psychiatric Association. (1994). *Diagnostic and statistical manual of mental disorders* (4th ed.). Washington, DC: Author. Reprinted with permission from the American Psychiatric Association.

as dizziness, weakness, tremors, nausea, and drowsiness. (For more information on LSD, see Gold, 1996.) PCP is injected or sprinkled onto smoking material, such as tobacco or marijuana. The neurologic effects of PCP include ataxia, tremors, muscular hypertonicity, and hyperflexion. PCP also can el-

---

Table 2.3
DSM-IV CRITERIA FOR SUBSTANCE INTOXICATION

A. The development of a reversible substance-specific syndrome due to recent ingestion of (or exposure to) a substance (Note: Different substances may produce similar or identical syndromes)

B. Clinically significant maladaptive behavioral or psychological changes that are due to the effect of the substance on the central nervous system (e.g., belligerence, mood lability, cognitive impairment, impaired judgement and impaired social or occupational functioning) and that develop during or shortly after use of the substance

C. The symptoms are not due to a general medical condition and are not better accounted for by another medical disorder

---

Source: American Psychiatric Association. (1994). *Diagnostic and statistical manual of mental disorders* (4th ed.). Washington, DC: Author. Reprinted with permission from the American Psychiatric Association.

---

evate the systolic and diastolic blood pressures. At higher dose levels, it can cause muscle twitching or spasm, continuous seizures, coma, psychosis, and even heart failure (Stude, 1993).

Opioids And Opiates:

Opiates are naturally occurring products derived from the opium poppy and include morphine, codeine, and thebaine. Opioids, which are entirely synthetic, include methadone hydrochloride. Both the opiates and opioids share morphine-like pharmacologic properties. They usually are taken through intravenous injection. All opioids and opiates have the effect of relieving pain, insomnia, anxiety, cough, and diarrhea; a negative effect of opioids and opiate at large dose levels is

Table 2.4
DSM-IV Criteria for Substance Withdrawal

A. The development of substance-specific syndrome because of the cessation of (or reduction in) substance use that has been heavy and prolonged

B. The substance-specific syndrome causes clinically significant distress or impairment in social, occupational, or other important areas of functioning

C. The symptoms are not due to a general medical condition and are not better accounted for by another mental disorder

Source: American Psychiatric Association. (1994). *Diagnostic and statistical manual of mental disorders* (4th ed.). Washington, DC: Author. Reprinted with permission from the American Psychiatric Association.

respiratory depression. Persons who use opioids and/or opiates will develop tolerance immediately; however, the lethal dose level does not change. When a person with an opioid and/or opiate dependence stops taking the drug, withdrawal symptoms may occur within 4 to 24 hours and worsen within 24 to 72 hours, with acute symptoms ending within 4 to 10 days (Stude, 1993).

Cocaine:

Cocaine is extracted from the cocoa leaf as an active alkaloid and is consumed by snorting. Recently, "crack" cocaine has become popular. Cocaine produces an immediate, intense feeling of euphoria; however, its effects are brief, usually lasting for only a few minutes. Side effects of large doses include agitation, insomnia, loss of appetite, convulsions, and paranoia. Chronic use of cocaine may produce negative physical symptoms, including constriction of blood vessels, degeneration of the nasal septum, pulmonary dysfunction, blood pressure problems, and a variety of infections. Persons who use crack cocaine may experience severe depression and suicidal ideation after cessation of use (Stude, 1993).

Sedatives:

Sedatives include mostly alcohol, barbiturates, benzodiazepines (Librium, Valium, Xanex), and glutethimide (Doriden). These drugs tend to reduce anxiety and induce sleep. The major psychological effects of this class of drugs are to inhibit or impair transmission of nervous impulses and to increase the onset and duration of sleep. Suppression of rapid eye movement sleep often results in excessive dreaming, with occasional vivid nightmares. The therapeutic effects of sedatives usually are short; tolerance can develop with a single dose. Chronic users need continually larger doses to achieve the desired effect. Withdrawal symptoms include delirium tremens, convulsions, tachycardia, hallucinations, and delusions (Stude, 1993).

Amphetamines:

Amphetamines may be taken orally or injected intravenously. Their effect on the central nervous system often results in increased blood pressure. Larger doses result in increased heart rate and irregular heart beat. Behaviorally, amphetamines result in increased alertness, elevated mood accompanied by increased self-confidence, and psychomotor hyperactivity, which lead to an inability to rest or sleep. Two types of psychoses may result from amphetamine use: toxic psychosis, which usually improves within a few days of termination of drug use, and psychosis with schizophreniform, affective, or paranoid features, which may persist even for weeks (Stude, 1993).

Volatile Solvents-Inhalants:

When inhaled as gases or vapors, several substances found

around the home and the workplace (e.g., benzene from coal, petroleum, hydrocarbons and chloroform, found in cleaning solvents and degreasers) may result in substance intoxication. The effects of these solvents and inhalants are similar to alcohol in terms of their intoxication and result in depression of the central nervous system. Severe systemic changes may occur (e.g., cardiac arrhythmias, chronic nervous system damage, hypertension, dizziness, and tachycardia). Many of these substances also lessen a person's sexual inhibition (Stude, 1993).

CONCEPTUAL MODELS OF SUBSTANCE-RELATED DISORDERS

Most substance abuse assessment and treatment programs in this country tend to follow the disease model often treated with the 12-step principles developed by Alcoholics Anonymous (AA) (Barbor, 1993; Chiauzzi, 1991; Marlatt & Gordon, 1985; Miller & Hester, 1989). However, other models (e.g., the moral model, the self-medication model, the relapse prevention model, and the biopsychosocial model) are discussed in the literature. In this chapter, we will limit our discussion to the disease, relapse prevention, and biopsychosocial models.

The Disease Model:

In the disease model, biologic and genetic predispositions are thought to cause substance-related disorders. Persons who are labeled "alcoholics" or "addicts" are considered qualitatively different from moderate users. This model views substance-related disorders as progressive, irreversible diseases that ultimately result in death if left untreated. Abstinence is the primary goal of treatment, and clients are cautioned to maintain vigilance against relapse. Recovery is considered never ending.

Several implications of this model may be problematic in treating relapse. First, the disease model focuses primarily on biologic factors, even though the preponderance of relapse precipitants are psychological and social (Chiauzzi, 1991; Marlatt, 1985). Second, there is a paradox involving self-control in the disease model: the client diagnosed with a substance-related disorder is unable to exert control over the use of psychoactive substances, but he or she is told that the only way to curb the problem is to refrain from using psychoactive substances and to maintain total abstinence for an indefinite period (Marlatt, 1985). Third, the disease model implies that the provider and the client have an inherently unequal relationship; the client is placed in a submissive position waiting for treatment. Fourth, the belief that one has a disease may be interpreted as a total waiver of responsibility if a relapse occurs. Fifth, the belief in loss of control may result in a self-fulfilling prophecy in which a client diagnosed with a substance-related disorder may use the loss of control concept as an excuse to continue using psychoactive substances.

The Relapse Prevention Model:

The relapse prevention model views addictive behavior as an acquired habit that can be modified or eliminated by applying the laws of learning theory; therefore, the client also is considered capable of self-control. In this view, addictions develop from a combination of classic conditioning (e.g., morning drinking to combat withdrawal) and operant conditioning (e.g., improved social functioning when drinking). Recovery is seen as a learning task for which the client diagnosed with alcohol dependence or another substance-related disorder takes responsibility. There is a deemphasis on the "alcoholic" and "addict" labels.

The process of change occurs in three steps. The first step is to *commit to change* rather than making impulsive decisions; long-term "maintainers" exhibit a readiness for and understanding of the implications for change. The second step is to *implement change;* this step may involve treatment and/or self-change. The third step, in which relapse prevention skills are paramount, is *maintenance.* This is not only the longest and most challenging step; it involves the most trials and errors. During this stage, recovery includes the incremental learning and refinement of coping skills (Miller & Hester, 1989).

Cummings, Gordon, and Marlatt (1980) compared clients diagnosed with alcohol dependence, heroin dependence, nicotine dependence, and gambling and overeating disorders. They found remarkable consistency in major relapse episodes and evaluated a number of high-risk situations that encompassed emotional, social, and psychological factors. Negative emotional states, social pressures, and interpersonal conflicts were found to be related to relapse.

There are several cognitive factors that mediate a person's ability to cope with high-risk situations. Bandura (1977) believes that self-efficacy, or a person's perception that he or she can cope with a prospective high-risk situation, determines the nature and power of coping behavior in response to a threat. Another factor is outcome expectancy, which refers to a person's perception of the effects of his or her behavior. Expectancies are affected by social and cultural beliefs, self-esteem, and environmental factors. If a person has low expectancies, he or she is at high risk of relapse because the person does not expect to be effective.

Barbor's General Model:

Barbor (1993) recently proposed a general biopsychosocial framework for conceptualizing substance-related disorders in which risks, harmful consequences, and dependence are separate but potentially interrelated diagnostic categories. According to Barbor's model, the differential risks of experiencing the adverse effects of substance abuse can be divided into two components: vulnerability and exposure.

Some people are more vulnerable than others to developing substance abuse problems based on their physiologic, psychologic, and social traits. For example, Hesselbrock, Stabenau, Hesselbrock, Meyer, and Barbor (1982) reported that persons with attention deficit disorder, childhood conduct disorder, and a family history of substance abuse problems are most likely to develop problems related to substance abuse.

Social antecedents also may be considered vulnerability factors. Exposure to substances is a major risk factor. Because frequent consumption of large amounts of alcohol or other psychoactive substances is a general prerequisite to addiction, persons who belong to cultural groups in which high intake of these substances is the norm are more vulnerable to develop substance-related disorders. For example, socially learned drinking customs, such as those commonly found on university campuses, may cause large segments of a target population (e.g., college students) to drink excessively in response to social pressures. Exposure can be measured in terms of quantity per occasion, frequency of use, and variability of consumption.

However, risk behaviors are modified by many factors, such as how fast an alcoholic beverage is consumed, the purity of the substances, the direction of change in the blood-alcohol concentration curve, the presence or absence of other drugs in the body, the amount of food the person ate, and the social context of the drug use or drinking occasion (Barbor, 1993). Dependence can be influenced by the risk factors, modifying variables, and harmful consequences of substance use.

SUBSTANCE ABUSE ASSESSMENT

The key to treating rehabilitation clients with coexisting substance-related disorders is to identify, recognize, and treat substance-related problems as early as possible. Traditionally, substance abuse assessment procedures have been directed toward a binary diagnosis: either you *are* a substance abuser or you *are not* (Budziack, 1993). The focus is to identify common signs and symptoms of disease and use these characteristics to confirm a diagnosis. Only after establishing a diagnosis are related factors such as gender, ethnicity, and circumstances of the client considered in formulating a treatment plan (Blume, 1983). However, Budziack (1993) strongly advocated for substance abuse assessments to move from a binary diagnostic labeling to a multidimensional functional assessment.

A comprehensive assessment should not only address alcohol and other drug use and problems in areas of life that are caused by and contribute to substance abuse; it should also focus on differences among persons who abuse drugs and how these differences can be used to develop individualized and prescriptive treatment plans. The most valuable plan will have clear implications for differential treatment and will explicitly point out the links between the situation and characteristics of the client and specific treatment recommendations (Graeber, Gardner, Chan, & Wang, 1995).

To detect potential substance abuse problems among clients with other disabilities, rehabilitation counselors should be aware of some of the clinical signs of substance abuse, the kinds of medical examinations that can be used, and psychometric instruments that may help to identify substance abuse problems early in the rehabilitation process.

Clinical Signs:

Rehabilitation counselors are advised to look for clinical signs of intoxification or other substance-related symptoms, such as slurred speech, bloodshot eyes, lack of coordination, memory lapse, and the smell of alcohol. Disruptions in a client's regular routine or fluctuations in mood states also may be indicative of problematic substance use. These include: keeping irregular hours, employment difficulties, unusual financial problems, frequent mood changes, family conflict, legal problems, submissive or remorseful feelings for engaging in inappropriate behavior, changes in friends and/or leisure activities, missing/losing valuable items (e.g., jewelry), and failure to keep appointments. When substance abuse is suspected, rehabilitation counselors should inquire about clients' substance use patterns, family history, friends/social life, lifestyle, employment history, legal problems, and health problems.

Medical Examinations:

In addition to direct questioning, physical methods for detecting substance abuse include blood analysis to indicate signs of chronic use, breath analysis to detect alcohol use within 24 hours, and urinalysis to detect alcohol and other drugs. Laboratory examinations are important considering the high rates of polysubstance use among persons with disabilities, especially among persons with mental illness and substance-related disorders.

Psychometric Instruments:

Psychometric instruments have been developed to detect substance abuse problems. Two of the most commonly used instruments in the field are the *Michigan Alcoholism Screening Test* (MAST) and the *MacAndrew Alcoholism-Revised Scale* (MAC-R) (Ingraham et al., 1992).

The MAST is one of the most well-known screening devices to detect alcohol use. It consists of 25 yes/no questions focusing on areas such as physical symptoms associated with alcohol dependence, marital problems resulting from drinking, hospitalization related to drinking, legal problems, and psychological problems. For each "yes" response, a numerical value ranging from 0 to 5 is assigned to the item, depending on the severity of the problem. In general, a 4-point score suggests the client may have an alcohol abuse problem, and a total score of 5 or above places the client in an "alcoholic" category (Selzer, 1971). However, practitioners in the field traditionally have used slightly higher cutoff scores than those suggested by the MAST. Ingraham and associates (1992) suggested the use of 4 and below as suggestive of no problem, a score of 5 to 7 as suggestive of a potential problem, and 8 or higher as suggestive of alcoholism.

It has been reported that the MAST measures "self-identified" alcohol-dependent clients. However, there are difficulties with persons who do not admit to problem drinking or who exaggerate alcohol problems to gain attention (Graeber et al., 1995). The MAST has been used in general military hospitals, with clients who are hospitalized for alcohol dependence, for psychiatric clients, and with social drinkers. It has been found to have high levels of discriminative validity (0.90) and reliability (0.95) (Selzer, 1971).

The *MacAndrew Alcoholism Scale* (MAC) was developed originally by contrasting the Minnesota Multiphase Personality Inventory (MMPI) responses between 200 men suffering from alcoholism and 200 nonalcoholic men in a psychiatric facility (Graham, 1990). For differentiating between the two groups (the MAC-R is the MMPI-2 version of the MAC), 49 items were found to be useful. The MMPI-2 eliminated 4 of the original MAC items and replaced them with 4 new items. According to Graham (1990), a MAC-R raw score of 28 or above indicates a strong possibility of substance abuse, scores of 24 to 27 are somewhat suggestive of substance use, and a score of 23 or less strongly contraindicates substance abuse. False-positive results are common among clients with an extroverted activity-oriented style and among Black Americans. The internal consistency of the MAC-R is not particularly impressive (0.56 for men and 0.45 for women) (Graham, 1990). The test-retest reliability of the MAC-R is modest (0.62 and 0.78 respectively for subsamples of men and women in the MMPI-2 normative samples) (Graham, 1990). In general, the MAC and MAC-R were useful in distinguishing persons addicted to alcohol from those who are not. Persons addicted to drugs and persons addicted to gambling scored similarly to persons addicted to alcoholism on the MAC.

SUBSTANCE ABUSE TREATMENT

There are three types of treatment intervention: cognitive remediation, skill building, and lifestyle modification. Cognitive remediation includes positive self-statements, enhancement of outcome expectancy and self-efficacy, coping imagery, self-talk, and distraction. Skill building includes role-playing, self-monitoring, refusal skills, and relapse rehearsal. Lifestyle modification includes exercise, relaxation techniques, and effective time management.

Treatment Programs:

Effective substance use disorder treatment programs for clients with disabilities should incorporate a team approach that focuses on the overall needs of individual clients. Both inpatient and outpatient treatment programs should be accessible; include detoxification facilities; and incorporate education regarding substances, disability issues, and the interactive effects of the substances with specific disabilities. The educational component should employ audiocassettes, as well as visual and tactile aids such as pictures and checklists that are available in braille. Treatment programs also should offer a range of modalities, including individual, family, couples, and group therapy.

Inpatient Treatment Programs

Most traditional treatment programs promote 28-day inpatient treatment. This type of treatment is program driven; each day is programmed with a set of predetermined group activities from early morning through the evening. It almost invariably follows a strict 12-step orientation (Budziack, 1993).

Intensive Outpatient Treatment Programs

Intensive outpatient programs typically involve 4 to 6 hours of treatment activities per day for 5 to 6 days per week for 3 to 6 weeks. These programs also usually are program driven and use abbreviated versions of the treatment schedules followed in 28-day inpatient programs.

Therapeutic Communities

The philosophy of therapeutic communities is based on a

social learning approach to prevention that emphasizes skills training, self-help orientation stressing client responsibility, and the principles of the therapeutic community such as credible role models and community building (Wexler, Magura, Beardsley, & Josepher, 1994). Cognitive-behavioral training is applied to self-help groups in a therapeutic community drug treatment program. Examples of the behavioral skills training include overcoming social anxieties, dealing with nonverbal experience, and anger management (Egelko & Galanter, 1993). The self-help concept is formed by using the collective resources of members to mobilize peer pressure. Therapeutic communities foster a sense of safety, structure, and a supportive environment. They also foster confrontation among clients, teaching by using reality therapy for reasoning approaches, and existential thought (Bratter, Bratter, Radda, & Steiner, 1993).

Halfway Houses

Halfway houses are used to integrate clients into the social environment on the basis of outpatient monitoring and create specific preconditions for restoration and social status. This type of setting usually is used for clients in transition from a hospital to society. Halfway houses consist of two types: highly structured or minimally structured treatment regiment (Pekarik & Zimmer, 1992).

Self-Help Groups

The structure of substance abuse treatment programs in this country is dominated by the disease model concept often treated with the 12-step principles of recovery, which come from AA. To initiate recovery, AA members believe that a person must:

> Step 1: Admit that he or she is powerless over alcohol and that his or her life has become unmanageable.

Step 2: Believe that a power greater than oneself can restore him or her to sanity.

Step 3: Decide to turn his or her will and life over to the care of God.

Step 4: Make a searching and fearless inventory of oneself.

Step 5: Admit to God, to oneself, and to another human being the exact nature of one's wrongs.

Step 6: Be entirely ready to have God remove all defects of character.

Step 7: Humbly ask God to remove his or her shortcomings.

Step 8: Make a list of all persons he or she has harmed and be willing to make amends to them.

Step 9: Make direct amends to such people wherever possible, except when to do so would injure them or others.

Step 10: Continue to take personal inventory and, when wrong, promptly admit it.

Step 11: Through prayer and meditation, seek to improve one's conscious contact with God.

Step 12: Have a spiritual awakening as a result of these steps, try to carry this message to other alcoholics, and practice these principles in all affairs.

The success of AA has fostered other self-help groups, most based on the 12-step program, including Narcotic Anonymous, Cocaine Anonymous, and Rational Recovery. The facilitator of a self-help group should be informed about the issues surrounding the specific disability and what can be expected from the client. The facilitator also should be able to assess clients who are likely to benefit from the 12-step approach (Budziack, 1993).

Programs for Families

Family members affected by addictions often need a chance to begin to grow, as well. The first step in this process is a period of exploration and experimentation to make up for lost experiences (Schlesinger & Horberg, 1993). The goal is to help family members define their problems concretely in terms that promote family action. Treatment can be conceptualized as a 5-step process: (a) identify family problems, (b) separate facts from opinions, (c) identify facts related to addiction, (d) identify feelings associated with these facts, and (e) identify family strengths (Schlesinger & Horberg, 1993). To aid families in their support of each other, treatment programs should offer or refer family members to Al-Anon, Alateen, and groups offering education regarding disability and substances.

When referring clients for substance abuse treatment, counselors should identify programs that are willing and able to provide individualized treatment (Budziack, 1993), and they should work closely with substance abuse treatment providers to meet the needs of clients with disabilities.

CURRENT TRENDS IN ASSESSMENT AND TREATMENT

The substance abuse treatment field is beginning to shift away from dogmatic approaches to traditional assessment and treatment. Based on results of rigorous research (Budziack, 1993), the assumption that persons with alcohol and substance-related problems form a homogeneous group who have a unitary disease caused solely by a genetic defect is increasingly questioned.

The traditional approach of using the disease model and the 12-step principles developed by AA, which requires clients to follow a prescribed sequence of activities and to experience a spiritual reawakening to initiate recovery, is thought to be too rigid (Budziack, 1993) and unyielding to accommodate the personal characteristics and treatment needs of the full range of substance abuse clients. Because of their religious overtone, these principles may create problems for some clients with substance use problems. Furthermore, the expectation of the 12-step principles (i.e., only *one* treatment approach is appropriate for *all* people with substance abuse problems) also may be problematic. Frequently, clients who found the traditional treatment program a mismatch for their needs were labeled as uncooperative and dropped from treatment. This dogmatic approach does not provide sufficient flexibility for matching treatment to clients' individual characteristics and needs.

Budziack (1993) contended that "despite claims of proven approaches, most traditional treatment procedures are based on clinicians' personal experiences and preferences rather than objective evidence from controlled research." He challenged the scientific base of the major assumptions of traditional substance treatment programs (e.g., the homogeneity assumption). For example, to justify the need for a universal core treatment, traditionalists frequently proclaimed that alcoholism is inherited (i.e., passed from parents with alcohol problems through a genetic vulnerability to alcohol) and that all persons with alcohol problems share a genetic flaw (Budziack, 1993). Landmark studies conducted by Goodwin (1988, 1993) are cited frequently as proof that genetic makeup is more important than psychosocial factors in determining vulnerability for drinking problems. Goodwin found that children of parents with alcohol problems were more likely to develop alcohol problems, even when raised by adopted parents. However, in a careful review of Goodwin's work, Budziack found that the interpretation of the data had been exaggerated. In fact, Goodwin (1988) was very cautious in presenting his findings and stated that his research "suggests that severe forms of alcohol abuse may have a genetic predisposition but that heavy drinking itself... reflects predominately nongenetic factors."

Additionally, the homogeneity assumption can be challenged further, based on recent psychological research. Evidence (DiClemente, 1991; Prochaska & DiClemente, 1992; Prochaska, DiClemente, & Norcross, 1992) suggests that people change problem behaviors along a 5-stage continuum (transtheoretical model): precontemplation, contemplation, preparation, action, and maintenance. They originally validated the stages-of-change concept with psychotherapy clients. They demonstrated that the use of differential treatments closely matched to a particular stage of change of a client were more effective than a nonmatching approach. This model also has been found to be applicable to patients with brain injuries and persons with addictive behaviors (e.g., smoking, drinking, and eating problems) (DiClemente, 1991; Prochaska & DiClemente, 1992; Prochaska et al., 1992).

As a result of additional research, substance abuse assessment is beginning to move from a binary (yes/no) diagnostic labeling of substance abuse to a multidimensional functional assessment, with a focus on both substance use and problems in other life areas that contribute to substance abuse. Likewise, the substance abuse treatment field is moving rapidly from the traditional dogmatic approach to a flexible, client-centered, individualized treatment plan. The pertinent question today seems to be: Which approach works best for whom under what conditions? The current research focus is on the development of empirically tested treatments to complement the traditional approach.

SUBSTANCE ABUSE AND BRAIN AND SPINAL CORD INJURIES

Despite the prevalence of alcohol and substance abuse problems among persons with brain and/or spinal cord injuries and their association with vocational rehabilitation failure and poor rehabilitation outcome, these problems often are not identified in the assessment, rehabilitation, development, or treatment implementation phases. Because of these factors, clients' uses of alcohol and other substances must be assessed and monitored throughout all phases of their rehabilitation.

Brain Injury:

A traumatic brain injury occurs every 15 seconds in the United States. More than 2 million brain injuries occur each year with 500,000 severe enough to require hospital admission (Chan, 1995). The incidence of intoxication at injury is approximately 50%.

Between 25% to 50% of patients with traumatic brain injury use alcohol and drugs in spite of the restrictions imposed by the type of medications they are prescribed or the type of care facility in which they reside (Chan, 1995). Frequently, patients with brain injury continue to use alcohol and other drugs because of a premorbid history of substance abuse. Other patients with brain injury begin to use alcohol or drugs as a way of coping with impairments, changes in their lives, or the emotions they are experiencing. Because of cognitive, behavioral, and functional deficits, survivors of brain injuries pose unique challenges to professionals in the field of substance abuse treatment.

Continued alcohol or drug use not only increases the risk of a second or third brain injury, alcohol use also complicates the injury and recovery. Typically, blood-alcohol levels at the time of injury are negatively correlated with the level of consciousness and positively correlated with the length of coma. In other words, the higher the blood-alcohol level, the lower the level of consciousness and the longer the coma. Lower levels of consciousness and longer coma durations are associated with poorer rehabilitation outcomes. Furthermore, patients who are intoxicated at the time of injury typically have longer hospital stays and rehabilitation phases.

The following four physiologic actions have been proposed

to negatively affect neurologic functioning and recovery from brain injury:

1. Alcohol in the body at the time of the injury leads to greater swelling of the brain, causing more severe cell damage.

2. Alcohol negatively affects blood clotting and makes capillaries increasingly fragile. During a brain injury, there is a greater chance of capillaries breaking, and more time is required for blood to clot.

3. Alcohol causes a reduction in blood pressure and a decrease in the body's tolerance of blood loss. Combined, these problems reduce the amount of oxygen sent to the brain. Lack of oxygen (hypoxia) can result in further destruction of brain cells.

4. Alcohol impairs a person's ability to fight off infection. Secondary infections can result in extensive damage to brain tissue.

Spinal Cord Injury:

Approximately 10,000 traumatic spinal cord injuries are reported to occur in the United States each year (Yarkony, 1993). These injuries are most commonly caused by motor vehicle accidents, sports (e.g., diving), violence (gun shots and knife wounds), and falls (Yarkony, 1993). The prevalence of substance use among patients with traumatic spinal cord injuries is alarmingly high (Heinemann, 1986; Heinemann et al., 1989).

Heinemann (1986) cautioned rehabilitation professionals to be vigilant for signs of prescription medication misuse and substance use problems. He indicated that diazepam (Valium) and propoxyphene (Darvocet) are the most often misused medications among patients with spinal cord injuries and that the misuse of these medications is associated with depression and poor psychological adjustment. Also, patients with spinal cord injuries and substance-related problems spend more time in quiet activities, such as sleeping and resting, and less time in productive activities, such as rehabilitation therapies, during hospitalization. Therefore, substance use may have detrimental effects on rehabilitation outcome because patients do not prepare themselves adequately for life in their communities. Heinemann (1986) found that employed persons are less likely than unemployed persons to use alcohol, diazepam, marijuana, or cocaine.

Heinemann and colleagues (1989) suggested that an effective substance abuse treatment program for patients with spinal cord injuries should include assessment, postinjury education, exploration of coping techniques, and a team approach that considers the needs of the whole patient.

Factors in Assessing Post-Injury Use and Abuse:

There are many areas of concern related to postinjury substance abuse that must be assessed. Accurate knowledge of these areas will help develop rehabilitation and treatment plans for alcohol and substance abuse. These areas of concern include:

- *Pre-injury use*: Past behavior is the best predictor of future behavior. If alcohol and/or substance problems existed before injury, there is a greater chance they will continue after the injury.

- *Past social activities*: After suffering a traumatic injury, many patients maintain an alcohol- and drug-free existence while in acute or residential care. However, once they return to the community, they have greater opportunity and independence in activities. Patients whose previous lifestyle included alcohol and substance abuse often return to similar social situations when discharged into the community.

- *Awareness*: After a traumatic brain injury, patients typically have less insight into themselves and their problems, which makes changing the alcohol or substance abuse problem more difficult.

- *Coping skills*: There are many physical, cognitive, behavioral, and emotional consequences to brain injury. In reaction to these changes and with diminished coping skills, many patients may begin to use and abuse substances, including alcohol, illegal drugs, and prescription medications.

- *Prescription medication*: Patients may have many physiologic conditions (e.g., seizures in brain injured patients) that require medication. The use of alcohol or drugs in conjunction with prescription medication can alter the treatment effects (e.g., lower seizure thresholds) and may have potentially life-threatening consequences.

Difficulties with Typical Treatments:

Three problems have been identified with traditional alcohol and substance abuse programs that make them less successful for patients with traumatic brain injury. First, traditional treatments, such as individual therapy or groups (e.g., AA), are oriented primarily toward using cognition and insight to get clients to recognize and understand alcohol and substance use. Because of reduced cognitive functioning following a traumatic brain injury, patients may have greater difficulty becoming aware of and changing problems. Second, most inpatient drug and alcohol treatment programs operate within a short time frame. Because of impairments in learning and executive functioning, patients with traumatic brain injury require more time to process and acquire information and often need more time than these programs typically allow. Third, few professionals are trained in both substance abuse and traumatic brain or spinal cord injury issues.

After a comprehensive review of the literature related to substance abuse and brain injury rehabilitation, Chan and associates (1995) provided the following recommendations. (Patients with brain injury share many characteristics with patients with spinal cord injuries; these recommendations should be considered for this patient population, as well.)

- Incorporate alcohol and substance abuse history into the assessment phase; if the problem is not identified, it cannot be treated.

- Merge the treatment of traumatic brain injury with the treatment of alcohol and substance abuse problems. In many situations, one cannot succeed without the other.

- Emphasize behavioral interventions in the treatment of this problem, and make things more concrete and observable so there is a greater chance of the information being understood and learned (e.g., through pictures and videos).

- Select short-term goals geared toward the client's success; for example, instead of aiming for complete abstinence, try reducing the number of drinks consumed.

- Develop special support groups for patients with traumatic brain injury; for example, support groups modeled after AA have been set up using a modified version of the 12-step principles.

- Develop staff training programs for professionals that incorporate traumatic brain injury and alcohol and substance abuse issues.

IMPLICATIONS FOR REHABILITATION COUNSELING

Rehabilitation counselors can play an important role in working with clients with substance abuse problems. These clients constitute a large portion of many rehabilitation counselors' caseloads (either as a primary or secondary disability) (Goodwin, 1993; Schwab & DiNitto, 1993). Rehabilitation counselors must develop competence in substance abuse assessment and treatment so they can detect signs of substance abuse among their clients and intervene in a timely manner.

Recent research (Deren & Rendell, 1984) demonstrates that clients in treatment who are not working have greater difficulty reintegrating into their communities as productive and contributing members. Evidence also suggests that employment status is positively related to abstinence from substance use upon successful treatment (Livingston, Rendell & Wolkstein, 1990; Schwabb & DiNitto, 1993). In this sense, vocational rehabilitation may be regarded as a "pull factor" and can be distinguished from other "push factor" therapies, such as psychotherapy and participation in AA.

Certification in Substance Abuse Treatment:

Since the mid 1980s, there has been increased interest among rehabilitation educators in training rehabilitation counselors to work in the substance abuse treatment field. In response, the Commission on Rehabilitation Counselor Certification (CRC) recently approved the substance abuse counselor (SAC) specialty for certified rehabilitation counselors who have received the appropriate didactic and clinical training in substance abuse counseling.

Requirements for Certification:

For rehabilitation counselors who are interested in receiving a certificate in substance abuse counseling, the three requirements for the CRC-SAC credential are:

1. *Education*: A minimum of 12 semester hours of coursework (6 of which are at the graduate level) covering areas such as the foundations of substance abuse counseling (an introductory course on drugs/ alcohol abuse), substance abuse diagnosis/ assessment, clinical substance abuse counseling, and substance abuse and special populations (e.g., teens, women, the elderly, minorities, and athletes).

2. *Acceptable employment*: A minimum of 12 months of supervised acceptable work experience. To be acceptable, at least 50% of an applicant's job activities must have involved providing direct substance abuse services.

3. *Acceptable supervision*: Documentation of employment supervision by a person with CRC-SAC credential, a person with a graduate degree in rehabilitation counseling who also holds a state or national certification in substance abuse counseling, or a person with a graduate degree in a health and human service profession who also holds either a specialty certification in substance abuse services or a state or national certification in substance abuse counseling.

CONCLUSION

Research indicates that substance abuse both contributes to an increased incidence of disability and undermines rehabilitation gain. However, many rehabilitation counselors may lack sophistication concerning the dual problems of substance abuse and disability because of unfamiliarity and inadequate training in this area. Rehabilitation counselors also should be aware of trends in substance abuse assessment and treatment such as the use of the multidimensional functional assessment approach over the binary diagnostic approach, and the change from the traditional dogmatic treatment approach to a person-centered individualized treatment plan. These new approaches appear to be more flexible than the traditional assessment and treatment approaches, and may be more appropriate for rehabilitation clients.

REFERENCES

American Psychiatric Association. (1994). *Diagnostic and statistical manual of mental disorders* (4th ed.). Washington, DC: Author.

Bandura, A. (1977). Self-efficacy: Toward a unifying theory of behavior change. *Psychology Review, 84,* 191–215.

Barbor, T. F. (1993). Substance use and persons with physical disabilities: Nature, diagnosis, and clinical subtypes. In A. W. Heinemann (Ed.), *Substance abuse and physical disability* (pp. 43-56). Binghamton, NY: The Haworth Press.

Blume, S. (1983). *The disease concept today.* Minneapolis: The Johnson Institute.

Bratter, B. I., Bratter, T. E., Radda, H. T., & Steiner, K. M. (1993). The residential therapeutic caring community. Special issue: Psychotherapy for the addictions. *Psychotherapy, 30,* 299–304.

Budziack, T. J. (1993). Evaluating treatment services. In A. W. Heinemann (Ed.), *Substance abuse and physical disability* (pp. 239-255). Binghamton, NY: The Haworth Press.

Burke, W. H., Wesolowski, M. D., & Gruth, W. L. (1988). Comprehensive head injury rehabilitation: An outcome evaluation. *Brain Injury, 2,* 313–322.

Brismar, B., Engstrom, A., & Rydberg, V. (1983). Head injury and intoxication: A diagnostic and therapeutic dilemma. *Acta Chirurgica Scandinavica, 149,* 11–14.

Brownell, K. D., Marlatt, G. A., Lichenstein, E., & Wilson, G. T. (1986). Understanding and preventing relapse. *American Psychologist, 41,* 765–782.

Chan, F., Cunningham, J., Kwok, L., Dunlap, L., Kobayashi, R., & Tanquery, M. (1995). *Solving the vocational assessment puzzle: Pieces to meet the challenge with people having traumatic brain injury* [computer software]. Chicago: Rehabilitation Institute of Chicago.

Chiauzzi, E. J. (1991). *Preventing relapse in the addictions: A biopsychosocial approach.* New York: Pergamon Press.

Cummings, C., Gordon, J. R., & Marlatt, G. A. (1980). Relapse: Strategies of prevention and prediction. In W. R. Miller (Ed.), *The addictive behaviors* (pp. 231-321). Elmsford, NY: Pergamon Press.

Deren, S., & Rendell, J. R. (1984). *Increasing program utilization of vocational services.* Rockville, MD: National Institute on Drug Abuse.

DiClemente, C. C. (1991). Motivational interviewing and the stages of change. In W. Miller & S. Rollnick (Eds.), *Motivational interviewing preparing people to change addictive behavior* (pp. 191-199). New York: Guilford Press.

Egelko, S., & Galanter, M. (1993). Introducing cognitive-behavioral training into a self-help drug treatment program. *Psychotherapy, 30,* 214–221.

Goodwin, D. W. (1988). *Is alcoholism hereditary?* New York: Ballentine Books.

Goodwin, L. R. (1993). Special interest network in substance abuse. *Journal of Rehabilitation Counseling, 24,* 58–62.

Gold, M. S. (1996). Trends in hallucinogenic drug use: LSD, "ecstasy," and the rave phenomenon. In *The Hatherleigh guide to treating substance abuse, part I* (pp. 129-152). New York: Hatherleigh Press.

Graeber, J., Gardner, W. J., Chan, F., & Wang, M. H. (1995). *Substance abuse rehabilitation* [computer software]. Madison, WI: Department of Rehabilitation and Special Education, University of Wisconsin—Madison.

Graham, J. R. (1990). *MMPI-2: Assessing personality and psychopathology.* New York: Oxford University Press.

Greer, B. G. (1986). Substance abuse among people with disabilities: A case of too much accessibility. *Journal of Rehabilitation, 52,* 34-38.

Greer, B. G. (1989). Alcohol and other drug abuse by the physically impaired: A challenge for rehabilitation educators. *Alcohol Health Research World, 13,* 144.

Harrington, S. S. (1994). *The validity of the McAndrew Alcoholism Scale and the Substance Abuse Proclivity Scale in detecting substance abuse among adolescents hospitalized for psychiatric problems.* Unpublished doctoral dissertation, University of Wisconsin-Madison, Madison, WI.

Heinemann, A. W. (1986). Substance abuse and disability: An update. *Rehabilitation Report, 2,* 3-5.

Heinemann, A. W., Doll, M., & Schnoll, S. (1989). Treatment of alcohol abuse in persons with recent spinal cord injuries. *Alcohol Health Research World, 13,* 110-117.

Heinemann, A. W., Keen, M., Donohue, R., & Schnoll, S. (1988). Alcohol use by persons with recent spinal cord injury. *Archives of Physical Medicine and Rehabilitation, 69,* 619-624.

Hesselbrock, V. M., Stabenau, J. R., Hesselbrock, M. N., Meyer, R. E., & Barbor, T. F. (1982). The nature of alcoholism in patients with different family histories for alcoholism. *Progress in Neuro-physchopharmacology and Biological Psychiatry, 6,* 607-614.

Ingraham, K., Kaplan, S., & Chan, F. (1992). Rehabilitation counselors' awareness of client alcohol abuse patterns. *Journal of Applied Rehabilitation Counseling, 23,* 18-22.

Lam, C. S., Chan, F., & McMahon, B. T. (1991). Factorial structure of the change assessment questionnaire for individuals with dead injuries. *Rehabilitation Psychology, 36,* 189–199.

Livingston, P., Rendell, J. R., & Wolkstein E. (1990). A work-study model for rehabilitation counselor education in substance abuse. *Journal of Applied Rehabilitation Counseling, 21,* 16–20.

Lowenfels, A. B., & Miller, T. T. (1984). Alcohol and trauma. *Annals of Emergency Medicine, 13,* 1056–1060.

Marlatt, G. A., Gordon, J. R. (1985). *Relapse prevention.* New York: Guilford Press.

Miller, W. R., & Hester, R. K. (1989). Self-control training. In W. R. Miller & R. K. Hester (Eds.), *Handbook of alcoholism treatment approaches: Effective alternatives* (pp. 141-149). New York: Pergamon Press.

National Institute on Alcohol Abuse and Alcoholism, Department of Health and Human Services. (1982). *Statistical report on National Institute on Alcohol Abuse and Alcoholism funded treatment programs for calendar year 1980.* Rockville, MD: Author.

National Institute on Disability and Rehabilitation Research. (1990). Rehabilitation brief. In *Substance abuse and disability* (p. 12). Washington, DC: National Institute on Disability and Rehabilitation Research.

O'Donnel, J., Cooper, J., Cessner, J., Shehan, I., & Ashely, J. (1981-1982). Alcohol, drugs, and spinal cord injury. *Alcohol Health Research World,* 227-229.

Pekarik, G., & Zimmer, L. (1992). Relation of client variables to continuance in five types of alcohol treatment settings. *Addictive Behaviors, 17,* 105-115.

Prochaska, J. O., DiClemente, C. C. (1992). Stages and processes of self-change of smoking: toward an integrative model. *American Psychologist, 47,* 1101-1114.

Prochaska, J. O., DiClemente, C. C., & Norcross, J. C. (1992). In search of how people change: Applications to addictive behavior. *American Psychologist, 47,* 1101-1114.

Schlesinger, S. E., & Horberg, L. K. (1993). Comprehensive treatment of addictive families. In A. W. Heinemann (Ed.), *Substance abuse and physical disability* (pp. 217-237). Binghamton, NY: The Haworth Press.

Schwab, A. J., & DiNitto, D. M. (1993). Factors related to the successful vocational rehabilitation of substance abusers. *Journal of Applied Rehabilitation Counseling, 24,* 11-20.

Selzer, M. L. (1971). The Michigan Alcoholism Screening Test: The quest for a new diagnostic instrument. *American Journal of Psychiatry, 127,* 1653-1658.

Stude, E. W. (1993). Drug abuse. In M. G. Brodwin, F. Tellez, & S. Browdin (Eds.), *Medical, psychological, and vocational aspects of disability* (pp. 51-57). Athens, GA: Elliot & Fitzpatrick.

Texas Rehabilitation Commission. (1990). The high cost of substance abuse. *Texas Business Today,* June, 4.

Wexler, H. K., Magura, S., Beardsley, M. M., & Josepher, H. (1994). An AIDS education and relapse prevention model for high-risk parolees. *Journal of Addictions, 29,* 361-386.

Yarkony, G. M. (1993). Medical complications in rehabilitation. In A. W. Heinemann (Ed.), *Substance abuse and physical disability* (pp. 93-103). Binghamton, NY: The Haworth Press.

AUTHORS' AFFILIATIONS

Ms. Cardoso is a doctoral student, Dr. Chan is a Professor and Co-Director of the Rehabilitation Research and Training Center, and Dr. Thomas is a Professor in the Rehabilitation Psychology Program at the University of Wisconsin—Madison.

Dr. Roldan is Assistant Professor in the Department of Psychology, Illinois Institute of Technology.

Mr. Ingraham is a Senior Rehabilitation Counselor for the Illinois Department of Rehabilitation Services in Elgin, IL.

3

Substance Abuse in Pregnancy

Mindy Thompson Fullilove, MD, and Isabelle Dieudonné, MD

Dr. Fullilove is Associate Professor of Clinical Psychiatry and Public Health at Columbia University and New York State Psychiatric Institute, New York, NY. Dr. Dieudonné is Assistant Professor of Pediatrics and a neonatologist at the New York Hospital-Cornell Medical Center, New York, NY.

KEY POINTS

- Because of the risks for fetal harm, even minimal use of a psychoactive substance during pregnancy can be appropriately considered substance abuse.

- Scorned by society and health care providers, drug-using pregnant women often avoid getting the medical attention they need. Counseling these women presents challenges that the professional must meet.

- Research indicates that a smaller proportion of women use illicit drugs than men. The results of studies comparing the education levels, ethnicity, and age of first-time mothers who use substances are also reported.

- The effects on fetuses resulting from the abuse of substances are discussed for the following substances: alcohol; tobacco; marijuana; heroin, methadone, and other opiates; and cocaine.

- Principles that are helpful in the treatment of women who abuse substances include using a woman-sensitive treatment setting and making an early diagnosis.

- Guidelines for managing drug withdrawal during pregnancy are presented.

- All women who abuse drugs, regardless of race, class, or drug of choice, need counseling to establish a drug-free pregnancy.

INTRODUCTION

According to the fourth edition of the *Diagnostic and Statistical Manual of Mental Disorders* (DSM-IV) (American Psychiatric Association, 1994), substance abuse is "a maladaptive pattern of substance use manifested by recurrent and significant adverse consequences related to the repeated use of substances" (p. 182). A key feature of maladaptive use is the continued use of substances in situations in which it is physically hazardous. Because of the risks for fetal harm, even minimal use of a psychoactive substance during pregnancy can be appropriately considered substance abuse, although such zero tolerance might not be appropriate at other points in a woman's life.

In addition to the problems of abuse and dependence, the use of psychoactive substances can cause a wide range of organic psychological disorders, including psychosis, anxiety, panic disorder, and mood disorders. The diagnosis of these disturbances related to substance use requires mastery of the differential diagnosis of organic and functional illnesses. The treatment of these illnesses requires care for the primary addictive condition as well as other concurrent mental disorders.

The stigmatization and social rejection drug users may experience also can bring on psychological illnesses, although they would not necessarily fit a specific diagnostic category in the nomenclature. Rather, the literature suggests that social rejection can lower self-esteem, injure the development of appropriate narcissistic defenses, and cause disorders such as anxiety and paranoia. The psychological damage that results from social rejection requires aggressive treatment to return the suffering person to full, productive functioning.

The complexity of the psychological disorders related to psychoactive substance use is magnified by the problems inherent in treating those drug users who are also pregnant. The health care team must confront the array of dangers such drug use poses for the developing fetus as well as the intense societal disdain for women who are viewed as endangering the unborn child. Scorned by society and by health care providers, drug-using women often flee from needed medical attention to the detriment of their own health and that of the fetus. Assisting drug-using women through pregnancy challenges our counseling skills and knowledge, as well as our capacity to work with the socially despised.

In addition to the primary psychological illnesses related to substance use disorders (e.g., substance abuse or dependence, organic psychiatric disorders, and stigmatization), health care providers who work in addiction services have recognized that other psychological illnesses often present simultaneously with the addictive disorder and also require medical attention. These cases of dual diagnoses have often focused on clients with major mental illnesses such as schizophrenia and bipolar disorder. However, recent research has shown that many other psychopathologic disorders can accompany addiction. For example, posttraumatic stress disorder (PTSD), an illness that produces intense dysphoria, can lead to drug or alcohol addiction. In fact, trauma, such as that experienced in the course of childhood sexual abuse, may be an important etiologic agent for many cases of addiction (Bollerud, 1990). Those who have experienced trauma require treatment for both the trauma disorder and the addictive disorder to achieve a full and lasting recovery.

EPIDEMIOLOGY OF DRUG USE AMONG WOMEN

The psychoactive substances considered in this chapter are alcohol, tobacco, marijuana, opiates, and cocaine. It is important—before discussing the extent of drug use among women (especially pregnant women)—to address an unspoken concern of some readers that we have erred by "lumping together" such substances as heroin and tobacco. After all, how can the havoc wrought by heroin addiction be compared with smoking a few cigarettes?

The drugs are comparable, we would argue, because of the addictive state they produce. The legal status of nicotine makes it seem less insidious, but the drug itself can be deadly. Narcotics Anonymous ([NA], 1988) describes the commonality of addiction this way:

> All of us, from the junkie snatching purses to the sweet little old lady hitting two or three doctors for legal prescriptions, have one thing in common: we seek our destruction a bag at a time, a few pills at a time, or a bottle at a time until we die. This is at least part of the insanity of addiction. The price may seem higher for the addict who prostitutes for a fix than it is for the addict who merely lies to a doctor. Ultimately both pay for their disease with their lives. Insanity is repeating the same mistakes and expecting different results.

The use of alcohol, marijuana, and tobacco is widespread in American society, but women's use of licit and illicit drugs differs from the patterns seen among men. For example, although the prevalence of smoking has declined among all Americans, Pirie, Murray, and Luepker (1991) noted:

> The prevalence of smoking and the burden of smoking-related illness in this country are beginning to shift toward women. . . . Smoking prevalence rates in the youngest groups of adult women are beginning to exceed those in men, at least among whites, and overall smoking rates among women are projected to exceed those among men by the latter part of the 1990s.

Data from the National Institute on Drug Abuse (NIDA) National Household Survey, an annual representative sample of the household population of the United States, also suggest that women's patterns of illicit drug use differ from those seen among men. Table 3.1 shows that a smaller proportion of women (32%) use drugs than men (42%). Over the time period examined in the table, 1985–90, no significant increase was found in those reported ever having used illicit drugs (lifetime drug use). As for examining reports of illicit drug use in the past year, the table documents a substantial decline for men (from 24% in 1985 to 16% in 1990) and a significant decline — less substantial than that seen for men — for women (from 16% in 1985 to 11% in 1990).

TABLE 3.1 TRENDS IN PREVALENCE OF ANY ILLICIT DRUG USE BY GENDER		
IN PERCENTAGES		
1985 (n=8038)	1988 (n=8814)	1990 (n=9259)
Lifetime		
Men 42.0	40.0	42.4
Women 32.2	33.4	32.1
Past Year		
Men 23.7	16.4	15.5*
Women 15.8	12.0	11.4*
Past Month		
Men 15.2	9.0	7.9*
Women 9.4	5.8	5.1*

* Difference between 1985 and 1990 statistically significant at the .05 level

Table 3.2 demonstrates changes in the use of cocaine, which had reached epidemic proportions by the mid-1980s. Men are more likely to report lifetime use of cocaine (14% in 1990) than are women (9% in 1990). Reports of use show a significant decline between 1985 and 1990, from 8% of men reporting use of cocaine in 1985 to 4% in 1990, and 4% of women reporting such use in 1985, with a decline to 2% in 1990.

To examine the use of drugs during pregnancy, Abma and Mott (1991) analyzed data from a major national study, the

TABLE 3.2
TRENDS IN PREVALENCE
OF COCAINE USE BY GENDER

IN PERCENTAGES

	1985 (n=8038)	1988 (n=8814)	1990 (n=9259)
Lifetime			
Men	15.3	13.1	13.8
Women	8.2	8.5	9.0
Past Year			
Men	8.4	5.6	4.3*†
Women	4.4	2.8	2.0*†
Past Month			
Men	3.9	2.0	1.1*†
Women	2.0	1.0	0.5*†

* Difference between 1985 and 1990 statistically significant at the .05 level
† Difference between 1988 and 1990 statistically significant at the .05 level

Source: NIDA Household Survey of Drug Abuse, December 11, 1990

National Longitudinal Study of Youth, which interviewed 11,400 young people in 1979 and has since resurveyed them annually. From that large sample, the researchers selected 1664 young women who had had a baby, whose first child had been born after the original interview in 1979, and whose files contained information on drug use during the period of the pregnancy. The results showed that 45% of these young mothers had used cigarettes, alcohol, or marijuana at some time during pregnancy. As shown in Table 3.3, white women are much more likely than Latina or African-American women to smoke tobacco. White women are also more likely than Latina or African-American women to drink liquor or to smoke marijuana, but the differences are less striking. Education varied in its effects on drug use. The least-educated women were most likely to smoke tobacco or marijuana, but least likely to drink alcohol. The most highly educated women were

Table 3.3
PERCENTAGE OF FIRST-TIME MOTHERS
WHO SMOKED CIGARETTES, DRANK ALCOHOL,
OR SMOKED MARIJUANA DURING PREGNANCY
(BY SELECTED BACKGROUND CHARACTERISTICS)

Characteristic	N	Cigarettes	Alcohol	Marijuana
Race/Ethnicity				
Latina	299	18.6	3.7	9.8
African-				
American	436	25.0	7.6	11.0
White/other	929	40.7	11.7	13.5
Education				
<12 years	545	46.9	5.5	17.9
12 years	667	41.5	12.3	15.0
>12 years	452	21.4	11.2	5.6
Age at First Birth				
<20	526	39.5	5.8	18.9
20–22	542	41.5	10.5	16.1
>22	596	31.4	13.2	6.9
Total	**1664**	**36.7**	**10.5**	**12.9**

Source: Abma, J. C., & Mott, F. L. (1991). Substance use and prenatal care during pregnancy among young women. *Family Planning Perspectives, 23*(3), 117–123.

markedly less likely to smoke cigarettes or marijuana but were average in their use of alcohol during pregnancy. Age, too, showed marked variation. Those who were oldest at first birth (i.e., older than 22 years of age) were least likely to smoke cigarettes or marijuana during pregnancy but were more likely to drink alcohol during pregnancy. The complexity of the pattern of drug use suggests that groups defined by race, age, and education all participate in drug use but differ on the choice of drug.

VARIATIONS IN DRUG USE

Cultural variation in drug choice has been documented in

other studies from around the country. Chasnoff, Landress, and Barrett (1990) conducted a study in Pinellas County, Florida, and found that 15.4% of white women had a positive urine test for alcohol, marijuana, cocaine, or opiates, whereas 14.1% of African-American women had a positive urine toxicology. Although the rates of positive urine screening were similar, the white and African-American women chose different drugs. A study of drug use among middle class white women revealed that 5% admitted using narcotics during pregnancy (Hoegerman & Schnoll, 1991). It is important to note that these studies describe variation in patterns of substance use throughout society, but they confirm that use is common and is not limited to any one racial group or social class.

Drug use behaviors also show marked variation by region. For example, a household survey of neighborhoods in San Francisco found that, in 1987, 56% of respondents had used marijuana, 31% had used cocaine, and 9% had used crack (Golden et al., 1990)—levels of drug use much higher than those noted in the NIDA household surveys. The crack epidemic, in particular, has been a highly localized event, spreading from city to city but not affecting all major urban areas or all areas within a specific urban center (U.S. Department of Justice, 1988). In epicenters of the crack epidemic, the effects of drug use have been severe and have caused disruption in family, social, health, and legal systems (Marzuk et al., 1990; Mieczkowski, 1988; Rolfs, Goldberg, & Sharrar, 1990).

A recent report issued by the Unified Court System of the State of New York named the period 1985–90 "The Crack Years." The report clearly showed that the impact of the cocaine/crack epidemic had been devastating in the inner city. It linked the following trends to substance abuse—and especially to crack use—in the state of New York:

- The incidence of intrafamily violence has risen 400% in the past 5 years along with a 650% rise in cases of neglect over the decade, and a 147% increase in child protective cases.

- The juvenile homicide rate is rising five times faster than the adult rate.

- The foster care population has more than doubled in the past 5 years.

- An estimated 467,000 children of addicted parents live in New York State.

The report argued that the crack epidemic had overwhelmed the judicial system in New York City as well as in other parts of New York State. Several features of the epidemic appear to be responsible for its massive impact on social structures. First, crack dealers, predominantly men, were involved in internecine warfare to establish sales territories. Dealers were also involved in violent encounters with law enforcement officials. For complex reasons that are as yet poorly understood, men at all levels of crack sales and crack use were also physically and sexually abusive to women in a fashion that has been unprecedented in inner-city communities (Amaro et al., 1990).

Second, marketing of crack was directed toward women and adolescents. Because the drug is rapidly addictive, many who experimented with it became trapped in addiction. It is clear that crack users in the course of a drug-taking binge are unable to care for themselves or others, and will neglect health, welfare, and personal hygiene while engaged in drug-seeking behavior (*Crack Cocaine Epidemic*, 1991). The consequences of women's heavy involvement in crack use have been disastrous for inner-city neighborhoods, where women typically have been pillars of community stability (Chasnoff et al., 1989; Cherukuri et al., 1988; Nobles et al., 1987). One example of this shift in roles is the increase in the number of infants born to substance-abusing mothers in New York City: between 1980 and 1989 (the latest year for which data are available), the rate of substance abuse increased fivefold, from 7/1000 to 35/1000. The localization of the crack epidemic, and its severe effects on women, appear to be closely tied to recent socioeconomic changes in inner-city communities in the United States.

FETAL EFFECTS OF SUBSTANCES OF ABUSE

Alcohol:

Alcohol is the most common teratogen to which a fetus may be exposed. Fetal alcohol syndrome (FAS) was first described in the late 1960s in the babies of women who drank during their pregnancies (Smith, 1982). The incidence of FAS is 1–3/1000 live births. FAS is now recognized as the leading cause of mental retardation (Fanaroff & Martin, 1992; Pietrantoni & Knuppel, 1991).

FAS encompasses growth retardation, microcephaly (abnormal smallness of the head), a flat midface, a thin upper lip, short palpable fissures, renal and cardiac anomalies, and mental retardation (Smith, 1982). To be defined as having FAS, the Fetal Alcohol Study Group (1991) of the Research Society on Alcoholism proposed that one anomaly from each of the following categories must be included:

1. Prenatal or postnatal growth retardation, failure to thrive

2. Neurologic abnormalities (irritability, hyperactivity), developmental delay, mental retardation

3. At least two of the following dysmorphologies:

    a. Microcephaly

    b. Microphthalmia (abnormal smallness of one or both eyeballs) or short palpable fissures

    c. Poorly developed filtrum, thin upper lip, and flattening of the maxilla

Many infants of mothers who drink do not develop complete FAS, but may still display features associated with prenatal effects of alcohol. In fact, less than one third of the offspring of alcoholic women are normal at birth (Creasy & Resnik, 1989; Hoyme, 1990). A relationship seems to exist between the amount of alcohol consumed and the severity of the syndrome (Fanaroff & Martin 1992; Pietrantoni & Knuppel, 1991). A reduction of alcohol intake, even at the end of the second trimester, can improve neonatal outcome (i.e., birth weight) (Fanaroff & Martin, 1992).

Mild FAS has been induced by 1 oz of alcohol or two drinks daily and most often includes low birth weight (LBW) as one of its features (Pietrantoni & Knuppel, 1991). Infant anomalies have been found even when alcohol intake is of short duration (Pietrantoni & Knuppel, 1991). Of women who drank moderately (1–1.5 oz/day) in the first trimester, 11% bore children with alcohol-related abnormalities (Creasy & Resnik, 1989; Hoyme, 1990). Approximately 30%–40% of infants born to alcoholic mothers developed the complete FAS. This was observed when 2–2.5 oz of alcohol were consumed daily during the first trimester (Pietrantoni, & Knuppel, 1991). Among mothers who were heavy drinkers, 32% of the infants had congenital malformation with 16% having major malformations. The Collaborative Perinatal Study reported that 44% of infants born to alcoholic mothers are mentally retarded and that 17% of these infants die (Fanaroff & Martin, 1992). The frequency of partial expression of FAS (called alcohol-related birth defects) was 3–5/1000 live births (Fanaroff & Martin, 1992; King & Fabro, 1983; Pietrantoni & Knuppel, 1991). Other complications included an increase in the rate of premature delivery and spontaneous abortions among heavy drinkers (Fanaroff & Martin, 1992; King & Fabro, 1983; Pietrantoni & Knuppel, 1991).

The growth retardation observed when alcohol intake exceeded 1 oz/day continues throughout childhood (Fanaroff & Martin, 1992). The average intelligence quotient (IQ) for those born to chronic alcoholics was 60–70 (Fanaroff & Martin, 1992; Hoyme, 1990; Pietrantoni & Knuppel; Smith, 1982).

Finally, alcohol withdrawal, although uncommon, has been described in the newborn. The infant will be agitated and hyperactive, with increased tremors for 72 hours followed by 48 hours of lethargy before returning to normal activity. The newborn breath will have the odor of alcohol, and seizures may occur (Fanaroff & Martin, 1992).

Tobacco:

Although the influence of smoking seems to be greater during the last 4 months of gestation, women who smoke have an increased frequency of spontaneously aborting a chromosomally normal conceptus (Fanaroff & Martin, 1992; King & Fabro, 1983). Smoking during pregnancy produces infants who are 200 g lighter on average than those born to nonsmokers (Creasy & Resnik, 1989; Fanaroff & Martin, 1992; Hoyme, 1990). In addition, the more a woman smokes during pregnancy, the lower the weight of her newborn at delivery will be (Creasy & Resnik, 1989; Fanaroff & Martin, 1992; King & Fabro, 1983). One study reported that 4.7% of nonsmokers gave birth to infants weighing less than 2500 g (LBW); 7.7% of women who smoke less than one pack of cigarettes per day gave birth to LBW infants as opposed to 12% of women who smoke more than one pack per day (King & Fabro, 1983). When a woman stopped smoking during pregnancy, the risk of delivering a LBW infant was similar to that of a nonsmoker (Creasy & Resnik, 1989; Fanaroff & Martin, 1992; King & Fabro, 1983).

Although LBW infants born to smokers show a greater weight gain and increase in head circumference during the first year of life compared with infants of mothers who are nonsmokers, infants of smokers remain smaller. Smokers also have an increased rate of abruptio placentae and placenta previa. The increase in abruptio placentae is associated with greater perinatal mortality (Fanaroff & Martin, 1992; King & Fabro, 1983).

Sudden infant death syndrome (SIDS) is strongly associated with maternal smoking during pregnancy as well (Hoffman & Hillman, 1992; King & Fabro, 1983). Studies have shown that neurologic behavioral abnormalities such as minimal cerebral dysfunction and hyperactivity are more common among children born to women who smoke (Fanaroff & Martin, 1992; King & Fabro, 1983). These children are somewhat behind other children in reading, mathematics, and general ability (Creasy & Resnik, 1989; Fanaroff & Martin, 1992).

Marijuana:

Reports of marijuana's effect on the size of infants at birth, the length of gestation, and neonatal behavior are inconclusive. Among them, one study found an increase in body movement and a decrease in quiet sleep when marijuana was used by the mother during all trimesters. In general, no morphologic abnormalities have been correlated with marijuana use (Day & Richardson, 1991).

Heroin, Methadone, and Other Opiates:

Most information on the effects of opiate use comes from the study of methadone use in pregnancy (Deren, 1986; Hoegerman & Schnoll, 1991). The study of the specific effects of heroin or methadone on the infant is complicated by two factors: (a) the use of multiple drugs, some of which are known but poorly documented (e.g., cigarettes and alcohol) and some of which are unknown (e.g., quinine used to cut heroin); and (b) the presence of multiple social factors that contribute to poor pregnancy outcome, such as poverty, malnutrition, decreased access to medical care, disruption of the family unit, and violence.

Maternal opiate abuse is associated with an increased risk of LBW (50% of the offspring are LBW and 50% of these are small for gestational age) and presence of withdrawal symptoms, which occurred in 70%–90% of their newborns (Creasy

& Resnik, 1989; Deren, 1986; Fanaroff & Martin, 1992). Infants of narcotic-addicted mothers have a higher mortality rate and a higher incidence of SIDS (Deren, 1986; Fanaroff & Martin, 1992; Hoffman & Hillman, 1992).

Other neonatal and pediatric complications associated with maternal opiate abuse include infections (such as acquired immunodeficiency syndrome [AIDS]) associated with intravenous drug use, prematurity and its complications (i.e., intraventricular hemorrhage, membrane disease, etc.), asphyxia (suffocation), and long-term learning and behavioral sequelae. Although studies have been inconsistent, many believe the behavioral consequences are the most devastating outcome of opiate addiction (Deren, 1986; Fanaroff & Martin, 1992; Hoegerman & Schnoll, 1991).

Withdrawal of a pregnant addict can be dangerous for the fetus (Fanaroff & Martin, 1992). Opiate withdrawal can result in increased oxygen consumption by the mother and the fetus and possible fetal compromise ranging from mild asphyxia to fetal death (Hogerman & Schnoll, 1991). Newborns usually start withdrawing 24–72 hours after birth. Symptoms include irritability, tremors, hyperactivity, high-pitched cry, frantic sucking, and sleeping and feeding problems. More than two thirds of babies born to opiate-addicted mothers will show signs of withdrawal (Fanaroff & Martin, 1992). Although the peak of symptoms usually occurs at 3–5 days of age after the last dose of opiate, symptoms can peak at 2–3 weeks of age for methadone (a longer-acting agent). The intensity of symptoms is directly related to the mother's dose of opiate prior to and at delivery. Greater than 70% of infants show signs of central nervous system (CNS) irritability. Fifty percent show signs of respiratory abnormalities such as increase in respiratory rate and signs of gastrointestinal abnormalities (e.g., vomiting and diarrhea). Seizures are rare, but sneezing and sweating are frequent (Hoegerman, & Schnoll, 1991).

The above withdrawal symptoms have been described as neonatal abstinence syndrome. However, symptoms can be observed several months after birth; this has been described as subacute withdrawal syndrome.

Infants born to methadone-maintained mothers seem to have higher birth weights than infants born to heroin-addicted mothers (Creasy & Resnik, 1989; Fanaroff & Martin, 1992; Hoegerman & Schnoll, 1991). Many believe methadone to be the management of choice for heroin-addicted mothers because of decreased incidence of fetal death and neonatal complications with its use. However, studies have demonstrated that the symptoms of neonatal withdrawal are more severe with methadone than with heroin (Creasy & Resnik, 1989; Fanaroff & Martin, 1992).

In the first few months of life, infants born to opiate-addicted mothers may be found to be less interactive with their mothers and more irritable and less consolable (Deren, 1986). Studies have also shown these infants to experience sleep disturbances; increase in muscle tone; and weak visual, motor, and perceptual skills (Deren, 1986; Hoegerman & Schnoll, 1991).

Follow-up studies revealed postnatal growth deficiencies and microcephaly (Creasy & Resnik, 1989; Fanaroff & Martin, 1992). Children born to opiate-addicted mothers performed less well on the Bailey Developmental Scale (Deren, 1986). Their testing on perceptual abilities and capacity for organization was inferior (Creasy & Resnik, 1989; Fanaroff & Martin, 1992), and their social and school adjustment was poor even though IQ scores remained unaffected. They had attachment difficulties and were hyperactive with impaired attention spans and aggressive behavior (Chasnoff, 1991b; Deren, 1986; Hoegerman & Schnoll, 1991).

Cocaine:

In pregnancies affected by cocaine, spontaneous abortions and premature separation of the placenta are common (Chasnoff, 1991b; Fanaroff & Martin, 1992; Hoyme, 1990; Jones,

1991; Rosenak et al., 1990). Cocaine produces possibly up to 10 times more stillbirths than are found in the normal population (Rosenak et al., 1990). Intrauterine growth retardation, prematurity, fetal distress at delivery, neurobehavioral changes, and SIDS frequently are seen as well (Berhman & Vaughan, 1987; Chasnoff, 1991b; Fanaroff & Martin, 1992; Hoffman & Hillman, 1992; Rosenak et al., 1990). The anomalies observed are urogenital, neurologic, and skeletal in nature (Chasnoff, 1991b; Jones, 1991).

A spasm of uterine arteries with alterations of the passage of oxygen and nutrients to the fetus is thought to be caused by the increased sympathetic tone associated with cocaine use. That, in turn, leads to a cardiovascular response in the fetus (increasing blood pressure and heart rate) through fetal hypoxemia followed by a release of fetal catecholamines (e.g., adrenaline) (Fanaroff & Martin, 1992; Jones, 1991; Rosenak et al., 1990). In addition, stimulation of the pregnant uterus causes it to contract. This constriction of uterine vessels and the uterine muscle may be an effect of cocaine on the uterus and the fetus, resulting in an increased rate of prematurity, growth retardation, microcephaly, and congenital anomalies (King & Fabro, 1983). Jones (1991) further explains the etiology of these congenital defects: hemorrhages are associated with a rise in systemic and cerebral blood pressure, hypoperfusion, and hypoxia, and may result in intracranial hemorrhage and infarction, intestinal infarction, limb reduction defects, and urinary tract anomalies (Chasnoff, 1991b; Reed, 1987).

Neurobehavioral defects in infants result from the direct effect of cocaine on a developing CNS (Chasnoff, 1991b). Sleep disturbances, tremors, feeding difficulties, vomiting, sneezing, and high-pitched cry are changes that have been observed in infants born to cocaine users. Some of these changes— including feeding difficulties and somnolence—have been observed through the first year of life (Rosenak et al., 1990). Follow-up studies that used the Brazelton Neonatal Behavioral Assessment Scale noted "depression of interactive behavior and poor organizational response to environmental stimuli" (Jones, 1991). Cocaine-exposed children may have stronger anxiety reactions and disturbances in the capacity for organization (Rosenak et al., 1990).

Cocaine can affect the fetus at any time through gestation. Long-term effects of cocaine use are not yet well known; but the seriousness of its effects on the fetus and the newborn are now being documented more clearly.

TREATMENT OF SUBSTANCE USE DISORDERS DURING PREGNANCY

Despite differences in the drugs of abuse, the following principles are helpful in the treatment of women addicts.

Woman-Sensitive Treatment Setting:

A woman-sensitive treatment setting is one geared to the needs of women with children. These mothers typically need social support for every aspect of their role as mothers. They need child care to keep appointments, and they need training in parenting skills. In addition, they need adequate housing and income supports (Reed, 1987).

Women also want social situations to be structured in a manner that allows for interpersonal processes and mutual support. The confrontational style of treatment developed in the 1970s in work with young men addicted to heroin has little relevance to the treatment needs of women addicts. Women's communication is geared around "talking things over" in a setting that is peer oriented.

Women also have many responsibilities outside the treatment setting: for the household, for other kin, and for friends and relatives. Treatment settings that impose long, rigorous schedules make it difficult for women to function effectively in the life roles they occupy. The problem is no different from that confronted by working women who must juggle a rigid work schedule with the demands of home and children. In any event, such rigidity is to be avoided in the design of woman-sensitive treatment.

Early Diagnosis:

The process of denial that appears to cloud the early stages of addiction encompasses not only the user and her family, but also those who are health providers (Chasnoff, 1991a; Chavkin, 1991). As we improve training in the treatment of substance abuse disorders, more and more providers will be able to make such diagnoses and begin to recommend treatment earlier in the course of the illness. In general, all encounters with the health care system should include routine questioning about drug and alcohol use. The physical examination should include inspection for drug use stigmata, such as yellowing of the fingertips from cigarette smoke and needle marks from drug injection. During all stages of pregnancy, routine monitoring of the urine for drugs and alcohol is recommended. Any evidence of drug use should be thoroughly explored in the clinical setting.

Improved recognition does not imply that clients will be able to recognize the effects of drug use and to accept responsibility for treatment. Health care providers have relatively little expertise in this aspect of treatment. Rather, addiction unfolds with increasing social, economic, and legal havoc, until the chaos in the user's life forces her to seek help.

The following strategies may improve the effectiveness of early intervention: (a) intensive education of the client in the nature and course of addictive disorders, (b) education of the family and the support system in their role in the progress of the addiction, (c) persistence in the discussion of the substance use problems, and (d) employment of coercion when it is clear that the woman's drug use is endangering herself or others.

Coercion of substance users into treatment has always been a controversial issue (Garcia, 1990). For many years, some who worked in addiction services felt that people mandated to seek treatment would not benefit from it; rather, people had to be "ready" for treatment before it could work. Experience has shown, however, that many of those mandated to treatment did improve. The enforced sobriety provided an opportunity to establish and maintain abstinence. However, all who have achieved substantial sobriety—whether mandated to treatment or not—report that they finally accepted personal responsibility for staying clean. To quote NA (1988), "We are not responsible for our disease, but we are responsible for our recovery."

DRUG WITHDRAWAL

Withdrawal from drug use may present a problem, depending on the level of the woman's use and, more importantly, the type of drug used. The risks of drug withdrawal are increased for all those who are frequent users consuming substantial amounts of drugs. Table 3.4 outlines the drugs of abuse, the dangers to the fetus from abrupt drug withdrawal, and the treatments in current use to facilitate withdrawal in pregnancy. We must underscore the limits of medical knowledge on safe withdrawal from drug use during pregnancy. The risks of intervention must be weighed against the risks of continued drug use and women should be fully informed of the relative risk/benefit ratio. Despite the many problems associated with drug withdrawal, we believe a drug-free pregnancy is an important goal.

For women who use cigarettes and marijuana, withdrawal can be assisted with behavior modification and psychosocial supports. For cocaine, only a few pharmacologic treatments are in current use. Probably the most widely used is desipramine (Pertofrane), but its safety in pregnancy is not established. For alcohol withdrawal, benzodiazepines are used, but studies have suggested that they can cause congenital malformations in the first trimester. Methadone (Dolophine), widely used by those addicted to heroin, causes pediatric, medical,

Table 3.4
MANAGEMENT OF DRUG WITHDRAWAL DURING PREGNANCY

Substance	Risk to Fetus from Abrupt Withdrawal	Possible Treatments for Mother's Withdrawal
Cigarettes	No known problems	Behavior modification
Marijuana	Unknown	Behavior modification
Alcohol	Possible transient symptoms, similar to those seen in newborn	Benzodiazepines[t] Acupuncture[‡]
Cocaine	Possible transient symptoms, similar to those seen in newborn	Desipramine[§] Acupuncture
Opiates*	Increased oxygen requirement for the fetus, in some cases leading to death	Methadone** Acupuncture

* Based largely on information about methadone
t May cause congenital malformations and are used in the first trimester
‡ Body acupuncture or electro-ear acupuncture may cause miscarriage
§ Safety in pregnancy is not established
** Known to cause medical, obstetric, and pediatric complications

TABLE 3.5
COMPLICATIONS IN OPIOID-DEPENDENT PREGNANCIES

	Obstetric	Medical	Pediatric
Methadone plus illicit drugs	31.6%	28.4%	80.0%
Methadone alone	28.6%	14.3%	83.3%

Source: Hoegerman, G., & Schnoll, S. (1991). Narcotic use in pregnancy. *Clinics in Perinatology, 18*(1), 51–76.

and obstetric complications, as shown in Table 3.5 (Hoegerman & Schnoll, 1991).

Ear acupuncture, which is a physiologic intervention, but not a pharmacologic one, appears to be safe for withdrawal from a wide range of drugs during pregnancy (American Hospital Association, 1991). Ear acupuncture treatments are given once a day and use four or five needles placed at specific points on the ear. The needles, once inserted, are left in place for 45 minutes while the patient sits quietly. The use of needles at points on the body away from the ear or the use of electro-acupuncture to the ear are not recommended for use during pregnancy because such treatments might cause miscarriage. No congenital malformations or teratogenesis related to use of acupuncture during pregnancy has been reported. Broader use of this modality for drug withdrawal during pregnancy is worthy of further clinical and research evaluation.

ETHICAL ISSUES

The specter of poor African-American women abusing cocaine and neglecting their children has been given much publicity in the lay and scientific press. The problems caused by women's use of alcohol and cigarettes attract much less attention and, some have argued, are viewed with less anger. This discrepancy creates a serious ethical problem for society. Indeed, the problems of substance use — including the danger to the fetus — are serious ones. But inappropriate focus on one drug or one group of women will cause more harm than good in treating the problems of addiction.

The major implication for the counselor is that all women, regardless of race, class, or drug of choice, need our care and attention to establish and carry a drug-free pregnancy. It is important to emphasize to the client that drug addiction is a disease rather than a crime. Within that context, the careful and complete diagnosis of addictive disorders should be a routine part of the care offered to all women. Once the diagnosis of an addictive disorder is established, the full complement of necessary therapies should be placed at the woman's disposal. Pregnancy offers an opportunity to encourage women to adopt positive health behaviors (Chasnoff, 1991c; Phibbs, Bateman, & Schwarz, 1991).

REFERENCES

Abma, J. C., & Mott, F. L. (1991). Substance use and prenatal care during pregnancy among young women. *Family Planning Perspectives, 23,* 117–123.

Amaro, H., et al. (1990). Violence during pregnancy and substance use. *American Journal of Public Health, 80,* 575–579.

American Hospital Association. (1991). *Hospital and community partnerships: Prenatal, infant care, and pediatric models for underserved women.* Chicago: Author.

American Psychiatric Association. (1994). *Diagnostic and statistical manual of mental disorders* (4th ed.). Washington, DC: American Psychiatric Press.

Berhman, R., & Vaughan, V. C. (1987). *Nelson textbook of pediatrics.* Philadelphia: W. B. Saunders.

Bollerud, K. (1990). A model for the treatment of trauma-related syndromes among chemically dependent inpatient women. *Journal of Substance Abuse Treatment, 7,* 83–97.

Chasnoff, I. J. (Ed.). (1991a). Chemical dependency and pregnancy: Clinical and methodologic issues. *Clinics in Perinatology, 18,* 113–123.

Chasnoff, I. J. (1991b). Cocaine and pregnancy: Clinical and methodologic issues. *Clinics in Perinatology, 18,* 113–123.

Chasnoff, I. J. (1991c). Drugs, alcohol, pregnancy and the neonate: Pay now or pay later. *Journal of the American Medical Association, 266,* 1567–1568.

Chasnoff, I. J., et al. (1989). Temporal patterns of cocaine use in pregnancy. *Journal of the American Medical Association, 261,* 1741–1744.

Chasnoff, I. J., Landress, H. J., & Barrett, M. E. (1990). The prevalence of illicit drug or alcohol use during pregnancy and discrepancies in mandatory reporting in Pinellas County, FL. *New England Journal of Medicine, 322,* 1202–1206.

Chavkin, W. (1991). Mandatory treatment for drug use during pregnancy. *Journal of the American Medical Association, 266,* 1156–1161.

Cherukuri, R., et al. (1988). A cohort study of alkaloidal cocaine ("crack") in pregnancy. *Obstetrics and Gynecology, 72,* 147–151.

Crack Cocaine Epidemic: Health Consequences and Treatment. (1991). Washington, DC: United States Government Printing Office.

Creasy, R. K., & Resnik, R. (1989). *Maternal-fetal medicine.* Philadelphia: W. B. Saunders.

Day, N. L., & Richardson, G. A. (1991). Prenatal marijuana use: Epidemiology, methodologic issues, and infant outcome. *Clinics in Perinatology, 18,* 77–91.

Deren, S. (1986). *Children of substance abusers: Review of the literature.* Albany: New York State Division of Substance Abuse Services, Bureau of Research and Evaluation.

Fanaroff, A. A., & Martin, R. J. (1992). *Neonatal-perinatal medicine.* (5th ed.). New York: C. W. Mosby.

Garcia, S. A. (1990). Birth penalty: Societal responses to perinatal chemical dependency. *Journal of Clinical Ethics, 1,* 135–140.

Golden, E., et al. (1990). Crack use, sexual behavior, and the risk for heterosexual transmission of HIV infection. Presented at American Public Health Association Annual Meeting, New York.

Hoegerman, G., & Schnoll, S. (1991). Narcotic use in pregnancy. *Clinics in Perinatology, 18,* 51–76.

Hoffman, H. J., & Hillman, L. S. (1992). Epidemiology of the sudden infant death syndrome: Maternal, neonatal, and postneonatal risk factors. *Clinics in Perinatology, 19,* 717–737.

Hoyme, H. E. (1990). Teratogenically induced fetal anomalies. *Clinics in Perinatology, 17,* 547–567.

Jones, K. L. (1991). Developmental pathogenesis of defects associated with prenatal cocaine exposure: Fetal vascular disruption. *Clinics in Perinatology, 18,* 139–145.

King, J. C., & Fabro, S. (1983). Alcohol consumption and cigarette smoking: Effect on pregnancy. *Clinical Obstetrics and Gynecology, 26*(2), 437–447.

Marzuk, P. M., et al. (1990). Prevalence of recent cocaine use among motor vehicle fatalities in New York City. *Journal of the American Medical Association, 263,* 250–256.

Mieczkowski, T. (1988). Crack distribution in Detroit. Presented at American Society of Criminology Annual Meeting, Chicago.

Narcotics Anonymous. (1988). Van Nuys, CA: NA World Service Office.

Nobles, W. W. , et al. (1987). *The culture of drugs in the black community.* New York: Black Family Institute.

Phibbs, C. S., Bateman, D. A., & Schwarz, R. M. (1991). The neonatal costs of maternal cocaine use. *Journal of the American Medical Association, 266,* 1521–1526.

Pietrantoni, M., & Knuppel, R. A. (1991). Alcohol use in pregnancy. *Clinics in Perinatology, 18,* 93–111.

Pirie, P. L., Murray, D. M., & Luepker, R. V. (1991). Gender differences in cigarette smoking and quitting in a cohort of young adults. *American Journal of Public Health, 81,* 324–327.

Reed, B. G. (1987). Developing women-sensitive drug-dependence treatment services: Why so difficult? *Journal of Psychoactive Drugs, 19,* 151–164.

Rolfs, R. T., Goldberg, M., & Sharrar, R. G. (1990). Risk factors for syphilis: Cocaine use and prostitution. *American Journal of Public Health, 80,* 853–857.

Rosenak, Y., et al. (1990). Cocaine: Maternal use during pregnancy and its effect on the mother, the fetus, and the infant. *Obstetrical and Gynecological Survey, 45,* 348–359.

Smith, D. W. (1982). *Recognizable patterns of human malformation.* (3rd ed.). Philadelphia: W. B. Saunders.

U. S. Department of Justice, Drug Enforcement Administration. (1988). *Crack cocaine availability and trafficking in the United States.* Washington, DC: Author.

4

Clinical Profile and Evaluation of Comorbid Major Depression and Alcoholism

Jack R. Cornelius, MD, MPH, Ihsan M. Salloum, MD, MPH, Dennis C. Daley, MSW, and Michael E. Thase, MD.

Dr. Cornelius is Associate Professor of Psychiatry, Dr. Salloum and Mr. Daley are Assistant Professors of Psychiatry, and Dr. Thase is Professor of Psychiatry, Western Psychiatric Institute and Clinic of the University of Pittsburgh, Pittsburgh, PA.

KEY POINTS

- The comorbid presence of major depression and alcohol use disorders is one of the most prevalent comorbid conditions in the United States; it should be differentiated from alcohol-induced depression.

- Depressed alcoholics have many symptoms in common with both nonalcoholic major depressed patients and nondepressed alcoholics. Some symptoms are more severe in this dual-diagnosis population than in nonalcoholic major depressed patients, including suicidality, impulsivity, low self-esteem, unstable relationships, and self-neglect.

- Evaluation of depressed alcoholics should focus on both alcohol-related and psychiatric problems.

- Depressed alcoholics are most commonly male, unmarried, and of low socioeconomic status.

- The majority of depressed alcoholics report that depressive symptoms precede their increased alcohol use and that depression is a bigger problem for them than alcoholism. Most use alcohol as a form of self-medication to escape from depression.

- To date, there is no clear pharmacologic "treatment of choice" for depressed alcoholics.

BACKGROUND

The comorbid presence of major depression and alcohol use disorders is among the most prevalent comorbid conditions in the United States (Helzer & Pryzbeck, 1988; Lewis, Helzer, Cloninger, Cronghan, & Whitman, 1982; Peace & Mellsop, 1987; Regier et al., 1990; Ross, Glaser, & Germanson, 1980). According to a report from the Epidemiologic Catchment Area (ECA) Study (Helzer & Pryzbeck, 1988), alcoholism and depression were the first and fourth most prevalent major DSM-III (*Diagnostic and Statistical Manual of Mental Disorders* [American Psychiatric Association, 1980]) disorders in the United States, respectively. Comorbidity between these two disorders occurs more commonly than would be expected by chance alone. Another report from the ECA study found that affective disorders were roughly twice as common among those with an alcohol use disorder as among those without an alcohol use disorder (Regier et al., 1990). Furthermore, individuals treated in mental health and addictive disorder clinical settings have a greater likelihood of having comorbid disorders than those in the community (Regier et al., 1990). Thus, comorbidity between alcoholism and depressive disorders is particularly common in clinical populations.

Despite the prevalence of patients with comorbid major depression and alcohol use disorders (hereinafter referred to as "depressed alcoholics"), the clinical profile of these patients remains unclear. Previously published reports describing this dual-diagnosis population had almost exclusively involved patients treated in facilities for alcohol rehabilitation, whereas those treated at psychiatric hospitals were largely excluded (Ross et al., 1980). Depressive symptomatology in alcohol rehabilitation facilities is generally less severe than that found in dual-diagnosis patients in psychiatric hospitals (Cornelius, Salloum, Mezzich et al., 1995; Salloum et al., 1995). Comparisons between depressed alcoholics and nonalcoholic major depressed patients were scarce, primarily because of the lack of reports from psychiatric hospitals, which contain both alcoholic and nonalcoholic major depressive populations. Comparisons between dual-diagnosis populations and single diagnosis comparison groups (i.e., nondepressed alcoholics and nonalcoholic major depressed patients) also have been frequently limited by small sample size.

In the last couple of years, the first few papers have been published comparing large samples of depressed alcoholics to both nonalcoholic major depressed patients and nondepressed alcoholics (Cornelius et al., 1996; Cornelius, Jarrett et al., 1995; Cornelius, Salloum, Mezzich et al., 1995; Salloum et al., 1995). These studies have provided the first comprehensive description of the clinical features that distinguish this dual-diagnosis group from both of the two relevant single-diagnosis populations.

In this chapter, the clinical features that characterize depressed alcoholics are reviewed. This description includes definitions of major depressive disorder and of alcohol dependence (American Psychiatric Association [APA], 1994), as well as an enumeration of the most prominent symptoms of depressed alcoholics. In addition, clinical correlates are presented concerning demographic characteristics, psychosocial stressors, level of functioning, personal and social history markers, and family history of depressed alcoholics as opposed to those of the single-diagnosis comparison groups. The evaluation, treatment, and clinical course of depressed alcoholics are reviewed briefly. The etiology and pathogenesis of this population also are discussed. Finally, future directions in the understanding of this population are presented.

DEFINITION AND DSM-IV DIAGNOSTIC CRITERIA

In this chapter, *depressed alcoholics* will be defined as patients with both comorbid major depressive disorder and alcohol dependence. According to the DSM-IV (APA, 1994), the essential feature of major depressive disorder is a clinical course that is characterized by one or more major depressive episodes without a history of manic, mixed, or hypomanic episodes. A major depressive episode must exhibit five or more of the following nine symptoms during the same 2-week period:

1. Depressed mood

2. Diminished interest or pleasure

3. Significant weight loss

4. Insomnia or hypersomnia

5. Psychomotor agitation or retardation

6. Fatigue or loss of energy

7. Feelings of worthlessness or guilt

8. Decreased concentration

9. Recurrent suicidal ideation or a suicide attempt

According to the DSM-IV, the essential feature of *alcohol dependence* is a maladaptive pattern of alcohol use, leading to a clinically significant impairment or distress, as manifested by three or more of the following symptoms, occurring at any time in the same 12-month period:

• Tolerance (need for increased amounts for intoxication)

• Withdrawal syndrome or use to relieve or avoid withdrawal

• Unsuccessful efforts to decrease drinking

• Drinking in larger amounts

- Giving up on important activities

- Much time spent obtaining alcohol or recovering from its effects

- Continued drinking despite physical or psychological problems

CLINICAL FEATURES

As would be expected, the dual-diagnosis population of depressed alcoholics has many symptoms in common with both nonalcoholic major depressed patients and nondepressed alcoholics. However, the acute symptom profile of hospitalized depressed alcoholics tends to resemble that of major depressed patients more than that of alcoholics. Symptoms of depression in these patients, in decreasing order of prominence, include depressed mood, low self-esteem, hyposomnia, suicidality, social withdrawal, decreased appetite, decreased motor activity, poor concentration, decreased weight, general anxiety, and decreased libido. Alcohol-related symptoms include excessive alcohol use, impulsivity, lack of insight, and illicit substance use. A variety of associated symptoms also may be seen, such as auditory and visual hallucinations, confusion, disorientation, and poor memory (Cornelius, Salloum, Mezzich et al., 1995; Salloum et al., 1995).

Several symptoms are more severe in depressed alcoholics than in nonalcoholic major depressed patients. These include suicidality, impulsivity, low self-esteem, unstable relationships, and self-neglect. The symptom that most clearly distinguishes depressed alcoholics from nonalcoholic major depressed patients is level of suicidality, despite the fact that most depressive symptoms do not distinguish between these diagnostic groups. Suicidal behavior is especially marked in the dual-diagnosis group as compared to nonalcoholic major depressed patients (Cornelius, Salloum, Mezzich et al., 1995;

Salloum et al., 1995). By contrast, a wide variety of depressive symptoms are more prominent in depressed alcoholics than in nondepressed alcoholics, whereas level of alcohol use, violent behavior, lack of insight, and impulsivity are more prominent in nondepressed alcoholics.

The clinical profile of depressed alcoholics is influenced by factors such as gender and ethnicity. For example, generalized anxiety, reversed neurovegetative symptoms (e.g., increased sleep and increased appetite), and minor tranquilizer abuse are more common in female depressed alcoholics. Other factors are more prominent in male depressed alcoholics, including level of alcohol use, drug use other than minor tranquilizer abuse, and antisocial behavior (Cornelius, Jarrett et al., 1995; Hesselbrock, Meyer, & Keener, 1985). Reversed neurovegetative symptoms (also called atypical depressive symptoms) are more common in Caucasian than in African-American depressed alcoholics, but the level of alcohol and drug use is higher among African-American depressed alcoholics (Cornelius, Fabrega et al., 1996).

The association between alcoholism and depression in depressed alcoholics is complex and has fomented much debate (Schuckit, 1986). Some authors have described the relationship between these two disorders to be an example of the "chicken and the egg" phenomenon (Meyer, 1986). Others have concluded that the distinction between primary versus secondary depression is an important distinction and should be made whenever possible (Powell, Read, Penick, Miller, & Bingham, 1987). Hesselbrock and associates (1985) reported that depression tends to precede alcohol abuse in women, whereas the reverse pattern is more common among men. Cloninger and colleagues (Cloninger, 1987; Cloninger, Bohman, & Sigvardsson, 1981) developed the type 1/type 2 classification system of alcoholics based on factors including gender, inheritance pattern, severity and recurrence of alcoholism, environmental reactivity, and criminality. The type 1/type 2 classification system significantly overlaps with the primary/secondary classification of alcoholics (Anthenelli, Smith, Irwin, & Schucki, 1994). However, significant variability occurs in assigning diagnoses of type 1 and type 2 alcoholism with the use of current methods (Anthenelli et al., 1994). Thus, to date, no single subtyping system has sustained wide acceptance for subtyping depressed alcoholics or alcoholics in general.

CLINICAL COURSE

The age of onset of first alcohol abuse is generally slightly younger than the first depressive episode (Cornelius, Ehler et al., 1995). However, most depressed alcoholics report that depressive symptoms precede their increased alcohol use in a typical episode, and a majority report that depression is a bigger problem for them than alcoholism. Most report using alcohol as a form of self-medication to escape from depression (Cornelius, Salloum, Cornelius et al., 1995). However, the patient's report of depression preceding pathologic alcohol use often conflicts with reports from family or outpatient therapists, who report that increased drinking was apparent before an observable increase in depressive symptoms and who often see drinking as the patient's primary problem. Consequently, family members often view the patient's report of depression preceding increased alcohol use as evidence of the patient's denial of the alcoholism.

Most depressed alcoholics exhibit mild depressive symptoms and occasional light drinking between major symptom exacerbations. Symptom exacerbations often are triggered by prominent psychosocial stressors, such as loss of a significant other or loss of a job (Murphy, Wetzel, Robins, & McEvoy, 1992). Following the stressor or stressors, the patient's alcohol use and depression may increase relatively quickly, resulting in prominent depressive symptoms in conjunction with a heavy alcohol binge. An increase in comorbid illicit substance use also may occur during these episodes. Suicidal ideations are common during such episodes, and actual suicide attempts are fairly common (Hawton, Fagg, & McKeown, 1989; Klatsky & Armstrong, 1993; Schuckit, 1985). Prominent depressive symptoms or an actual suicide attempt often lead to psychiatric hospitalization, on either a voluntary or involuntary basis. Depressive symptoms often decrease following detoxification but frequently worsen on discharge from the hospital in conjunction with relapse of drinking unless additional treatment is provided. Over their lifetime, many depressed alcoholics require multiple psychiatric hospitalizations and multiple episodes of treatment in a detoxification center. Multiple lifetime suicide attempts are not uncommon (Cornelius et al., 1993; Cornelius, Ehler et al., 1995). The lifetime risk for completed suicide attempt is high in depressed alcoholics (Barraclough, Bunch, Nelson, & Sainsbury, 1974; Cornelius et al., 1993; Lesage et al., 1994; Nicholls, Edwards, & Kyle, 1974; Roy & Linnoila, 1986).

DEMOGRAPHIC CHARACTERISTICS

Depressed alcoholics are primarily men, which is more similar to the gender distribution of alcoholism rather than that of major depression. Comorbid depression and alcoholism are more prevalent among hospitalized African-Americans than among hospitalized Caucasians. Depressed alcoholics are similar in age to nonalcoholic major depressed patients and are older in general than nondepressed alcoholics. A large proportion of depressed alcoholics are unmarried, which is similar to the pattern seen in nondepressed alcoholics. Conversely, the proportion of depressed alcoholics who are single, divorced, separated, or widowed is high. The social class of depressed alcoholics is typically low to very low, which is similar to that of nondepressed alcoholics and lower than that seen in nonalcoholic major depressed patients. Thus, in general, the demographic profile of depressed alcoholics is more similar to that of nondepressed alcoholics than to that of nonalcoholic major depressed patients, with the exception of age distribution, which is more similar to that of nonalcoholic major depressed patients (Cornelius, Salloum, Mezzich et al., 1995; Salloum et al., 1995).

PSYCHOSOCIAL STRESSORS AND LEVEL OF FUNCTIONING

Psychosocial stressors often are severe before a relapse into drinking or depression among depressed alcoholics. Specifically, interpersonal loss, family discord, poor social support, living alone, unemployment, financial trouble, and serious medical illness often are seen in depressed alcoholics, especially at times when the patient makes a suicide attempt (Murphy et al., 1992). Depressed alcoholics have more stressors in the areas of employment and of bereavement than either of the single-diagnosis comparison groups (Salloum et al., 1995).

Long-term level of functioning among depressed alcoholics is typically poor, which is similar to that seen among nondepressed alcoholics and lower than that seen among nonalcoholic major depressed patients. However, all three populations are impaired during acute relapses (Cornelius, Salloum, Mezzich et al., 1995; Salloum et al., 1995).

PERSONAL HISTORY MARKERS AND FAMILY HISTORY

Depressed alcoholics are similar to nondepressed alcoholics on their personal history profile, with both populations displaying a high level of abnormalities. These abnormalities are not limited to variables that may have resulted from consequences of alcoholism, such as difficulties in employment or lack of social support, but include variables that usually predate drinking behavior, such as being raised in a broken family, behavioral problems at school, and academic difficulties. In contrast, depressed alcoholics demonstrate significantly higher levels of most personal history abnormalities than nonalcoholic major depressed patients, including perinatal problems, developmental delays, growing up in a broken home, behavioral problems at school, academic problems, difficulties during military service, considerable periods of unemployment, history of marital disharmony, arrests with convictions, and lack of social support (Cornelius, Salloum, Mezzich et al., 1995; Salloum et al., 1995).

Few studies have been conducted evaluating the family history of patients with comorbid major depressive disorder and alcoholism. Depressed alcoholics reportedly have high rates of both major depression and alcoholism in their family history (Salloum et al., 1995). Thus, depressed alcoholics may bear a double burden of familial disorders.

EVALUATION

Evaluation of depressed alcoholics should always focus on both alcohol-related and psychiatric problems. A history of alcohol-related problems should include a careful history of alcohol and drug use patterns, neurologic signs, cognitive deficits, seizures, history of head trauma, and a history of various treatments for alcoholism. A history of psychiatric problems should include a careful history of depressive symptoms, with a particular focus on suicidal ideation and suicidal behavior, but also should include questions concerning hallucinations, delusions, and homicidal ideations. Nonmedical therapists and nonpsychiatric physicians should collaborate with psychiatrists in the evaluation of depressed alcoholics who demonstrate significant suicidal ideation or other significant psychiatric symptoms.

Hospitalization often is necessary for patients with significant suicidal ideation, suicidal behavior, or imminent risk of delirium tremens. Indeed, depressed alcoholics are more likely to be hospitalized than either nonalcoholic major depressed patients or nondepressed alcoholics (Salloum et al., 1995). Because of the prominence of both the depressive and the alcohol-related symptoms, hospitalization should ideally occur initially in a dual-diagnosis inpatient unit where special expertise in evaluating and treating depressed alcoholics is available. Initial treatment for dual-diagnosis patients in less restrictive settings, such as in day treatment programs, frequently is unsuccessful (Case, 1991). Hospitalization for relapses of depression and drinking may be relatively brief, despite the initial prominent symptom severity, because several studies indicate that depressive symptoms often decrease substantially within a few weeks of admission (Cornelius et al., 1993; Dackis, Gold, Pottash, & Sweeney, 1986; Gibson & Becker, 1973; Kranzler et al., 1995; Overall, Reilly, Kelley, & Hollister, 1985).

TREATMENT

Depressed alcoholics often receive group therapy, disulfiram, and anticonvulsant treatment, all of which are commonly used in nondepressed alcoholics. However, depressed alcoholics also are treated with a variety of treatments commonly used in nonalcoholic major depressed patients; these treatments include individual psychotherapy, antidepressant medication, and minor tranquilizers (Salloum et al., 1995). The effectiveness of these treatments, either individually or in combination, in depressed alcoholics has received little attention until recent years.

Preliminary placebo-controlled studies suggest that selective serotonin agonists such as fluoxetine decrease the drinking and the depressive symptoms of depressed alcoholics; however, these studies have not yet been confirmed (Cornelius, Salloum et al., 1993; Cornelius, Salloum, Cornelius et al., 1995; Cornelius et al., 1996; Kranzler et al., 1995). The efficacy of tricyclic antidepressants recently has been evaluated in a few studies involving depressed alcoholics (Mason & Kocsis, 1991; Mason, Kocsis, Ritvo, & Cutler, 1996; McGrath et al., 1996). These studies report modest efficacy for tricyclic antidepressants in treating the depressive symptoms of depressed alcoholics but report no significant efficacy for tricyclic antidepressants in treating the excessive alcohol use of these patients. Treatment with tricyclic antidepressants also is limited by their anticholinergic side effects, by their potential for fatality when taken in overdose amounts, by their complicated titration schedule, and by their need for periodic medication blood levels. Consequently, the efficacy and clinical utility of tricyclic antidepressants remain unclear in depressed alcoholics.

The efficacy of naltrexone also has been evaluated in a couple recent studies involving alcoholics (O'Malley et al., 1992; Volpicelli et al., 1992). These studies have reported efficacy for naltrexone in treating the excessive alcohol use of nondepressed alcoholics. However, none of these studies involving naltrexone have included *depressed* alcoholics, so it is unclear whether naltrexone is efficacious in treating either the drinking or the depression of depressed alcoholics.

In conclusion, the only class of medications that has been reported to effectively treat both the drinking and the depression of depressed alcoholics are the selective serotonin antagonists. However, it should be noted that these reports of efficacy for selective serotonin antagonists in depressed alcoholics are preliminary and unconfirmed. In contrast, tricyclic antidepressants effectively treat the depressive symptoms of depressed alcoholics but do not effectively treat the excessive alcohol use of these patients. Naltrexone effectively treats the excessive alcohol use of nondepressed alcoholics, but no studies to date have been performed with naltrexone in depressed alcoholics, so no efficacy has been shown for the depressive symptoms or excessive alcohol use of these patients. Consequently, so far no definitive pharmacologic "treatment of choice" exists for depressed alcoholics.

ETIOLOGY AND PATHOPHYSIOLOGY

The etiology and pathophysiology of the depressive disorder and the alcohol use disorder of depressed alcoholics is not fully understood. Studies evaluating cerebrospinal fluid 5-hydroxyindoleacetic acid (5-HIAA) levels and brain stem 5-HIAA levels implicate low serotonergic functioning in the etiology of suicidality (Asberg, Traskman, & Thoren, 1976; Mann, Stanley, McBride, & McEwen, 1986; Traskman, Asberg, Bertilsson, & Sjostrand, 1981), excessive alcohol use (Ballenger, Goodwin, Major, & Brown, 1979; Banki, 1981; Banki, Arato, Papp, & Kurcz, 1984; Takahashi, Yamane, & Tani, 1974), and impulsivity (Moss, 1987; Soubrié, 1986), all of which characterize depressed alcoholics. Consequently, it is possible that the clinical association of suicidality, pathologic alcohol use, and impulsivity in depressed alcoholics is explained by the fact that these symptom domains are associated with serotonergic dysfunction. For example, Takahashi and colleagues (1974) speculated that abnormality of brain serotonin metabolism might be a factor causing both the psychological abstinent symptoms and the depressive mood symptoms—including suicidal ideation—that are commonly found among alcoholics. Ballenger and co-workers (1979) further speculated that the pathophysiology of alcoholism might involve preexisting low brain serotonin levels that are transiently increased by acute alcohol consumption, which eventually leads to a further depletion of brain serotonin levels. These speculations are consistent with later studies that show that alcohol-preferring lines of rats have lower brain levels of serotonin and 5-HIAA than nonpreferring lines of rats (Murphy, McBride, Lumeng, & Li, 1982). These basic scientific studies may help explain the apparent clinical efficacy of serotonergic medications in depressed alcoholics. However, to date, the precise role of serotonin and other neurotransmitters in depressed alcoholics remains unclear.

FUTURE DIRECTIONS

The prevalence and clinical importance of dual disorders only recently has begun to be realized. Much remains to be investigated concerning depressed alcoholics and other dual disorders. For example, little is known about the etiology, pathophysiology, or long-term course of these disorders. Further studies are warranted to clarify the role of serotonin and of other neurotransmitters in the etiology and pathophysiology of depressed alcoholics. Such studies may help explain the apparent clinical efficacy of serotonergic medications in these patients. The nature of the relationship between the depression and the alcoholism of depressed alcoholics remains unclear. Furthermore, little is known about the treatment response of depressed alcoholics to various classes of medications. Longer-term medication studies, such as continuation trials, are particularly scarce. Virtually nothing is known about potential predictors of response (e.g., gender, ethnicity, severity of depression, or severity of alcohol use) to various treatments. Finally, it is unclear which combination of treatments, such as medication plus psychotherapy, is most useful for different subpopulations of depressed alcoholics. Further studies are warranted to answer these questions.

REFERENCES

American Psychiatric Association. (1980). *Diagnostic and statistical manual of mental disorders* (3rd ed.). Washington, DC: Author.

American Psychiatric Association. (1994). *Diagnostic and statistical manual of mental disorders* (4th ed.). Washington, DC: Author.

Anthenelli, R. M., Smith, T. L., Irwin, M. R., & Schucki, M. A. (1994). A comparative study of criteria for subgrouping alcoholics: The primary/secondary diagnostic scheme versus variations of the type 1/type 2 criteria. *American Journal of Psychiatry, 151,* 1468–1474.

Asberg, M., Traskman, L., & Thoren, P. (1976). 5-HIAA in the cerebrospinal fluid. *Archives of General Psychiatry, 33,* 1193-1197.

Ballenger, J. C., Goodwin, F. K., Major, L. F., & Brown, G. L. (1979). Alcohol and central serotonin metabolism in man. *Archives of General Psychiatry, 36,* 224-227.

Banki, C. M. (1981). Factors influencing monoamine metabolites and tryptophan in patients with alcohol dependence. *Journal of Neural Transmission, 50,* 89-101.

Banki, C. M., Arato, M., Papp, Z., & Kurcz, M. (1984). Biochemical markers in suicidal patients. *Journal of Affective Disorders, 6,* 341-350.

Barraclough, B., Bunch, J., Nelson, B., & Sainsbury, P. (1974). A hundred cases of suicide: Clinical aspects. *British Journal of Psychiatry, 125,* 355-373.

Case, N. (1991). The dual-diagnosis patient in a psychiatric day treatment program: A treatment failure. *Journal of Substance Abuse Treatment, 8,* 69-73.

Cloninger, C. R. (1987). A systematic method for clinical description and classification of personality variants. *Archives of General Psychiatry, 44,* 573-588.

Cloninger, C. R., Bohman, M., & Sigvardsson, S. (1981). Inheritance of alcohol abuse: Cross-fostering analysis of adopted men. *Archives of General Psychiatry, 38,* 862-868.

Cornelius, J. R., Ehler, J., Jarrett, P., Levin, R., Cornelius, M. D., Mann, J. J., & Black, A. (1995). Patterns of alcohol abuse and suicidality in alcoholics with major depression. *Alcoholism, Clinical and Experimental Research, 19,* 108A.

Cornelius, J. R., Fabrega H., Cornelius, M. D., Mezzich, J., Maher, P. J., Salloum, I. M., Thase, M. E., & Ulrich, R. F. (1996). Racial effects on the clinical presentation of alcoholics at a psychiatric hospital. *Comprehensive Psychiatry, 37,* 102-108.

Cornelius, J. R., Jarrett, P. J., Thase, M. E., Fabrega, H., Haas, G. L., Jones-Barlock, A., Mezzich, J. E., & Ulrich, R. F. (1995). Gender effects on the clinical presentation of alcoholics at a psychiatric hospital. *Comprehensive Psychiatry, 36,* 435-440.

Cornelius, J. R., Salloum, I. M., Cornelius, M. D., Perel, J. M., Ehler, J. G., Jarrett, P. J., Levin, R. L., Black, A., & Mann, J. J. (1995). Preliminary report: Double-blind placebo-controlled study of fluoxetine in depressed alcoholics. *Psychopharmacology Bulletin, 31,* 297-303.

Cornelius, J. R., Salloum, I. M., Cornelius, M. D., Perel, J. M., Thase, M. E., Ehler, J. G., & Mann, J. J. (1993). Fluoxetine trial in suicidal depressed alcoholics. *Psychopharmacology Bulletin, 29,* 195-199.

Cornelius, J. R., Salloum, I. M., Ehler, J. G., Jarrett, P. J., Cornelius, M. D., & Black, A. (1996). Fluoxetine versus placebo in suicidal depressed alcoholics. *Alcoholism: Clinical and Experimental Research, 20,* 94A.

Cornelius, J. R., Salloum, I. M., Mezzich, J., Cornelius, M. D., Fabrega, H., Ehler, J. G., Ulrich, R. F., Thase, M. E., & Mann, J. J. (1995). Dispro-portionate suicidality in patients with comorbid major depression and alcoholism. *American Journal of Psychiatry, 152,* 358-364.

Dackis, C. A., Gold, M. S., Pottash, A. L., & Sweeney, D. R. (1986). Evaluating depression in alcoholics. *Psychiatry Research, 17,* 105-109.

Gibson, S., & Becker, J. (1973). Changes in alcoholics' self-reported depression. *Quarterly Journal on the Study of Alcoholism, 34,* 829-836.

Hawton, K., Fagg, J., & McKeown, S. (1989). Alcoholism, alcohol, and attempted suicide. *Alcohol and Alcoholism, 24,* 3-9.

Helzer, J. E., & Pryzbeck, T. R. (1988). The co-occurrence of alcoholism with other psychiatric disorders in the general population and its impact on treatment. *Journal of Studies on Alcohol, 49,* 219-224.

Hesselbrock, M. N., Meyer, R. E., & Keener, J. J. (1985). Psychopathology in hospitalized alcoholics. *Archives of General Psychiatry, 42,* 1050-1055.

Klatsky, A. L., & Armstrong, M. A. (1993). Alcohol use, other traits, and risk of unnatural death: A prospective study. *Alcoholism, Clinical, and Experimental Research, 17,* 1156-1162.

Kranzler, H. R., Burleson, J. A., Korner, P., Del Boca, F. K., Bohn, M. J., Brown, J., & Liebowitz, N. (1995). Placebo-controlled trial of fluoxetine as an adjunct to relapse prevention in alcoholics. *American Journal of Psychiatry, 152,* 391-397.

Lesage, A. D., Boyer, R., Grunberg, F., Vanier, C., Morissette, R., Menard-Buteau, C., & Loyer, M. (1994). Suicide and mental disorders: A case-control study of young men. *American Journal of Psychiatry, 151,* 1062-1068.

Lewis, C. E., Helzer, J., Cloninger, C. R., Cronghan, J., & Whitman, B. Y. (1982). Psychiatric diagnostic predisposition to alcoholism. *Comprehensive Psychiatry, 23,* 451-461.

Mann, J. J., Stanley, M., McBride, P.A., & McEwen, B. S. (1986). Increased serotonin$_2$ and beta-adrenergic binding in frontal cortices of suicide victims. *Archives of General Psychiatry, 43,* 954-959.

Mason, B. J., & Kocsis, J. H. (1991). Desipramine treatment of alcoholism. *Psychopharmacology Bulletin, 27,* 155-161.

Mason, B. J., Kocsis, J. H., Ritvo, E. C., & Cutler, R. B. (1996). A double-blind placebo-controlled trial of desipramine for primary alcohol dependence stratified on the presence or absence of major depression. *Journal of the American Medical Association, 275,* 761-767.

McGrath, P. J., Nunes, E. V., Stewart, J. W., Goldman, D., Agosti, V., Ocepek-Welikson, K., & Quitkin, F. M. (1996). Imipramine treatment of alcoholics with primary depression: A placebo-controlled clinical trial. *Archives of General Psychiatry, 53,* 232-240.

Meyer, R. E. (1986). How to understand the relationship between psychopathology and addictive disorders: Another example of the chicken and the egg. In R. E. Meyer (Ed.), *Psychopathology and addictive disorders* (pp. 3-16). New York: Guilford Press.

Moss, H. B. (1987). Serotonergic activity and disinhibitory psychopathology in alcoholism. *Medical Hypothesis, 23,* 353-361.

Murphy, J. M., McBride, W. J., Lumeng, L., & Li, T. K. (1982). Regional brain levels of monoamines in alcohol-preferring and nonpreferring lines of rats. *Pharmacology, Biochemistry and Behavior, 16,* 145-149.

Murphy, G. E., Wetzel, R. D., Robins, E., & McEvoy, L. (1992). Multiple risk factors predict suicide in alcoholism. *Archives of General Psychiatry, 49,* 459-463.

Nicholls, P., Edwards, G., & Kyle, E. (1974). Alcoholics admitted to four hospitals in England: General and cause-specific mortality. *Quarterly Journal on the Study of Alcoholism, 35,* 841-855.

O'Malley, S. S., Jaffe, A. J., Chang, G., Schottenfeld, R. S., Meyer, R. E., Rounsaville, B. (1992). Naltrexone and coping skills therapy for alcohol dependence. A controlled study. *Archives of General Psychiatry, 49,* 881-887.

Overall, J. E., Reilly, E. L., Kelley, J. T., & Hollister, L. E. (1985). Persistence of depression in detoxified alcoholics. *Alcoholism, Clinical and Experimental Research, 9,* 331-333.

Peace, K., & Mellsop, G. (1987). Alcoholism and psychiatric disorders. *Australian and New Zealand Journal of Psychiatry, 21,* 94-101.

Powell, B. J., Read, M. R., Penick, E. C., Miller, N. S., & Bingham, S. F. (1987). Primary and secondary depression in alcoholic men: An important distinction. *Journal of Clinical Psychiatry, 48,* 98-101.

Regier, D. A., Farmer, M. E., Rae, D. S., Locke, B. Z., Keith, S. J., Judd, L. L., & Goodwin, F. K. (1990). Comorbidity of mental disorders with alcohol and other drug abuse. *Journal of the American Medical Association, 264,* 2511-2518.

Ross, H. E., Glaser, I. B., & Germanson, T. (1980). The prevalence of psychiatric disorders in patients with alcohol and drug problems. *Archives of General Psychiatry, 45,* 1023-1031.

Roy, A., & Linnoila, M. (1986). Alcoholism and suicide. *Suicide and Life-Threatening Behavior, 16,* 244-273.

Salloum, I. M., Mezzich, J., Cornelius, J. R., Day, N. L., Daley, D., & Kirisci, L. (1995). Clinical profile of comorbid major depression and alcohol use disorders in an initial psychiatric evaluation. *Comprehensive Psychiatry, 36*(4), 260-266.

Schuckit, M. A. (1985). The clinical implications of primary diagnostic groups among alcoholics. *Archives of General Psychiatry, 42,* 1043-1049.

Schuckit, M. A. (1986). Genetic and clinical implications of alcoholism and affective disorder. *American Journal of Psychiatry, 143,* 140-147.

Soubrié, P. (1986). Reconciling the role of central serotonin neurons in humans and animal behavior. *Behavioral and Brain Sciences, 9,* 319-364.

Takahashi, S., Yamane, H. K., & Tani, K. (1974). CSF monoamine metabolites in alcoholism: A comparative study with depression. *Folia Psychiatrica Neurologica Japonica, 28,* 347–354.

Traskman, L., Asberg, M., Bertilsson, L., & Sjostrand, L. (1981). Monamine metabolites in CSF and suicidal behavior. *Archives of General Psychiatry, 38,* 631-636.

Volpicelli, J. R., Alterman, A. I., Hayashida, M., O'Brien, C. P. (1992). Naltrexone and the treatment of alcohol dependence. *Archives of General Psychiatry, 49,* 876-880.

5

Overcoming Adolescent Addiction: Working with Families and the Role of 12-Step Programs

Robert L. DuPont, MD

Dr. DuPont is President, Institute for Behavior and Health Inc, Rockville, MD, and Clinical Professor of Psychiatry, Georgetown University School of Medicine, Washington, DC.

KEY POINTS

- Treating addiction in adolescent clients often requires participation in an addiction treatment program with a solid foundation. Programs such as the 12-step approach of Alcoholics Anonymous (AA) provide the necessary structure, climate of honesty, and group support crucial to ending harmful addictions.

- Once a family concedes the necessity of external intervention by specialists in substance abuse, counselors should help parents find the most appropriate addiction treatment program. The 12-step path represents an adolescent patient's best chance for a successful long-term recovery.

- Family members of clients suffering from addictions frequently develop co-dependence. Counselors should regard addiction holistically (i.e., both as an individual and a familial problem rather than the exclusive failure and responsibility of the substance abuser).

- Families should establish their own clearly defined rules for family life — including what terms are acceptable for alcohol and drug use — and consequences for violating such rules.

- Counselors can learn about addiction by working through issues of addiction with their clients and by attending 12-step meetings.

INTRODUCTION

Preventive measures, drug testing, and even professional counseling sometimes are not sufficient to prevent or cure addiction in adolescent clients. Addiction treatment programs with a solid foundation, such as the 12-step approach of Alcoholics Anonymous (AA), provide the necessary structure, climate of honesty, and group support to end harmful addictions. Mental health professionals and substance abuse counselors are uniquely positioned to refer addicted adolescents to the 12-step programs, to help them adopt and adjust to a treatment regimen, and to present them with opportunities to strengthen their self-esteem in a drug-free life.

THE ROLE OF ADDICTION TREATMENT

Counseling adolescents and setting up a family program to deter substance abuse often does not end adolescent addiction. When addiction persists after these initial interventions, it is appropriate to refer the teenager and the family to an addiction treatment program. Addiction treatment is now available on both an inpatient and outpatient basis. Costs range from a few thousand dollars to as much as $30,000. Some health insurance plans cover addiction treatments, but insurers are becoming less amenable to subsidizing addiction treatment and other forms of mental health care.

Once a family concedes the necessity of external intervention by specialists in substance abuse, counselors should inform parents of the most appropriate addiction treatment programs, as well as apprise them of which choices are the most geographically and financially accessible. Counselors also may help parents through the often-grueling process of sharing authority over their children with these programs by reminding them that they are taking steps integral to their child's recovery and that formal addiction treatment is a relatively short part of the teenager's life. Whether it lasts 2–6 weeks (as many inpatient programs do) or 10–15 weeks (as many intensive outpatient addiction treatment programs do), addiction treatment is intensive and relatively brief.

Once a formal addiction treatment program ends, clients should be encouraged to enter *aftercare* to maximize the impact of that treatment. Aftercare commonly entails joining a 12-step fellowship (recommended for both the adolescent and the adolescent's family), participating in systematic drug testing, and undergoing continued counseling. The counselor may optimize the family's use of aftercare by integrating both the 12-step programs and addiction treatment into the life of the family in a manner similar to that of a primary care physician who helps patients and their families use hospital and specialist health care in cost-effective ways.

DEALING WITH PARENTAL ADDICTION AND OTHER FAMILY PROBLEMS

Regarding addiction holistically (i.e., as a familial problem rather than the exclusive failure and responsibility of the substance abuser) enables the counselor to generate a constructive family dynamic that mitigates the divisive impact of the disease and clears the path to a more thorough rectification of the problematic context that often precedes addiction. The family of a person suffering from an addiction will likely develop co-dependence (i.e., the loss of self in an all-consuming, external, needy, and emotional focal point) as the relations of family members become inextricably tied to the presence of addiction (DuPont & McGovern, 1996). Families with addicted adolescents usually require counseling and should be encouraged to attend Al-Anon meetings to overcome this co-dependence. Commendable addiction treatment programs include activities designed for families so that relatives of teenagers addicted to alcohol or other drugs can evaluate their own roles in the disease of addiction, as well as confront feelings of anger, bewilderment, and resentment without guilt or shame. Addictions thrive on repression and lies; a treatment program should expose and eradicate these weak foundations by stressing the liberation and empowerment that personal integrity and relational honesty make possible.

Addiction often has a genetic component. With this in mind, counselors must be prepared to help parents and siblings face not only their problems of co-dependence but also their own active addiction to alcohol or other drugs. Today, many families with relatively newly addicted adolescents have family members who have been active in 12-step fellowships. Because of these family members' experiential knowledge, often passionate conviction about the value of sobriety, and positions in the addicts' families, the counselor typically enlists their help in educating and supporting the related substance abuser struggling to recover from addiction.

Before they enter into active recovery, adolescents with substance abuse problems frequently cast blame for their problem-generating behaviors onto their parents and others. When I have encountered this attempt to deny self-accountability, I share sentiments widely held in the recovery community: "I respect your need to conduct your own research into addiction. I have a lot of experience, but I cannot foresee the future. Over time we will learn together about what works for you and what does not."

I use this same committed-but-detached approach with families that have remarkably different values from mine about teenage use of alcohol or other drugs. I definitely do not insist they adopt my views but am honored that my patients have sought my services and listened to my thoughts on the problems they face. I understand and respect that each family must find its own means of addressing its unique problems, and I welcome the fact that families have many sources of information in addition to me. As their counselor, I make myself available to help families engaged in their own research on addiction. I also acknowledge that their attempt to grapple with the addiction is a way of regaining a sense of control that has been lost and is vital to a successful recovery.

SETTING LIMITS WITHIN THE FAMILY

I strongly encourage families to establish their own rules for family life, including what is acceptable from a teenager when it comes to the use of alcohol or other drugs. No one rule is right for all families, but each family needs to have rules and clearly defined consequences for violating them. Modest penalties, such as restrictions on staying away from the home, curfews, and driving the family car, are usually sufficient to ensure that the adolescent abides by rules set by the family. For some teenagers, family teamwork with clear rules is all that is needed to stop alcohol and other drug use.

However, should such measures prove futile, the family members will have to think about what they must do if the adolescent fails to comply with family rules concerning alcohol or drug use. In worst case scenarios, parents may have to resort to drastic measures to make their substance-abusing adolescent aware of the gravity of the problem. As controversial as the use of drug tests for adolescents may seem, the so-called "tough love" approach (e.g., booting a substance-abusing teenager out of the home if he or she refuses to obey the family's rules for the use of alcohol or other drugs) presents a precarious and heart-wrenching challenge to parents.

It is seldom necessary to invoke the ultimate penalty: expulsion from the family home. Families should make every effort (through counseling, addiction treatment, and the families' own active involvement in Al-Anon) to avoid expulsion from the home without accepting ongoing use of alcohol or other drugs. If this conservative but challenging approach fails, as it sometimes does, then the family can turn to the legal system.

Indeed, the courts can stabilize seriously disrupted families confronting adolescent addiction. Rebellious, drug-using adolescents feel differently when faced with the prospect of jail if they do not meet the standards imposed by strict judges. However, if the courts also fail to stop the substance abuse, families may be forced to send the following message to their recalcitrant teenagers:

> We have our rules. If you cannot accept them, you are making a choice that your continued use of alcohol or other drugs is more important to you than living with us. By continuing to use drugs, you have chosen to leave our home. We will continue to love you and to stay involved in your life in any way that does not enable you to continue using alcohol or other drugs. The door to our family remains open for your return whenever you have decided to accept our rules. We will welcome you home whenever you are ready to accept those rules, which we are enforcing because we believe that they are essential to your maturing into a healthy, independent adult.

The most difficult part of this limit-setting process for most parents is summoning the courage to stop enabling their children's drug use by enforcing this Spartan measure. Once families take such a stand, they then face a second challenge: to be continuously loving and not rejective of or hostile to their rebellious children. I help my patients and their families by telling them that I have seen many adolescents go through similar learning experiences and that most of these youngsters, usually sooner rather than later, decide that their families are more valuable than drugs. Counselors can help families work through this difficult process, including the time when the adolescent is living outside the home. The 12-step fellowships can help both teenagers and their parents benefit from this painful experience.

Working with troubled adolescents and their families for many years, I have learned that success comes with humility and patience. I have learned to be hopeful at all times. Many desperate, seemingly hopeless addiction problems do find reasonably positive outcomes. For this reason, I emphasize to adolescents and their parents a sense of hope and reconciliation. Adolescents should be encouraged to do their own research on addiction and to find their own paths in life. Parents should never stop loving their children, no matter how wayward the children become. I encourage parents to stay involved with their children, attend Al-Anon meetings, and stick with their principles. The disease of addiction can be fatal, but more frequently it represents a tremendous growth opportunity for both adolescents and their families. Counselors often succeed if they reflect both elements of a tough love approach and hope for resilience in their work, especially in the most difficult cases (Wolin & Wolin, 1993).

TWO EXAMPLES OF COUNSELING SUBSTANCE-ABUSING ADOLESCENTS

The Case of Tom:

A family brought a rebellious, openly drug-using teenager to see me. Despite his high intelligence, Tom was performing terribly in school. He was not motivated to study and barely attended classes. He had moved his girlfriend into his bedroom at home as a permanent boarder to meet his sexual and housekeeping needs. His mother, a successful professional woman, was offended by how her son treated his girlfriend and by how the girl accepted Tom's open disrespect for her. Nevertheless, Tom's mother and father tolerated this behavior just as they tolerated his drug use and his poor school performance. They complained minimally and fought with each other over what to do, but they did not effectively address any of Tom's problems.

I suggested that the family initiate drug testing and set up a system to ensure that Tom did not continue to use drugs (or use their home as a "storage place" for his girlfriend). Tom's parents, both well-meaning and highly educated persons, explained that they had raised their children to be independent. Tom's mother informed me, "It is too late for us to set rules now." Despite his rebellious attitudes, which definitely included his view of me as part of his problems, Tom had no legal problems, was well liked at school, and had a job at a local store for more than 2 years in which he distinguished himself first as a water bed salesman and then as a supervisor of other water bed salesmen.

Several years after my brief sessions with Tom's family, Tom's parents came to see me about an unrelated marital problem. Before we worked on that, I asked for an update on their son. Tom's mother proudly announced that he was about to graduate from college within 4 years (an increasingly uncommon achievement), had reasonable grades, and had all but stopped smoking marijuana. He had received no treatment for his drug problem.

Tom was deeply interested in business and had started selling fancy rugs from his room at college, which netted him more than $10,000 a year. "He tells me that he is too busy to use drugs anymore. He talks about drug use as something he did to pass the meaningless years in high school. But he still lets us know that he thinks it is fine for him to smoke pot whenever he wants to."

Not only did Tom and his family neglect to pay attention to my advice, but Tom even appeared to thrive despite his drug use. How could this have happened, and, more importantly, what does that experience mean for the counseling of other drug-using adolescents?

There are some clues here for the concerned counselor. First, neither parent nor anyone in the family had a history of addiction to alcohol or other drugs. Second, Tom was progressing adequately, if barely, in school with no legal problems when I first saw him. Third, he was remarkably ambitious.

In retrospect, I think of Tom as an adolescent who was

living in an amazingly permissive environment. His drug use did not reflect a biologic disease of addiction; rather, it was indicative of a sad expression of the depths to which his hedonistic behaviors took him without risking either his self-perceived future prospects or effective parental limit-setting.

I wondered aloud with Tom's parents about what his life would have been like if he had not used drugs and if he had made better use of the academic and athletic opportunities available to him in high school and college. In my view, Tom could have attended a much better college had he worked harder in high school and not wasted so much of his time and brain capacity on marijuana. He learned far less than he could have if he had applied himself with a drug-free brain. Although I was less impressed than his parents by his success "on his own terms," I did express congratulations to them and Tom on beating some long odds, given his unfortunately permissive upbringing.

The Case of Sue:

> Sue's story is an altogether more common one. Her father and mother were heavy drinkers, but not full-blown alcoholics. Her maternal grandmother had died of alcoholism at the age of 60. Her older sister had been through a major addiction experience. At 13, Sue was rebellious and eager for the freedom she found at the local shopping mall, where there was no adult supervision. In addition, she was becoming promiscuous.

I worked with Sue and her family for 5 years. Sue used drugs for more than a year before she was expelled from school for the first time for truancy. Only at that time did she admit to her heavy use of alcohol and marijuana. Later, she was treated in two addiction treatment programs over the course of 1 year and went to a special public high school designed to meet the needs of drug-abusing students. Regular drug tests, AA meetings, and close supervision were part of this school's everyday routine. Her parents afforded Sue her own counselor, a female social worker, for over 2 years of individual counseling. Her parents had nearly separated over the conflicts generated by Sue's persistent reckless adolescent behaviors, most notably her substance abuse.

Sue later remarked that the key to her recovery was AA, which she found through her addiction treatment programs and her special high school program:

> For me, the turning point came when I had a real typical blow-up at my parents, and they said I had to find some place else to live. That was new for them. At first, I figured that they didn't mean it. When they held firm, I was sure that it would be easy and fun to live on my own — free of my bossy parents. I moved in with my boyfriend and his father. There were no rules there — but there was no family either. Finding food for meals became problematic, so I moved in with a girlfriend and her family. Rules at her home were more strict than I had faced with my own parents.
>
> Living on my own, which was no fun, taught me humility. I came home ready to accept my parents' rules. Funny thing, now that I have some clean time, I realize just how good the deal is that I have with my parents. I also know that I have cost them a lot of money and caused them a lot of pain. I figure that if I can make something good of my life that is the best way to pay them back, since they got into this mess with me because they love me.

Sue and her family were proud of her 18 months of sobriety before she went to college. In the last family counseling session before Sue left for college, Sue, her family, and I talked about how she now felt differently about what it meant to be an adult as compared with what she thought at the age of 14:

> At that time, I thought being an adult meant I could do whatever I wanted to do, anytime I wanted to do it. I didn't need a Nike commercial to tell me "just do it." That's how I lived my life, especially when it came to drugs and sex. Now I think of being on my own as an adult as scary. It means being respon-

sible for my own choices and my own behaviors. Being an adult means accepting the consequences when things work and when they don't.

We talked in that session about how odd it will seem for Sue to be in a college dormitory where some of her classmates undoubtedly will be abusing alcohol and/or other drugs, as well as participating in openly promiscuous sexual behavior. "I've done more than enough of that stuff to last a lifetime. I know where it leads, and it is not a good place for me to be." Sue was looking forward to attending AA meetings in her new college community and to finding a sponsor "to help me continue my recovery."

In stark contrast to Tom, Sue had the disease of addiction. Her behavior did not reflect a self-indulgent reaction to a permissive environment. Sue needed far more than a short lecture on the values of honesty and sobriety from me; she needed more than individual psychotherapy and drug tests. Sue ultimately made good use of in-school programs and of inpatient and outpatient addiction treatment services.

My work with Sue's family was neither magical nor brief. I kept my faith in Sue throughout numerous difficult phases, including serious suicide attempts and many late-night crises. Up to this point, her positive outcome has made it all worthwhile for me and her parents. Their joy as they prepared to send Sue to college—a goal that seemed virtually impossible even a year earlier—redeemed the costs incurred and the pain suffered during the 5 years of counseling.

LEARNING FROM ADDICTION

Addiction is a cunning, baffling, and powerful disease that is progressive and potentially fatal. Unlike Tom and Sue, some adolescents addicted to alcohol or other drugs do not recover. Some of the teenagers with whom I have worked died of their disease—in accidents, via an overdose, as homicide victims, or by committing suicide.

One way for counselors to learn about addiction is to work through the problems of addiction with their own clients. Over time, clients will learn through their pain and suffering, by trial and error, and they will unknowingly teach their counselors about this process—provided the counselors are open to learning. If counselors continue to support their substance-abusing clients through the process of finding their personal paths to recovery, they will be better equipped to help future clients.

Addiction is also a great teacher for adolescent clients and their families when they confront it truthfully. Addiction can be a relentless teacher. Counselors confronting addiction will find a tough test of their mettle and wisdom. As a lifetime student of the mysterious and marvelous human condition, I have found that addiction presents never-ending learning opportunities.

The Counselor's Role in 12-Step Programs:

One of the best ways to learn about addiction, especially adolescent addiction to alcohol and other drugs, is from people who have overcome it. In the 12-step fellowships, counselors can meet those who trully have grown as a result of their experiences with addiction (DuPont & McGovern, 1994). I have found open meetings of AA, Narcotics Anonymous, and Al-Anon remarkably enlightening. Counselors can find these programs listed in the telephone directory and can ask for the location and time of *open meetings* (i.e., those that are open to anyone who is interested in learning about addiction, as opposed to *closed meetings,* where attendance is restricted to members of the particular fellowship).

Counselors also can attend 12-step meetings with one or more of their own current or former clients. This process, called "sponsoring your therapist," is a major part of the public education effort of the 12-step fellowships. Appendix 5A lists the names and addresses of the national headquarters of the major 12-step fellowships and other mutual aid groups.

Most of them have useful free material for counselors, as well as for clients and their families.

My advice for counselors wanting to learn about the 12-step fellowships is as follows:

- Go to a 12-step meeting 15 minutes early and introduce yourself by your first name, saying that you are there to learn.

- Go alone to a few meetings so you can see what this experience is like for someone you refer to meetings.

- When you do refer clients to a 12-step fellowship, encourage them to go often (90 meetings in 90 days is the standard advice), to get a sponsor right away, and to "work the program."

Although I am not a member of any 12-step fellowships, I have witnessed the help offered by these programs to so many addicted people over the years that I cannot help but support them.

ADDICTION TREATMENT AND 12-STEP FELLOWSHIPS

As a practical matter, most addicted adolescents and their family members, cannot discover and approach the 12-step programs on their own. Denial and resistance are simply too great for them to overcome, often even with the help of a supportive counselor. Addiction treatment, either inpatient or outpatient, often is the necessary first step for many addicted persons and their families to overcome denial and to begin to understand the disease concept of addiction. The 12-step fellowships are usually integrated into the addiction treatment program. While undergoing an addiction treatment program, clients are encouraged to attend community 12-step meetings.

Thus, modern addiction treatment is not only a denial buster, but it is a powerful, often an absolutely necessary, introduction to the 12-step fellowships.

The 12-step method is not the only way to recover from an addiction. Some people who attend a few 12-step meetings do not benefit from them, and some addicted people who reject the 12-step programs do well without them, even over the long haul. On the other hand, I have never seen anyone who regularly attended 12-step meetings return to using alcohol or other addictive substances as long as they continued to attend meetings.

For the most part, these programs work for individuals and families who use them over long periods. The most common problem I encounter with the 12-step programs as a counselor is compliance: not all addicted adolescents and their families agree to use these programs, despite my best efforts. When they occur for people who have used a 12-step program, relapses almost always begin after — often weeks, months, or even years after — they have stopped going to the meetings.

I tell my teenage clients and their families that the 12-step approach represents their best chance for a successful recovery. If they choose another path, I work with them and encourage them, but each time they fail, I remind them where they are most likely to find help that will work: the 12-step programs.

"THE THIRTEENTH STEP"

Adolescents are vulnerable to being misled by some of the negative persons who cycle through 12-step programs. One dishonorable, unofficial tradition in 12-step programs is that older members occasionally take advantage of younger members. This is especially problematic for teenage girls, who may become targets for older men in the program. This process is sometimes called "The Thirteenth Step." Counselors and parents should help young members of the fellowships find safe and positive sponsors of the same sex who can provide guidance and support. When working with the 12-step fellow-ships, it is important to find the "winners" and to stick with them. Whatever may be said about the dangers for teenagers in 12-step fellowships—and dangers do exist—these dangers are far less in the worst 12-step encounter than those that occur every day as adolescents engage in their alcohol- and drug-using behaviors. It is important that these risks be considered and that neither these risks nor others commonly encountered deter counselors from making full use of the 12-step programs. In sorting through these problems, I find it useful to refer to *The Recovery Book* (Mooney, Eisenberg, & Eisenberg, 1992). I keep the book in my waiting room and frequently encourage adolescent patients and their family members to read it.

COUNSELOR CO-DEPENDENCE: A POTENTIAL PROBLEM

Most people in the counseling field have chosen their profes-sions because of an intense desire to help others in need. Some counselors who have grown up either in families dominated by addiction or in other types of dysfunctional families have (usually unconsciously) sought work as therapists as a way to resolve their own childhood problems, including feeling pow-erless to help their addicted or other dysfunctional family members (DuPont & McGovern, 1996).

This life experience of counselors often leads to co-depen-dence: in this case, the conviction that one's self-esteem and well-being depends on the success and happiness of some other person or persons, especially their clients. When such counselors work with addicted clients and their families, they are exposed to memories of their own painful childhood expe-riences in ways that can be both nonproductive and self-defeating.

Counselors concerned with the problem of co-dependence can find help by regularly attending meetings of Al-Anon, Adult Children of Alcoholics, or Co-Dependents Anonymous.

They need to make the 12-step program work for themselves, often with the help of a counselor-sponsor who is also a member of this fellowship. The goal of working with addicted clients is to "detach with love," which means being able to care and help while remaining personally detached. Counselors must be able to separate their clients' treatment outcomes from their self-esteem.

The counselor's role is important to clients and their families, but this role also is limited and defined by well-established professional and ethical boundaries. The greatest power in good counseling comes from a full appreciation for paradox, including the ability of counselors to be themselves and to encourage their clients' autonomy even as the counselors provide assistance, guidance, and support. Nowhere is this subtle and profound paradox more important than in rehabilitation work with addicted adolescents and their families.

REFERENCES

DuPont, R. L., & McGovern, J. P. (1994). *A bridge to recovery – An introduction to 12-step programs.* Washington, DC: American Psychiatric Press.

DuPont, R. L., & McGovern, J. P. (1996). Co-dependence. In *The Hatherleigh Guide to Issues in Modern Therapy* (pp. 69-92). New York: Hatherleigh Press.

Mooney, M. D., Eisenberg, A., & Eisenberg, H. (1992). *The recovery book.* New York: Workman Publishing.

Wolin, S. J., & Wolin, S. (1993). *The resilient self – How survivors of troubled families rise above adversity.* New York: Villard Books.

FOR FURTHER READING

DuPont, R. L. (1984). *Getting tough on gateway drugs: A guide for the family.* Washington, DC: American Psychiatric Press.

DuPont, R. L. (in press). *Learning from addiction*. Washington, DC: American Psychiatric Press.

Gold, M. S. (1991). *The good news about drugs and alcohol – Curing, treating, and preventing substance abuse in the new age of biopsychiatry*. New York: Villard Books.

Nowinski, J., & Baker, S. (1992). *The twelve-step facilitation handbook – A systematic approach to early recovery from alcoholism and addiction*. New York: Lexington Books.

Washton, A., & Stone-Washton, N. (1991). *Step zero – What to do when you can't take it anymore*. New York: HarperCollins.

APPENDIX 5A
12-STEP FELLOWSHIP AND OTHER MUTUAL AID GROUPS

Al-Anon Family Groups
International organization based on the 12 steps and 12 traditions adapted from AA. Founded in 1951 as mutual aid program of recovery for family and friends of alcoholics. More than 32,000 groups.

> 1600 Corporate Landing Parkway
> Virginia Beach, VA 23454
> (804) 563-1600
> (800) 344-2666 (Meeting information)
> (800) 356-9996 (General)

Alateen
International fellowship that is part of Al-Anon Family Groups. Founded in 1957 for teenagers and young adults affected by someone else's drinking. Adult member of Al-Anon serves as group sponsor. More than 4,100 groups.

> 1600 Corporate Landing Parkway
> Virginia Beach, VA 23454
> (804) 563-1600
> (800) 344-2666 (Meeting information)
> (800) 356-9996 (General)

Alcoholics Anonymous
International organization of men and women devoted to helping themselves and others overcome alcoholism by following the 12-step program to recovery. Founded in 1935. More than 94,000 groups.

> Box 459
> Grand Central Station
> New York, NY 10163
> (212) 870-3400

Adult Children of Alcoholics
International organization founded in 1976 and based on the 12 steps of AA. Mutual aid group for adults who grew up with alcoholic parents. More than 1800 groups.

> 1600 Corporate Landing Parkway
> Virginia Beach, VA 23454
> (804) 563-1600
> (800) 344-2666 (Meeting information)
> (800) 356-9996 (General)

Cocaine Anonymous
International mutual aid organization of men and women helping themselves and others achieve recovery from cocaine addiction. Founded in 1982. More than 1,500 groups.

> 3740 Overland Avenue, Suite C
> Los Angeles, CA 90034
> (310) 559-5833 (Business office)
> (800) 347-8998 (Meeting information)

Co-Dependents Anonymous, Inc.
National organization of men and women who grew up in dysfunctional families. About 3,500 groups. Founded in 1986.

National Service Office	*World Service Office*
P.O. Box 33577	P.O. Box 7051
Phoenix, AZ 85067-3577	Thomaston, GA 30286
(602) 277-7991	(706) 647-7736

Families Anonymous
International organization of family and friends of individuals with substance abuse or behavioral problems. Based on the 12 steps of AA. Founded in 1971. About 500 groups.

P.O. Box 3475
Culver City, CA 90231-3475
(800) 736-9805
(310) 313-5800

Nar-Anon Family Group
International organization based on the 12 steps of AA. Founded in 1967 for family and friends of drug addicts.

P.O. Box 2562
Palos Verdes Penninsula, CA 90274-0119
(310) 547-5800

Narcotics Anonymous
International organization based on the 12 steps of AA. Founded in 1953. Men and women hold community meetings to support one another in recovery from drug addiction. More than 22,000 groups.

P.O. Box 9999
Van Nuys, CA 91409
(818) 773-9999

Rational Recovery Systems
International nonspiritual mutual aid groups for individuals with chemical dependence problems. An alternative to 12-step programs. Membership groups use professional advisers. Founded in 1986. About 350 groups.

P.O. Box 800
Lotus, CA 95651
(916) 621-4374, 2667

Tough Love International
International mutual aid group for parents, children, and communities to support parents in taking a stand to help adolescent children take responsibility for their own behavior. Founded in 1979. Approximately 650 groups.

P.O. Box 1069
Doylestown, PA 18901
(800) 333-1069

APPENDIX 5B
SUGGESTED PUBLICATIONS

The following helpful publications are available from the National Clearing House for Alcohol and Other Drug Information, P.O. Box 2345, Rockville, MD 20852-2345, (800) 729-6686:

1. *Alcoholism tends to run in families.* Center for Substance Abuse Prevention, U.S. Department of Health and Human Services, 1992, Order Number PH 318.

2. *Growing up drug free: A parent's guide to prevention.* U.S. Department of Education, 1990, Order Number PHD 533.

3. *If someone close has a problem with alcohol or other drugs.* Center for Substance Abuse Prevention, U.S. Department of Health and Human Services, 1992, Order Number PH 317.

4. *10 steps to help your child say no: A parent's guide.* Center for Substance Abuse Prevention, U.S. Department of Health and Human Services, 1991, Order Number PH 229.

5. *What you can do about drug use in America.* Center for Substance Abuse Prevention, U.S. Department of Health and Human Services, 1991, Order Number PHD 587.

6

Physical Fitness Programming for Prevention and Treatment of Adolescent Substance Abuse

Thomas R. Collingwood, PhD, FACSM

Dr. Collingwood is Director, Fitness Intervention Technologies, Richardson, TX.

KEY POINTS

- Substance abuse in adolescents is a problem specific to at-risk youths. In addition to abusing substances to cope with peer pressure, stress, and physical changes, these adolescents are at risk of developing a variety of other problems; they may become violent, drop out of high school, or become pregnant.

- Substance abuse may be a symptom or expression of another problem in an adolescent's behavioral development. Thus, intervention goals should include enabling the adolescent to develop a healthy lifestyle by replacing health compromising behaviors with health-enhancing ones.

- Physical activity can play a major role in the management of substance abuse. The benefits of physical fitness include physiologic improvements, reduction of substance abuse risk factors, improvement in the adolescent's self-concept and sense of well-being, a significant decrease in multiple drug use, and an increase in abstinence.

- Physical fitness programming is a focused and structured intervention to alter risk factors and use patterns. For physical fitness intervention to be successful, the quality of the programming, staff leadership, and organizational factors is of critical importance.

INTRODUCTION

The extent and pattern of problems associated with adolescents, such as substance abuse, have received much attention. The U.S. Department of Health and Human Services (DHHS) first set specific national goals for promoting health and preventing disease in 1980 (DHHS, 1980). In 1983, the DHHS published *A Midcourse Review* (DHHS, 1983) with data indicating that many goals, especially in the adolescent area, were not being met. The most recent definition of national goals (DHHS, 1991) revised these objectives in light of realistic expectations.

The problem of substance abuse is categorized (along with other problems associated with adolescents) as a specific difficulty experienced by at-risk adolescents. The term *at risk* refers to one's developmental status, environment, physical status, family situation, and so forth. These adolescents are at risk of developing a variety of developmental problems, such as violent behavior, school dropout, pregnancy, and substance abuse. The adolescent period, with its stress, peer pressure, and physical changes, sets the context for the development of substance abuse behavior as one of many possible risk behaviors.

SUBSTANCE ABUSE AS A DEVELOPMENTAL PROBLEM

Substance abuse, delinquency, and other problems may be symptoms of the inability of adolescents to develop the skills necessary to become fully functioning and responsible persons. Adolescents have certain physical, emotional, and intellectual skills deficits that jeopardize them in terms of functioning successfully to meet their needs in many areas at home, in school, or in the community. Overcoming these deficits by acquiring certain physical, emotional, and intellectual skills can prepare adolescents to handle problems such as substance abuse more effectively.

Substance abuse may be a symptom or expression of another problem in behavioral development. The decisions regarding substance use at this developmental stage is an expression of the many behavioral crossroads of adolescent life. Some major points of this view are:

- Substance abuse behavior is *not* an isolated behavior; it is an integrated component of a health-compromising behavior cluster or syndrome.

- The adolescent is challenged with developmental choices between health-enhancing or health-compromising behaviors for physical, social, and psychological health.

- The adolescent stage of life represents a high-risk stage for developing a health-enhancing or health-compromising lifestyle. Various behaviors developed during adolescence are interrelated.

- Many developmental themes influence the choices made by adolescents: search for identity; development of a sense of autonomy, self-control, and accomplishment; peer pressure; stress; development of the concept of delayed gratification; and development of strategies to reduce physical and psychological pain. Substance abuse behavior may be an attempt to address these themes. However, it is related to a false sense of security in dealing with these issues and, in essence, is an avoidance behavior.

Given this developmental view, intervention goals include enabling the adolescent to develop a healthy lifestyle by replacing health-compromising behaviors with health-enhancing ones.

The recognition that substance abuse is a developmental and multifaceted lifestyle problem has led to a risk factor approach for predicting substance abuse (Newcomb,

Maddahian, & Bentler, 1986). (This approach is similar to the epidemiologic study of cardiovascular disease outlined by Meyer and Henderson [1974]). Studies have evaluated sequential patterns of substance abuse progression to ascertain predictive risk patterns (Bry, McKeon, & Pandina, 1982; Oetting & Beauvais, 1984; Yamaguchi & Kandel, 1984). Major factors isolated from these studies included delinquency, lack of self-esteem, maladjustment, depression, poor school performance, lack of religiosity, poor parental and peer relationships, early substance use, sensation seeking, peer and parental substance use, and cognitive beliefs. Steffenbarger (1980) has even suggested certain factors such as lack of self-esteem are the primary deficits that lead to substance abuse behavior. The results from these studies have led to a focused effort to prevent risk factors and eventual use.

PREVENTION/INTERVENTION MODELS

As a generic model, prevention emphasizes intervention aimed at all three elements: the host (immunization), agent (supply/control), and environment (contextual reinforcers). Although there are many models of intervention, Battjes (1985) categorized most prevention/intervention models into five broad areas: (a) information dissemination; (b) affective education; (c) alternatives; (d) social influences; and (e) social skills development. The majority of these approaches reflect the basic preventive mode of immunizing the host. Evaluations of these preventive approaches yielded mixed results. Studies of prevention programs indicated that the social influences, social skills, and self-esteem approaches appeared to have the most validity for influencing substance use patterns (Hawkins, Catalano, & Wells, 1986; Perry, 1987; Schaps, Bartolo, Moskowitz, & Palley, 1981). The efficacy of psychosocial programs also was supported by a metanalysis of a variety of prevention programs, indicating that the social influence, alternatives, and social skills programs demonstrated consistent positive outcomes (Tobler, 1987).

A prevention/intervention model that has had little formal evaluation but some validity involves providing adolescents with an alternative lifestyle (Carter, 1984). As far back as 1973, Cohen indicated that physical health and athletic activity were perceived by adolescents as major deterrents to substance abuse. Some of the latest federal initiatives note the need to develop healthy habits to counteract substance abuse behaviors (Bennett, 1986). Factor analytic studies indicate that health-related behaviors (e.g., exercise, adequate sleep, normal eating behavior, leisure activity) do not cluster with substance use behaviors (Hars, Stacy, & DeMatteo, 1984; Stocker, Retschald, Sollberger, Gass, & Abelin, 1978).

PHYSICAL FITNESS INTERVENTION

A specific lifestyle habit that has received little attention is physical activity leading to physical fitness. The adolescent substance abuser is but a subsample of the adolescent population. Surveys indicate that children and adolescents in the United States do not have the physical activity patterns or physical fitness levels recommended by the DHHS (1985). Data suggest that adolescent substance abusers have even lower levels of fitness than the general population, with fewer than 25% meeting performance standards (Collingwood, Reynolds, Kohl, Sloan, & Smith, 1991).

The Carnegie Council on Adolescent Development (1989) focused on the problem of preparing American youths for the 21st century. The report highlighted not only the problems of substance abuse and health behavior but also the problems of school-related behavior and poverty within the context of a wide array of adolescent problems. The report noted that health and fitness play a major role in the management of these problems. From a purely physiologic perspective, the physical fitness needs of this population must be addressed.

Beyond the need to develop fitness interventions for physiologic purposes, physical activity and fitness also have a beneficial impact on substance abuse risk factors. Summary articles consistently cited data demonstrating a relationship between physical fitness and a variety of factors, such as self-concept, depression, and anxiety (Doan & Schernan, 1987; Morgan & O'Conner, 1988). The National Institute of Mental Health consensus panel emphasized the beneficial emotional effect of exercise in all ages and both sexes (Morgan, 1987). In terms of substance abusers as a distinct population, research indicates that many personality factors related to fitness (i.e., decreased depression and increased self-confidence, well-being, and self-control) discriminate between substance abusers and nonabusers (Mayer, 1988).

The physical domain can be a valid area for assisting adolescents in developing deficit areas. It is uniquely suited for this purpose in that systematic physical training: (a) is a concrete and specific process, (b) involves goal orientation, (c) is active as opposed to passive, (d) teaches both leadership and teamwork, (e) is demanding (and can involve discomfort), (f) has delayed results, and (g) is a highly disciplined activity.

The notion of providing a physical fitness program as a treatment intervention has been applied in emotionally disturbed (Doyne, Chambless, & Beuler, 1982) and delinquent (Collingwood & Englesjgerd, 1977; Collingwood & Genthner, 1980; Hilyer, Wilson, & Dillon, 1982) populations. Data show the same positive relationships between physical fitness levels and affective factors such as improved self-concept and decreased depression and anxiety (Collingwood, 1972). The few studies of the benefits of exercise in adults suffering from alcoholism have demonstrated a short-term positive impact on self-esteem and consumption (Gary & Gurthrie, 1982; Murphy, Pagano, & Marlatt, 1986). An example of a fitness program schedule appears in Table 6.1.

An effort recently has been made to apply systematic fitness programs as prevention and treatment vehicles specifically aimed at reducing the extent of substance abuse in at-risk adolescents. Iterations of this approach have been made in a variety of settings such as community-based prevention settings for inner-city youths, school-based prevention programs, juvenile justice community and institutional settings, and

Table 6.1
EXAMPLE OF A FITNESS PROGRAM SCHEDULE

Every session should have an activity, education, and discussion component. Using a 1-hour class period as an example, the daily schedule would be as follows:

Warm-up	5	minutes
Flexibility stretching	5	minutes
Aerobic activity	15	minutes
Strength development	10	minutes
Cool-down	5	minutes
Education activity	10	minutes
Discussion activity	10	minutes

Fitness educational modules should cover these content areas in sequence over the course of 8–12 weeks:

Assessing health risks
Assessing fitness levels
Setting fitness goals
Planning warm-up and cool-down procedures
Designing a flexibility fitness plan
Designing an aerobic fitness plan
Designing a strength fitness plan
Designing a nutrition plan
Designing a relaxation exercise plan
Monitoring progress
Designing a motivational plan

rehabilitation residential centers. Evaluations of the program applications indicated that at-risk and substance-abusing adolescents who increased fitness demonstrated improved risk factors (self-concept and well-being) and significant decreases in multiple drug use with increased abstinence (Collingwood, Reynolds, & Jestor, 1992; Collingwood et al., 1991). Based on fitness programs serving more than 1000 at-risk adolescents, additional data indicated there were significant reductions in the use of nicotine, marijuana, alcohol, cocaine, and steroids (Collingwood, 1992; Collingwood, Sunderlin, & Kohl, 1994). Although these studies did not address the specific etiology by which these changes occurred, some speculations can be made. MacMahon (1990) overviewed the possible mechanisms by which exercise may have an impact on risk factors and use patterns to include psychological theories (e.g., self-control and mastery, deep relaxation, and recreational distraction) and physiologic theories (e.g., alterations in neurotransmitters and endorphin levels).

GUIDELINES FOR FITNESS PROGRAM IMPLEMENTATION

The three aspects of implementing physical fitness programs within a variety of community, educational, and rehabilitation settings for prevention and treatment of substance abuse are programming factors, staffing/leadership factors, and organizational factors.

Fitness Program Rationale:

Physical fitness programming is a focused and structured intervention to alter risk factors and use patterns (Collingwood, 1990; Collingwood et al., 1994); it is not a recreation "free time" or physical education program. The model uses a life skills approach to physical fitness, which provides a focused process for acquiring cognitive or behavioral control skills (e.g., problem solving, decision making, planning) to practice a health-enhancing, as opposed to a health-compromising, lifestyle.

The life skills fitness program is similar to the cognitive-behavioral social skills approach to substance abuse prevention (Botvin, Baker, Renick, Filazzola, & Botvin, 1984). In this context, the physical domain is the learning vehicle for acquiring life skills. A common program concept can be established whereby the development of fitness content as a life skill is conceptually parallel to the development of other life skills relating directly to the prevention of substance abuse. The rationale behind the model is also similar to that of Carkhuff and Berensons (1986), who viewed training as a treatment model for behavioral change.

The physical fitness program is designed to serve as a physical life skill that equips adolescents with an alternative lifestyle, habit, and leisure time activity. It emphasizes four major components for the development of exercise-fitness behavior: (a) cognitive and values development, (b) problem-solving and decision-making skills, (c) coping skills, and (d) self-control skills. Information is disseminated to establish meaning toward maintaining exercise and resisting influences not to exercise as an alternative lifestyle. The focus is on using the physical activity process to teach the values of self-discipline, responsibility, and respect. Problem-solving and decision-making skills are taught to aid adolescents in selecting exercise activity modes and to make more appropriate decisions as to when to exercise. Learning the application of relaxation and certain exercises provides avenues to counteract stress. Self-assessment, goal setting, planning, and responsibility for one's actions are taught by applying these skills to an activity program.

Programming Factors:

Programming factors, the elements that relate to the direct delivery of the fitness program, include:

- The physical fitness program must be structured, as opposed to being a free-time recreational activity.

- The physical activity must be systematically structured so that the demands on the participant are progressively more difficult.

- Adequate safety devices must be in place.

- The emphasis during activity sessions should be placed on disciplined achievement of goals.

- Physical activity classes should cover the major physical fitness areas of aerobic power, strength, flexibility, and body composition.

- Skills training (i.e., education) should focus on skills for developing and maintaining an individual program, such as major physical fitness assessment, goal setting, exercise planning (i.e., prescription), exercise monitoring, and reinforcement.

- There should be focused discussion group activity to consolidate learning from physical activity to substance abuse problems.

- Individualized follow-up fitness programs via a personal handbook should be used.

- Whenever possible, support for parent training (covering such topics as behavioral contracting, family fitness, and personal fitness activities) should be provided.

- If feasible, a peer fitness-leader training program should be used whereby selected participants are trained to serve as exercise "buddies" and role models for other adolescents.

- The sequence for activity components should be: warm up, flexibility stretching, aerobic activity, strength activity, and cool down.

- Special events such as fun runs and tournaments should be used to complement the basic program.

- A formal reinforcement system should be provided for participation and achievement.

- The educational sessions should be arranged on a modular basis for maximum integration into existing services.

- The fitness program should be configured into 8–12-week cycles.

Staff Leadership Factors:

Staff leadership factors, which involve the persons responsible for delivery of the fitness program, include:

- Organizations must dedicate staff time and resources to program delivery.

- Only physically fit role models should be selected to deliver the program.

- Fitness instructors must be trained or certified to deliver the fitness program.

- All activity should be led by a fitness instructor.

- Fitness instructors require ongoing training to upgrade and sustain skills.

Organizational Factors:

Organizational factors, the elements of a program that link the program to the participants, include:

- Fitness programs work best when they are integrated with existing services.

- Entry requirements and procedures for the fitness program must be made as convenient as possible for the participants.

- Organizations must integrate ongoing program evaluation.

- Organizations must have a program promotional plan.

- When possible, facility and exercise equipment should be provided.

CONCLUSION

Physical fitness programs are valid interventions for the prevention and treatment of substance abuse. However, such programs are successful only if a structured and valid physical training process is provided. A key rationale for fitness programming is not just to provide needed exercise for targeted adolescents but to capitalize on the physical domain as a learning area. Much can be taught through physical activity if the activity programming is structured to meet prevention and treatment objectives.

REFERENCES

Battjes, R. J. (1985). Prevention of adolescent drug abuse. *International Journal of the Addictions, 20*, 1113–1134.

Bennett, W. (1986). *What works: Schools without drugs*, Washington, DC: U.S. Department of Education.

Botvin, G. J., Baker, E., Renick, N. L., Filazzola, A. D., & Botvin, E. M. (1984). A cognitive-behavioral approach to substance abuse prevention *Addictive Behaviors, 9*, 137–147.

Bry, B. H., McKeon, P., & Pandina, R. J. (1982). Extent of drug use as a function of number of risk factors. *Journal of Abnormal Psychology, 91,* 273–279.

Carkhuff, R. R., & Berenson, B. G. (1986). *Teaching as treatment.* Amherst, MA: Human Resource Development Press.

Carnegie Council on Adolescent Development. *Turning points: Preparing youths for the 21st century.* New York: Carnegie Corporation.

Carter, J. (1984). Health promotion and disease prevention: Combatting substance abuse with healthy lifestyles. *Alabama Journal of Medicine and Science, 21,* 165–169.

Cohen, A. (1973). *Alternatives to drug abuse: Steps toward drug abuse prevention.* Washington, DC: National Institute for Mental Health, U.S. Government Printing Office.

Collingwood, T. (1972). The effects of physical training upon behavior and self attitudes. *Journal of Clinical Psychology, 28,* 71-75.

Collingwood, T. (1990). Youth fitness: A necessity to counteract drug abuse and develop citizenship. In L. Hale (Ed.), *Proceedings report of the national conference on military fitness* (pp. 97-100). Washington DC: U.S. Government Printing Office.

Collingwood, T. (1992). *Fitness intervention training: An evaluation of the installation of physical fitness programs for substance abuse prevention and treatment.* Springfield, IL: Illinois Department of Alcohol and Substance Abuse.

Collingwood, T., & Englesjgerd, M. (1977). Physical fitness, delinquency, and delinquency prevention. *Journal of Health, Physical Education, Recreation and Dance, 48,* 23.

Collingwood, T., & Genthner, B. (1980). Skills training as treatment for juvenile delinquents. *Professional Psychology, 11,* 591-598.

Collingwood, T., Reynolds, R., & Jestor, B. (1992). Enlisting physical education for the war on drugs. *Journal of Health, Physical Education, Recreation and Dance, 63,* 25-28.

Collingwood, T., Reynolds, R., Kohl, H., Sloan, S., & Smith, W. (1991). Physical fitness effects on substance abuse risk factors and use patterns. *Journal of Drug Education, 21,* 73–84.

Doan, R., & Schernan, A. (1987). The therapeutic effect of physical fitness on measures of personality: A literature review. *Journal of Counseling and Development, 66,* 28–35.

Doyne, E. J., Chambless, D. L., & Beutler, L. E. (1982). Aerobic exercise as a treatment for depression in women. *Behavior Therapy, 4,* 434–440.

Gary, V., & Guthrie, D. (1982). The effect of jogging on physical fitness and self-concept in hospitalized alcoholics. *Quarterly Journal Studies in Alcoholism, 29,* 292–303.

Hars, R., Stacy, A., & DeMatteo, M. (1984). Covariation among health-related behaviors. *Addictive Behaviors, 9,* 315–318.

Hawkins, J., Catalano, R., & Wells, E. (1986). Measuring effects of skills training interventions for drug abusers. *Journal of Consulting and Clinical Psychology, 54,* 661–664.

Hilyer, J. C., Wilson, D. G., & Dillon, C. (1982). Physical fitness training and counseling as treatment for youthful offenders. *Journal of Counseling Psychology, 33,* 1073–1078.

MacMahon, J. (1990). The psychological benefits of exercise and the treatment of delinquent adolescents. *Sports Medicine, 9,* 344–351.

Mayer, J. (1988). The personality characteristics of adolescents who use and misuse alcohol. *Adolescence, 23,* 383–404.

Meyer, A. J., & Henderson, J. B. (1974). Multiple risk factor reduction in the prevention of cardiovascular disease. *Preventative Medicine, 3,* 225–236.

Morgan, W. (Ed.). (1987). *Exercise and mental health.* New York: Hemisphere Press.

Morgan, W., & O'Connor, P. (1988). Exercise and mental health. In R. Dishman (Ed.), *Exercise adherence.* Champaign, IL: Human Kinetics Publishing.

Murphy, T. J., Pagano, R. R., & Marlatt, G. A. (1986). Lifestyle modification with heavy alcohol drinkers: Effects of aerobic exercise and meditation. *Addictive Behaviors, 11*, 175–186.

Newcomb, M., Maddahian, E., & Bentler, B. (1986). Risk factors for drug useamong adolescents: Concurrent and longitudinal analyses. *American Journal of Public Health, 76*, 525–531.

Oetting, E. R., & Beauvais, F. (1984). Common elements in youth drug abuse: Peer clusters and other psychosocial factors. *Journal of Drug Issues, 74*, 668–672.

Perry, C. (1987). Results of prevention programs with adolescents. *Drug andAlcohol Dependence, 20*, 13–19.

Schaps, E., Bartolo, R. D., Moskowitz, J., & Palley, C. S. (1981). A review of 127 drug-abuse prevention program evaluations. *Journal of Drug Issues, Winter*, 17–43.

Steffenbarger, R. (1980). Self-esteem theory of drug abuse. *National Institute of Drug Abuse Research Monograph Series, 30*, 157–163.

Stocker, H., Retschald, T., Sollberger, J., Gass, R., & Abelin, T. (1978). Influencing factors related to narcotic consumption and leisure sports in juveniles. *Sozial und Praventivmedizin, 23*, 246–247.

Tobler, N. S. (1987). Metanalysis of 143 adolescent drug prevention programs: quantitative outcome results of program participants compared to a control or comparison group. *Journal of Drug Issues, 16*, 537–567.

U.S. Department of Health and Human Services. (1980). *Promoting health/ preventing disease: Objectives for the nation.* Washington, DC: U.S. Government Printing Office.

U.S. Department of Health and Human Services. (1983). *A midcourse review.* Washington, DC: U.S. Government Printing Office.

U.S. Department of Health and Human Services. (1985). *National children and youth fitness study.* Washington, DC: U.S. Government Printing Office.

U.S. Department of Health and Human Services. (1991). *Healthy people 2000.* Washington, DC: U.S. Government Printing Office.

Yamaguchi, K., & Kandel, D. B. (1984). Patterns of drug use from adolescence to young adulthood, III: Predictors of progression. *American Journal of Public Health, 74,* 672–688.

7

Ethical Issues in Counseling Adolescents Who Abuse Alcohol and Other Drugs

Tomás José Silber, MD, MASS, and Daniel Silber, PhD

Dr. Tomás Silber is Director of Education and Training, Department of Adolescent and Young Adult Medicine, Children's National Medical Center, and Professor of Pediatrics, The George Washington University School of Medicine and Health Sciences, Washington, DC. Dr. Daniel Silber is Assistant Professor of Philosophy, Kent State University, Kent, OH.

KEY POINTS

- This chapter provides a framework for the ethics of counseling adolescent substance abusers. The authors discuss historical and legal changes that can illuminate our understanding of the place of adolescents in society in general and substance abuse counseling in particular, the counselor-adolescent client relationship, the characteristics of adolescent moral development, and the application of ethical theory.

- The ethical issues discussed in this chapter include autonomy, beneficence, paternalism, guidance, confidentiality, consent, availability of treatment, screening, and hospitalization.

- Endorsement of the following concepts may improve the care of adolescents: mutual participation as a goal of the counselor-client relationship, application of ethical theory to clinical practice, knowledge of the stages of adolescent moral development, and achievement of a reasonable balance between the support for adolescent autonomy and the limits placed by justified paternalism.

INTRODUCTION

The central moral issue in the treatment of adolescents is the conflict between the principle of autonomy and the principle of beneficence. Adults, including substance abuse professionals, exhibit a paternal desire to protect teenagers (and, in this process, exercise control); this must be balanced against the adolescent's need to make decisions autonomously (which implies a right to confidential counseling). An inherent tension exists between these two positions, and counselors often are forced to decide which principle applies best in a given circumstance. Moreover, treatments occur in a context of incongruent societal attitudes and contradictory institutional policies toward adolescents. As a result, the substance abuse profession has remained unresolved about how to balance autonomy and beneficence in the treatment of adolescent substance use (Silber, 1991a).

In attempting to ground the ethics of counseling adolescents, it is useful to consider the following: (a) historical and legal changes that can illuminate our understanding of the place of adolescents in society in general and substance abuse counseling in particular, (b) the counselor-adolescent client relationship, (c) the characteristics of adolescent moral development, and (d) the application of ethical theory.

HISTORICAL/LEGAL CHANGES

Adolescence, understood as the psychosocial adaptation to the biologic changes of puberty, has been recognized as a rather recent Western phenomenon. It is absent or rudimentary in times and places where the demands of child labor result in a premature transition from the expectations of childhood to the roles and responsibilities of adulthood. Therefore, one can speak of entire groups of teenagers who never really have experienced adolescence (Kett, 1993).

In colonial times, adolescents were not entitled to consent to their health care. Based on the concept of *parental sovereignty,* parents assumed a claim of ownership of their children. Adolescents had no rights to medical care because *all rights* were denied to them. This doctrine continues to be reflected in court rulings on custody, foster care, and adoption (Hofmann, 1980).

In the late 19th century, legal limits were imposed on parental ownership in circumstances in which children were considered to be in danger. This doctrine became known as *child welfare* and is clearly reflected in laws dealing with child abuse and compulsory education (Goldstein, Freud, & Solnit, 1980).

Despite their dissimilarity, these legal interpretations have a significant element in common: adolescents have no rights of their own; either the parent or the state determines what is in their best interest. The serious flaw of both doctrines is that neither distinguishes between the stages of complete dependency that characterize childhood and the capacity for autonomy that develops during adolescence. During the past three decades, a new philosophy emerged that dealt with the issue of the "civil rights" of adolescents, taking into account differences in age and maturity. This approach allowed parents or the state to represent minors' interests *only* as long as minors were not able to represent themselves (Hofmann, 1980).

A determining rule was proposed: the level of developmental capacity of the adolescent, rather than any arbitrary age or legal disposition, should be the deciding factor of competency for consent for treatment. Often referred to as the *mature minor doctrine,* this concept has been defined in the legal literature as such: "A 'mature' minor does make his or her decisions on daily affairs, is mobile, independent, and can manage financial affairs; can initiate own appointments, understands risks, benefits, and informed consent" (Brown & Truitt, 1979). The mature minor doctrine has been congruent with the viewpoint of specialists in child development and adopted by the Ameri-

can Academy of Pediatrics (AAP) (1973). As a societal definition, it acknowledges the changes that come with the increasing cognitive competence of teenagers and affirms that they
can make rational decisions and are therefore capable of giving informed consent (Silber, 1980).

THE COUNSELOR-ADOLESCENT CLIENT
RELATIONSHIP

Within the outlined historical context, a parallel change has
occurred in the nature of the counselor-adolescent client relationship, culminating in the gradual recognition that the adolescent, within the context of a family, is *the client*. This development implies a specific professional obligation to the individual adolescent, although the nature of the obligation to the
adolescent client has been the subject of controversy. However, most health care providers acknowledge that there is a
special dimension to their relationship with adolescent clients
in which they transcend the professional model and provide a
model of human interaction (Silber, 1980).

There are many possible variants in counselor-client relationships. A way of conceptualizing the essence of what goes
on in any given office visit consists of analyzing power equa-
tions. Three possible interactions have been identified: (a)
active-passive, (b) guidance-cooperation, and (c) mutual participation (Szasz & Hollander, 1956).

Active-Passive:

An active-passive relationship is forged when the counselor does something to the client and the client is unable to
respond. The clinical application of this model can be seen in
life-threatening situations, such as acute intoxication or severe
withdrawal symptoms, in which there is a total imbalance of
power. The prototype for this model is the *parent-neonate
relationship*.

Guidance-Cooperation:

In the guidance-cooperation relationship, the counselor tells the client what to do and the client obeys. The clinical application of this model is exemplified in the treatment of adolescents who have acknowledged a drug or alcohol problem. Although the client assumes some responsibility, the counselor clearly remains dominant. The main difference between the two participants pertains to power and its actual or potential use. It differs from the active-passive relationship in that both participants contribute actively to the relationship and its outcome. The prototype of this model is the parent-older child relationship.

Mutual Participation:

In the mutual participation relationship, the counselor's role is to help the client help himself or herself. The client's role is that of a participant in a partnership. The clinical application of this contract model can best be seen in working with recovering adolescents who are undergoing psychotherapy. The participants are of approximately equal power and need each other. In different ways, the relationship is satisfactory to both. The contractual model often used in adolescent health care approximates this model of mutual participation; its prototype is the adult-adult relationship.

Each of these counselor-client relationships is appropriate for certain circumstances and destructive for others. To decide which model best fits the health care needs of a particular teenager, one must begin by assessing how the developmental tasks of adolescence are being fulfilled by the individual. For example, a college student who is in denial of her alcoholism, has had two car accidents while driving under the influence, and has been lying to her family will require the active-passive approach involved in confrontation and detoxification. On the other hand, an adolescent who is working hard in counseling on issues of separation-individuation, has accepted a recom-

mended regimen of urine monitoring, and is an active member
of Narcotics Anonymous is readying himself for the mutual
participation modality.

Professionals need to fine-tune their ability to perceive
developmental transformations. To achieve a mutually constructive experience, counselors dealing with adolescents must
undergo a process of change in the relationship, similar to
another familiar process: "...the need for the parent to behave
ever differently toward his growing child" (Silber, 1980, p. 52).

ADOLESCENT MORAL DEVELOPMENT

Sooner or later, the counselor and the adolescent client will
begin to discuss issues such as substance or alcohol experimentation, sexual intercourse, and risk taking in general—all
of which lead to the exploration of moral dilemmas. When
such issues are addressed in treatment, it becomes necessary to
complement the knowledge of adolescent substance abuse
with an understanding of adolescent moral development.

There is no question that adolescents can be engaged in
moral reasoning when confronted with a moral dilemma,
despite their being ambivalent and unclear about their value
systems. To achieve clarity, consistency, and commitment in
this regard is one of the tasks of adolescence (Group for the
Advancement of Psychiatry, 1968). Although still controversial, the actual sequence of the stages of moral development
(Table 7.1) is based on the work of Kohlberg and Gilligan
(1971). Under stress, individuals may loose some of their
capacity for reasoning; this notion of moral developmental
steps must be considered when treating adolescents. The developmental stage should be matched by the guidance provided.

Guidance does not mean imposing values, and the reasons
for avoiding preaching are both ethical and practical. Imposing values violates the client's autonomy, deprives the adolescent of an opportunity to develop and exercise his or her own
moral code, and leads to a useless power struggle. The adoles-

---

Table 7.1
EXAMPLES OF STAGES OF MORAL DEVELOPMENT

Preconventional (generally preadolescence)
"Good" and "bad" are interpreted in terms of physical consequences (reward-punishment) or of the physical power of those that enunciate the rules: "Getting high is bad. My father told me that if I try crack again, he is going to kick me out of the house" (Melden, 1967).

Conventional (most common in early adolescence)
Maintaining the expectations and rules of the family, group, or nation is perceived as valuable in its own right. There is concern not only to conform but also to maintain and justify the social order: "I have decided againstsmoking pot. I'm a Catholic and that would go against the teaching of my church."

Postconventional (late adolescence, if ever, and beyond)
This stage is characterized by a strong impulse toward autonomous moral principles that carry their weight apart from the authority of the group or persons that follow them: "I have been throwing my life away. I agree to continue testing my urine. I think it is my duty to recover. It is all I can do for the kid I ran over. It hurts, but I now have a mission: to let others know."

---

cent should be encouraged to weigh decisions, investigate alternatives, and choose. By applying the Socratic method of teaching through questioning (Table 7.2), the counselor can identify the client's stage of moral development and continue asking questions to induce further reflection, which in turn may promote a higher level of moral functioning. This does not mean that a higher level of moral reasoning will produce a right answer or even a better one than derived at a lower level. The point is that we grow as our moral reasoning develops. One of the tragedies of adolescent addiction and intoxication is that when under the impact of stress and malaise, teenagers regress to lower levels of moral development.

Table 7.2
THE SOCRATIC METHOD

The Socratic Method:

- Consists of "grilling" a person to search for truth

- Implies a relentless series of questions and no allowance for contradictory replies

- Answers are met with confrontation, in pursuit of what is real and valuable

- May enhance the development (or rediscovery) of a value system

- Examples include: How do you see your life 5 years from now? Who is important in your life? What experiences (other than drugs or alcohol) have you valued in your life? What can give it meaning? (A follow-up on each of these questions can provide vast opportunity for reflection.)

THE APPLICATION OF ETHICAL THEORY

Ethical theory considers the obligation of clinicians and counselors to the parents of their adolescent clients. Parents often are worried and frightened. Within this context, counselors must choose among conflicting views of consent and confidentiality, autonomy and protection, and so on. Fortunately, the use of ethical theory can help achieve clarity and consistency in decision making.

Ethical theory can be described as an attempt to provide a rational account of morality. Ethical theory does not provide a concrete answer to specific problems; rather, it is a guide for obtaining an answer in a particular case, by determining which factors are relevant, and by testing for consistency (Melden, 1967). Because a variety of approaches have enriched moral philosophy, significant differences have evolved in the criteria used to decide what is appropriate, which has resulted in a multiplicity of philosophical schools. Some theories focus on the *consequence* of a behavior (consequential ethics); some see one particular end result — pleasure — as the deciding criterion (hedonism); and others look for a mathematical formula and embrace "the greatest happiness for the greatest number" (utilitarianism). The formalists appeal to the concept of *deontologic ethics* (from the Greek word for duty); they state that the rightness of the act does not flow from the goodness of the consequences of the act but rather from the *character* of the act. A completely different vantage point is taken in "self-development ethics," in which the "right" behavior is defined as the one that promotes self-realization. Somewhat related to this is the classic Aristotelian idea that it is the virtuous person who generates moral behavior.

Ethical theory applies to the adolescent client and counselor's responsibility in that morality is tested every day in our offices and hospitals. When we answer a moral problem, we obviously do not review all ethical theories. However, each of us has a set of moral principles and values that normally guide our actions. These principles are enmeshed in complicated ways, and we may not be fully conscious of them. They may or may not point toward a logical sequence. However, knowledge of ethical theory can assist us in bringing order and lending direction to many aspects of the treatment of adolescents.

What is ultimately at stake is the *nature* of the counselor's encounter with adolescents. A classic interpretation invokes a covenant between healer and client, establishing a fiduciary relationship (Ramsey, 1970). Although moving and eloquent, this theologic framework is not the only alternative to a moral commitment. For instance, one can support a secular model in which the adolescent, parents, and professional can agree on a handful of shared values: (a) respect for truth; (b) faith in the free play of critical intelligence; (c) respect for the basic worth, equality, and dignity of each individual; (d) understanding of the need for cooperative effort for the common good; and (e) recognition of the right of self-determination of each individual accepting the preceding constraints (Nye, 1967). These general ethical values can serve as guidelines and common ground in clinical work with adolescents and their parents.

RESOLVING MORAL DILEMMAS IN EVERYDAY PRACTICE

The counselor who treats adolescents knows that the parents often are in need of help and support as well. It is not unusual for the adolescent's substance abuse to coexist with other important — and sometimes threatening — events in the parents' lives, such as alcoholism, marital trouble, career difficulties, financial problems, and poor health. Every effort should be made to provide parents with answers to their questions and support for their endeavors.

But how can the obligation to the adolescent client be reconciled with the obligation to the parents? What happens when an adolescent shares information and then requests that his or her parents not be notified? May an otherwise dependent adolescent be considered independent when it comes to health care? These dilemmas and their resolution are crucial in the treatment of teenagers. They usually are expressed in terms of conflict around the issues of confidentiality and consent.

Confidentiality:

Confidentiality deals with the privileged nature of information provided to the counselor by the adolescent. Accordingly, the client's history cannot be shared with others, including parents, without the client's permission. However, when adolescents engage in activities that place their lives and health in grave danger, do the parents have a right to know?

A distinction must be made between adolescents who seek consultation on their own (and for whom the use of substances comes up in the context of a general assessment) and those who are brought to a counselor by their distraught parents or referred by an agency. Two principles used in trying to resolve these questions are the *principle of autonomy,* which states that a person should have a say in any action that is going to affect him or her, and the *principle of beneficence,* which states that whenever something good can be done for a person, it should be done, or at least no barriers should be placed to interfere with the attainment of that good.

Consent:

Consent is a contract between a client and a professional. The counselor must explain the nature of the treatment proposed as well as the existing alternatives, in return for which the client will give permission for treatment. However, in the case of an adolescent, who is neither a child nor an adult, who should give consent?

The principle of autonomy applied to an adolescent seeking psychological help rejects the formulation that the adolescent is being protected when parental consent is requested as a prerequisite for psychological care. It views insistence on parental consent as a denial of the adolescent's right as a separate person. The principle of beneficence also clearly lends support to a minor's search for treatment; many adolescents who seek mental health care would never do so if they knew prior parental consent would be required. Under this principle, it is also easy to see how confidentiality can be justified ethically: lack of confidentiality would constitute a barrier to health care.

This seems to contradict the tenet that parental involvement is an important and necessary part of the optimal health care for adolescents. The truth is that this is an apparent rather than a real contradiction. In fact, concerned counselors do not place themselves in an adversarial position in relation to parents when obtaining an adolescent's consent or when maintaining confidentiality. Professionals share the same goal as parents: to protect and restore the adolescent's health. Therefore, most counselors appropriately encourage their adolescent clients to seek support from their families, sometimes to the extent of acting as mediators in crisis situations, thereby helping to restore the organization of the family.

As with every rule, clear exceptions exist, such as the suicidal adolescent for whom confidentiality does not hold (but to whom we owe the acknowledgment of why it does not). The principle of protection also should prevail over the principle of autonomy in such cases as alcoholism, substance abuse (especially in cases of overdose), and physical or sexual abuse. These are more ambiguous, however, and any lack of clarity about the appropriate response to these situations may inhibit the consistency of the intervention and augment the risk that adolescents may not receive the care they need. Therefore, it must be clearly established that in the field of adolescent substance abuse, a common requirement is to rely on parental consent and to seriously limit the right to confidentiality.

Paternalism:

To deal with the difficult issue of insufficient or inappropriate care for adolescents who may need treatment against their will, a review of the notion of paternalism is needed. *Paternalism* has been defined as "a policy or practice of treating or governing people in a fatherly manner, esp[ecially] by providing for their needs without giving them responsibility" (*The American Heritage Dictionary*, 1991, p. 909). However, the word "paternalism" is usually interpreted in a more derogatory way; it is often used in a similar way as the word "sexism," suggesting a one-way distortion in a relationship. But unlike sexism, paternalism allows the distortion to be eliminated in cases in which it can be reasonably proved to be justified.

Buchanan (1978) argues that paternalism is an interference with a person's freedom of action or information that is justified as being for the good of the person who is interfered with or misinformed. Another explanation of paternalism stresses that next to the motivation and intention to prevent harm or benefit another person, there is a second feature, a "refusal to accept or acquiesce in an individual's choices, wishes, and actions.... It usurps a right of decision making on the grounds that someone else can make a better decision" (Childress, 1979). Thus, the emphasis is placed on the concept of violation of rights. Others have pointed out the coercive aspects of paternalism, including the role of parents who are seen as inclined to restrict their child's freedom in various ways (Dworkin, 1971). Gert and Culver (1976) injected yet another concept into the debate by highlighting that paternalism entails the violation of a moral rule. From this perspective, a counselor would be doing something morally wrong if he or she were to be involved in invading privacy and/or enforcing loss of liberty *unless* there were adequate justification for doing so; thus, paternalistic actions generally involve doing something that usually would be considered morally wrong.

The central issue, however, is often the opposite: that the adult's (i.e., parent's, teacher's, or counselor's) abdication of responsibility for an endangered adolescent will result in inadequate treatment. Therefore, it is proposed that those involved in adolescent health care need to nourish and promote adolescent autonomy yet consider justified paternalism as a respectable alternative to abandonment.

In the dialectic process of societal change, *justified paternalism* may emerge in the 1990s as a caring alternative to the "antipaternalistic" rights position of the 1960s (Silber, 1989). Justified paternalism should be testable and severely limited, because, by definition, it involves treating someone in a way that violates a moral rule (e.g., coercive deprivation of freedom or invasion of privacy). Paternalism can be justified only when the evil prevented is greater than the harm caused by the violation of the moral rule and, more important, if it can be justified universally under relevantly similar circumstances to treat all persons in this way (Beauchamp & Walters, 1978). These conditions must be fulfilled. In addition, care must be taken to be clear about the *sufficient* conditions to avoid the danger or temptation of accepting paternalism for too many cases. Adolescents should be allowed to experiment, make mistakes, and face the consequences of their acts; only in serious situations should the principle of justified paternalism be invoked.

Obviously, any debate on ethical issues relating specifically to adolescents is only one component of a much larger struggle in moral philosophy. Every society is a compilation of a number of different histories; each is the bearer of a highly particular kind of moral tradition. We must recognize the diverse origins of the premises that underlie our moral reasoning and continue working toward a fair, respectful, and protective synthesis.

DIAGNOSING AND TREATING ADOLESCENT SUBSTANCE ABUSE

Availability of Treatment:

Although some treatments of alcoholism or substance abuse in adolescents may be superior to others, adolescents in need of treatment often face obstacles in their quest for health care services. This may be because of external barriers (e.g., lack of appropriate insurance) or internal reluctance (caused by a mismatch between the services offered and the particular nature of adolescent development). Moreover, external obstacles, whether financial, legal, or institutional, often augment many adolescents' perception of lack of response to their specific needs, alienation, and distrust (Silber, 1991b).

The notion that adolescence is a time of good health is erroneous. The Office of Technology Assessment (1991) estimates that one in five adolescents suffers at least one serious health problem; alcoholism and substance abuse are prominent among these problems (O'Malley, Johnston, & Bachman, 1993). The magnitude of the health problems and the barriers to care have stimulated the Society for Adolescent Medicine (SAM) (1991) to present a position paper enumerating seven criteria that must be fulfilled to make adolescent health care a reality for all teenagers:

1. *Availability*. Age-appropriate services and trained health care providers must be present in all communities.

2. *Visibility*. Health services for adolescents must be recognizable and convenient and should not require extensive or complex planning by adolescents or their parents.

3. *Quality*. A basic level of service must be provided to all adolescents, and they should be satisfied with the care they receive.

4. *Confidentiality*. Adolescents should be encouraged to involve their families in health decisions, but confidentiality must be ensured. Appropriate exceptions, such as danger to life, need to be explained beforehand.

5. *Affordability*. Public and private insurance programs must provide adolescents with preventive and other services designed to promote health behaviors and decrease morbidity and mortality.

6. *Flexibility*. Services, providers, and delivery sites must consider the cultural, ethnic, and social diversity among adolescents.

7. *Coordination*. Service providers must ensure that comprehensive services are available to adolescents.

Screening:

Ethical concerns related to screening involve the issues of informed consent, confidentiality (parents, school, and insurers), and civil rights. Professional associations have developed screening guidelines (AAP, 1989, 1993; American Academy of Child and Adolescent Psychiatry [AACAP], 1990) and a consensus seems to be emerging. Although the AAP states that "parental permission is not sufficient for involuntary screening of the older competent adolescent," it concedes "consent from the older adolescent may be waived when there is reason to doubt competency or when the medical assessment suggests a high risk of serious damage due to substance use." Moreover, the AAP accepts that "parental consent may be sufficient for the involuntary screening of the younger adolescent who lacks the capacity to make informed judgment," (AAP, 1989). AACAP agrees that an adolescent client should be given the right of informed consent to drug and alcohol treatment but qualifies it by adding that "it may be appropriate, however, to obtain consent from the parents alone when the minor client exhibits poor judgment, cannot make a positive treatment alliance, is dangerous to himself or herself or to others, does not show concern for his or her condition, and/or refuses help" (AACAP, 1990). DuPont (1994) extends this indication by claiming, "The standard against which all counselor's actions should be judged is the teenager's best long-term interests." He raises concerns about legitimacy of making distinctions between drug abuse and recreational drug use or experimentation, because the latter also can be dangerous and even fatal (DuPont, personal communication, 1994). Finally, there is strength in a *limiting* argument that opposes routine screening on grounds of the distress it would produce on teenagers, as well as the low likelihood that this would result in therapeutic accomplishments (King & Cross, 1987).

There are three prerequisites for screening to be ethical:

1. It must be scientifically sound (Schwartz, 1993).

2. It should be agreed to by the adolescent, or there should be clinical grounds for requesting screening (Silber, 1991b).

3. It should be part of a therapeutic plan rather than for other nontherapeutic purposes (Tarter, 1993).

Hospitalization:

Although concern about the ethical problems raised by the lack of services has received much attention in the community and the lay press, less is known about the excesses of hospitalization, insurance fraud, and right violations (Wagner, 1992; Hoffman, Mee-Lee, & Arrowood, 1993). Alarm has been raised repeatedly about inappropriate inpatient placements: "large numbers of young people are being deprived of their liberty under the guise of receiving medical treatment without the benefit of due process or procedural safeguards," and "the quality of care in many hospitals is poor and abusive" (Schwartz, 1989, p. 473). The principle of beneficence requires that all counselors become involved in "soul searching" about their practices. Any abusive and degrading practices should be recognized as such and brought to an end. In a larger framework, legislative and administrative reforms should be endorsed whenever they help ensure that adolescents are protected by a system of checks and balances that allows the least restrictive optimal treatment. The adult professional community can and should protect adolescents, recognizing their voice and their rights (Melton, 1983). Finally, the profession has an obligation to "expose and, if possible, eliminate the false and misleading advertising about hospital child and adolescent psychiatric and substance abuse treatment programs," (Schwartz, 1989, p. 478). There is a clear role for monitoring community groups, in which the expertise of counselors would be an invaluable help.

Rights of Adolescents:

A look at today's world will show that the main threats to adolescents are war, poverty, and drugs. In the past decade, an estimated 1.5 million children and adolescents were killed and more than 4 million disabled (Schaller & Nightingale, 1992).

Five million children and adolescents are now in refugee camps because of war, and 12 million have lost their parents. Perversely, adolescents also have been made pupils of war and distributors of drugs, forced to participate as soldiers or pushers, often to kill members of their own community. War and the addictions also have an enormous socioeconomic impact, leading to a life of fear and destruction bereft of education and security.

In times of peace, poverty and neglect become the most visible outrage. In the United States a 3-year study (National Research Council Commission on Behavioral and Social Sciences, 1993) concluded that the institutions and settings that should be helping young people (including families, schools, and neighborhoods) instead were making it more difficult for many of them to become healthy responsible adults. The National Research Council Commission on Behavioral and Social Sciences argued that drug use, school failure, delinquency, and violence grew to tragic proportions partly because of the deteriorating environment in which the adolescents were raised. If this is the situation in one of the wealthiest nations in the world, it is easy to imagine how the current economic crisis is affecting the children and adolescents living in the poorer countries. This makes it more urgent to take into consideration, listen, and respond to the needs of adolescents (Hawkins & Fitzgibbon, 1993).

SUMMARY

Attitudes toward teenagers and professional response have undergone marked transformation over time and followed historical, social, and legal developments. Barriers to the treatment of adolescent substance abuse can be raised as much by an uncaring system that restricts access to care as by an abdicating, permissive one that neglects to offer treatment to those who need it but want to avoid it. Ethical issues are intimately related to these situations. Controversies about consent and confidentiality, autonomy and beneficence, and obligations to clients and parents often become the battlefield on which the type of adolescent health care provided by a society (or its absence) will be decided.

Endorsement of the following concepts may improve the care of teenagers: (a) mutual participation as a goal of the counselor-client relationship, (b) the application of ethical theory to clinical practice, (c) the knowledge of the stages of adolescent moral development, and (d) the achievement of a reasonable balance between the support for adolescent autonomy and the limits placed by justified paternalism.

Although counselors can guide individual substance abusing adolescents in the pursuit of health, this is not sufficient unless there is a far-reaching societal commitment to provide quality health care for all adolescents. As citizens, counselors need to add their voice and expertise to the development of policies that genuinely protect adolescents, encouraging them to develop into mature agents of their destiny.

REFERENCES

American Academy of Child and Adolescent Psychiatry. (1990). American Academy of Child and Adolescent Psychiatry position statement: Drug and alcohol screening. *AACAP Newsletter*, Summer, 31–32.

American Academy of Pediatrics. (1973). A model act providing for consent of minors for health services. *Pediatrics, 51,* 293.

American Academy of Pediatrics, Committee on Adolescence, Committee on Bioethics, and Provisional Committee on Substance Abuse. (1989). Screening for drugs of abuse in children and adolescents. *Pediatrics, 84,* 396–397.

American Academy of Pediatrics Committee on Substance Abuse. (1993). Role of the pediatrician in prevention and management of substance abuse. *Pediatrics, 91,* 1010–1013.

The American Heritage Dictionary (2nd college ed.). (1991). Boston: Houghton-Mifflin.

Beauchamp, T. L., & Walters, L. R. (1978). *Contemporary issues in bioethics.* Encino, CA: Dickensen Publishing.

Brown, R. H., & Truitt, R. B. (1979). Right of minors to medical treatment. *DePaul Law Review, 28,* 290.

Buchanan, A. (1978). Medical paternalism. *Philosophy Public Affairs, 7,* 370–374.

Childress, J. F. (1979). Paternalism and health care. In W. L. Robinson & M. S. Pritchard (Eds.), *Medical responsibility.* Clifton, NJ: Humana Press.

DuPont, R. L. (1994). Facing and preventing teenage alcohol and other drug use. *Directions in Substance Abuse Counseling, 2*(3), 6.

Dworkin, G. (1971). Paternalism. In R. Wesserstrom (Ed.), *Morality and the law.* Belmont, CA: Wadsworth Publishing.

Gert, B., & Culver, C. (1976). Paternalistic behavior. *Philosophy Public Affairs, 6,* 45–49.

Goldstein, J., Freud, A., & Solnit, A. (1980). *Beyond the best interest of the child.* New York: The Free Press.

Group for the Advancement of Psychiatry. (1968). *Normal adolescence.* New York: The Scribner Library.

Hawkins, D., & Fitzgibbon, J. J. (1993). Risk factors and risk behavior in prevention of adolescent substance abuse. *Adolescent Medicine: State of the Art Reviews, 4,* 249–262.

Hoffman, N. G., Mee-Lee, D., & Arrowood, A. A. (1993). Treatment issues in adolescent substance use and addictions: Options, outcome, effectiveness, reimbursement, and admission criteria. *Adolescent Medicine: State of the Art Reviews, 4,* 371–390.

Hofmann, A. (1980). A rational policy toward consent and confidentiality in adolescent health care. *The Journal of Adolescent Health Care, 1,* 9–13.

Kett, J. F. (1993). Discovery and invention in the history of adolescence. *The Journal of Adolescent Health Care, 14,* 605–612.

King, N. M., & Cross, A. W. (1987). Moral and legal issues in screening for drug use in adolescents. *Journal of Pediatrics, 111*, 249–250.

Kohlberg, L., & Gilligan, C. (1971). The adolescent as philosopher. *Daedalus, 100*, 1051–1055.

Melden, A. I. (1967). *Ethical theories: A book of readings with revisions.* Englewood Cliffs, NJ: Prentice-Hall.

Melton, G. B. (1983). Toward 'personhood' for adolescents: Autonomy and privacy as values in public policy. *American Psychologist, 38*, 99-103.

National Research Council Commission on Behavioral and Social Sciences. (1993). *Loosing generations: Adolescents in high-risk settings.* Washington, DC: National Academic Press.

Nye, I. (1967). Values, family, and a changing society. *The Journal of Marriage and Family, 22*, 241–244.

Office of Technology Assessment. (1991). *Adolescent health: Summary and policy options.* Washington, DC: United States Congress.

O'Malley, P., Johnston, L. D., & Bachman, J. G. (1993). Adolescent substance use and addictions: Epidemiology, current trends, and public policy. *Adolescent Medicine: State of the Art Reviews, 4*, 227–248.

Ramsey, P. (1970). *The Patient as person: Exploration in medical ethics.* New Haven, CT: Yale University Press.

Schaller, J. G., & Nightingale, E. D. (1992). Children and childhoods: Hidden casualties of war and civil unrest. *Journal of the American Medical Association, 268*, 642–644.

Schwartz, I. M. (1989). Hospitalization of adolescents for psychiatric and substance abuse treatment: Legal and ethical issues. *The Journal of Adolescent Health Care, 10*, 473–478.

Schwartz, R. H. (1993). Testing for drugs of abuse: Controversies and techniques. *Adolescent Medicine: State of the Art Reviews, 4*, 353–370.

Silber, T. J. (1980). Physician-adolescent patient relationship, the ethical dimension. *Clinical Pediatrics, 19*, 50-53.

Silber, T. J. (1989). Justified paternalism in adolescent health care. *The Journal of Adolescent Health Care, 10,* 499–502.

Silber, T. J. (1991a). Overcoming obstacles to care: Ethical issues. *Adolescent Medicine: State of the Art Reviews, 2,* 405–413.

Silber, T. J. (1991b). Parental request for a 'drug test': What should the caring pediatrician do? *Clinical Pediatrics, 30,* 643–645.

Society for Adolescent Medicine. (1991). Access to health care. *The Journal of Adolescent Health Care, 13,* 162–170.

Szasz, T., & Hollander, M. A. (1956). A contribution to the philosophy of medicine. *Archives of Internal Medicine, 97,* 585–589.

Tarter, R. E. (1993). An integrative approach for the evaluation and treatment of alcohol and drug abuse. *Directions in Substance Abuse Counseling, 1*(1), 3–13.

Wagner, R. (1992). Psychiatrists and administrators testify about abuse in psychiatric hospitals. *Psychiatric Times, 9,* 36–38.

8

Geriatric Alcoholism: Identification and Elder-Specific Treatment Programs

Jayne Reinhardt, MPH, and George Fulop, MD, MSCM

Ms. Reinhardt is Public Health Educator for the San Diego [CA] County Alcohol and Drug Services. Dr. Fulop is Associate Professor, Departments of Community Medicine, Geriatrics, and Psychiatry at The Mount Sinai School of Medicine, New York, NY.

KEY POINTS

- Approximately 10%–15% of the elderly population suffers from alcoholism.

- Three groups of elderly alcoholics are described: early-onset, late-onset, and intermittent.

- Elderly alcoholics present special problems that are not seen in younger substance abusers. The elderly are more sensitive to alcohol; they are more prone to liver disease, organ damage, cancer, and other illnesses.

- Geriatric alcoholics have higher rates of concurrent physical and psychological disorders, depres-

sion, suicide, and death than do nondrinkers of the same age group.

- Alcoholism is more difficult to detect in the elderly. Once their problem has been identified, however, geriatric alcoholics respond well to treatment.

- Several strategies are effective in the treatment of geriatric alcoholism. These modalities include inpatient and outpatient settings (elder specific, nonelder specific, or mixed aged) outreach strategies, peer support, and family involvement. Various treatment programs are described.

INTRODUCTION

Alcoholism is defined as the repetitive use of alcohol that causes physical, psychological, or social harm to the drinker or to others. The drinker typically denies the problem or refuses to deal with it effectively. It is estimated that 10%–15% of the elderly suffer from alcoholism (Robertson, 1992).

Three distinct groups of elderly alcoholics are commonly described: early-onset, late-onset, and intermittent. The early-onset alcoholic begins to drink before age 40 and continues to drink into old age. In persons with this condition, a family history of alcoholism and other medical problems is common.

Clients with late-onset alcoholism show no evidence of earlier drinking problems. For them, drinking is often a direct response to life stressors such as social isolation, limited family supports, physical and cognitive impairment, and financial limitations.

Intermittent alcoholics demonstrate occasional episodes of heavy drinking earlier in life, alternating with periods of sobriety. Again, late life stressors are probably major contributors.

In this chapter, the authors review the general physical, psychological, and social impacts of drinking and point out some of the characteristics specific to older clients. The elderly are more sensitive to alcohol; they often have higher rates of concurrent physical and psychological disorders, including depression and suicide. Because they often take prescription drugs, combining these with alcohol can induce detrimental side effects.

Alcoholism is commonly misdiagnosed or overlooked in the elderly, so all professionals should be especially alert to its possibility. The authors set forth principles of successful treatment approaches for elderly alcoholics that not only encourage sobriety, but must also attend to such daily concerns as loneliness, loss of independence, and declining health. Behavioral therapy models have been effectively used, and outreach strategies are important as well. Unconditionally offered support and ways to renew hope and self-esteem are critical recovery strategies.

Although alcohol abuse and dependence decline with increasing age, they continue to pose a serious public health problem and a challenge to the treating mental health specialist. Recognizing significant age-related characteristics of the elderly alcoholic can help identify elderly problem drinkers, implement elder-specific treatment plans, and help elderly alcoholics avoid the serious medical and social consequences of alcoholism. This chapter describes the number and types of elderly alcoholics and the diverse treatment programs available today.

EPIDEMIOLOGY OF ELDERLY ALCOHOLISM

According to Robertson (1992), approximately 10%–15% of elderly persons are alcoholics. As in younger alcoholic populations, men outnumber women. The National Institute on Alcohol Abuse and Alcoholism (NIAAA) estimates that approximately 10% of elderly men and 2% of elderly women are heavy or problem drinkers (Williams, 1984).

Problem drinking has been defined as the "repetitive use of [the] beverage alcohol causing physical, psychological or social harm to the drinker or to others" (Plaut, 1970, pp. 37–38). Regier and colleagues (1988) cite a 0.9% overall 1-month prevalence rate with 1.8% men and 0.3% women alcoholics among community-dwelling elderly. The fourth edition of the *Diagnostic and Statistical Manual of Mental Disorders* (DSM-IV) (American Psychiatric Association [APA], 1994) draws a distinction between alcohol "abuse" and "dependence." Both disorders include criteria that, despite knowing that within a 12-month period recurrent drinking of alcoholic beverages causes occupational, academic, home, physical, legal, and/or interpersonal problems, these individuals continue to drink excessively. Alcohol abusers do not meet the criteria for tolerance, withdrawal, or a pattern of compulsive use (inability to refrain) that define alcohol dependence (APA, 1994). The term *alcoholic* is used in this chapter to describe those individuals who have problems with alcohol, abuse alcohol, or are alcohol dependent.

CLINICAL SETTINGS

Researchers agree that active alcoholism in all age groups tends to be found more frequently in clinical settings than in community sites (Atkinson, 1984). Brody (1982) reports that among the elderly population, 10%–15% of all who seek medical attention for any reason have alcohol-related problems. In their random sample of 84 patients from a general medical geriatric outpatient clinic, Fulop and colleagues (1993) found that 4.8% of geriatric outpatients scored in the alcoholism range (>5) on the 25-question Michigan Alcohol Screening Test (MAST) (Seltzer, 1971). After analyzing the results of a survey designed to determine the characteristics of elderly alcoholics, as well as physicians' practice patterns for alcoholism in all major patient-care departments at the Johns Hopkins Hospital in Baltimore, Curtis and colleagues (1989) documented that 15%–26% of geriatric medical inpatients have alcohol-related problems. A report by the San Diego Association of Governments (1991) stated that one fourth of seniors in psychiatric wards are alcoholic.

AGE OF ONSET

Three distinct groups of elderly alcoholics with different ages of onset have been described: early-onset, late-onset, and intermittent (Atkinson, 1984; Bahr, 1969; Gomberg, 1982; Pruzinsky, 1987).

Early-Onset Elderly Alcoholism:

The early-onset elderly problem drinker began drinking before age 40 and, having survived the obstacles of alcohol abuse and dependence, continues drinking into old age. Some studies have indicated that these individuals are more likely to demonstrate life-long addictive patterns and have weak affiliations with family, employment, or voluntary agencies (Bahr, 1969). Family alcoholism is more common among early-onset drinkers than among people who began drinking after the age of 40 (Bienenfeld, 1987).

In reviewing the records of 216 elderly alcoholics who were admitted to the Alcoholism and Drug Dependence Unit (ADDU) at the Mayo Clinic in Rochester, Minnesota, between 1972 and 1983, Morse (1988) also found that the early-onset drinkers exhibited more medical problems than the other two groups of elderly alcoholics (late-onset and intermittent). The early-onset alcoholics had a greater number of diagnoses that included cirrhosis of the liver, peripheral neuropathy, and cerebellum degeneration.

Late-Onset Elderly Alcoholism:

Late-onset elderly problem drinkers begin abusing alcohol in later life, exhibiting no evidence of previous drinking problems. These excessive drinkers are more likely to have enjoyed high occupational status throughout most of their adult lives (Bahr, 1969) and report fewer family histories of alcoholism (Atkinson, Turner, Kofoed, & Tolson, 1985). Atkinson (1984) found that late-onset problem drinkers exhibited greater psychological stability and higher socioeconomic status than did early-onset drinkers.

The etiology of late-onset alcoholism remains controversial. Many researchers (Atkinson, 1988; Finlayson, Hurt, Davis, & Morse, 1988; Finney & Moos, 1984; Hurt, Finlayson, Morse, & Davis, 1988; Olsen-Noll & Bosworth, 1989) hypothesize that late-onset elderly alcoholism is a direct response to life stressors. These stressors include some of the social problems that often are present for all older adults such as social isolation, limited family supports, and physical and cognitive impairment—as well as financial limitations that may put restrictions on their activities (Weins, Menustik, Miller, & Schmitz, 1982–1983).

Finney and Moos (1984) defined life stress as a "component of one or more of several combinations of factors that may trigger or perpetuate drinking problems" (p. 267). They critically examined several studies that empirically associated life stressors with the late onset of problem drinking in the elderly as well as with the triggering of problem drinking in the elderly intermittent group. They concluded that much of the evidence acquired from these studies is consistent with the stress theory. However, because "the pervasiveness of the stress hypothesis in the alcoholism and gerontology fields derives more from its intuitive appeal than from empirical research," they believe that stress can only be considered one component among a combination of factors attributing to the late onset of excessive drinking in older people.

Finlayson and colleagues (1988) reviewed the medical records of the 216 elderly patients who had been treated for alcoholism between 1972 and 1983 at the ADDU. They found that various life events were associated with or exacerbated the early and late onset of problem drinking among 211 ADDU elderly patients. Stressors were attributed to the onset of their exacerbated drinking in 81% of the late-onset drinkers.

Intermittent Elderly Alcoholics:

A third group, intermittent alcoholics, have experienced occasional episodes of heavy or problem drinking earlier in their lives that alternated with periods of sobriety. Similar to the case of late-onset elderly alcoholism, relapse among the intermittent elderly problem drinker may also be considered a response to the stressors of growing older and losing various motivating factors for remaining sober such as job, spouse, and good health (Gomberg, 1982; Olsen-Noll & Bosworth, 1989; Pruzinsky, 1987).

EFFECTS OF PROBLEM DRINKING ON THE ELDERLY

In all age groups, the effects of alcohol can be severe. Alcohol slows brain activity and impairs mental alertness and judgment. In addition, alcohol use alters physical coordination and reaction time, which increases the risks of falling and having accidents. Over time, excessive drinking can cause permanent brain and central nervous system (CNS) damage, as well as impair the liver, heart, kidneys, and stomach (U.S. Department of Health and Human Services, National Institute on Aging, 1983).

Although problems associated with occupational functioning and interacting with friends and neighbors, as well as those related to the police, appear less often for elderly individuals, Hinrichsen (1984) reports that negative physiologic and societal implications are still pertinent; even limited use of alcohol among elderly persons may cause more significant problems than among individuals under the age of 60.

Alcoholism also creates other costs, not only to the alcoholic and significant others, but to innocent bystanders, such as car accident victims. The National Highway Traffic Society Administration (NHTSA) reports that in 1994, 16,589 people lost their lives in alcohol-related crashes. In addition, the NHTSA estimates that 40% of fatal crashes and 6% of all crashes involve alcohol (U.S. Department of Transportation, 1996).

Elderly alcoholic clients present special problems that are not seen in younger populations. Older adults' reactions to alcohol are much stronger than those of their younger counterparts. Because lean body mass decreases by about 10% from age 20 to age 70 and the body water component accounts for a smaller percentage of total mass, the amount of alcohol consumed is distributed to a smaller volume, resulting in a higher blood alcohol concentration (Olsen-Noll & Bosworth, 1988). Therefore, using quantity and frequency as criteria to diagnose elderly problem drinkers could be difficult and inaccurate. Moreover, the rates of concurrent medical disorders, death, depression, and suicide are higher among geriatric problem drinkers than among nondrinkers of the same age group.

Physiologic Complications:

Hurt and co-workers (1988) found that alcoholics had a higher frequency of psoriasis and peptic ulcer disease than did the general elderly population. Morse (1988) also reported that organic brain syndromes were the most "important psychiatric problems" of the alcoholic group.

Compared with their younger counterparts, elderly alcoholics are more prone to liver disease, cancers and other chronic illnesses, and organ damage (Grispoon, 1986). Excessive drinking can also double many common age-related physical ailments, such as occult cardiovascular disease, osteoporosis, hypoglycemia (an abnormally low concentration of glucose in the blood), hyperuricemia (enhanced blood concentrations of uric acid), and hypertriglyceridemia (elevated triglyceride concentrations in the blood) (Atkinson, 1984).

Studying alcohol use among a group of semi-independently living nonagenarian (> 90 years old) men and a group of 65–75-year-old men of similar demographic characteristics, Jensen and Bellecci (1987) found significant evidence that suggested alcohol use was related to the frequency of major medical illnesses among both groups. They reported that the heavier drinkers tended to have higher frequencies of major illnesses when compared with those who reported rarely or never drinking (3.8 versus 2.4). After studying 200 patients with liver disease, Potter and James (1987) reported that 28% of alcohol liver disease in persons 60 years or older was found to be related to alcoholism, with mortality rates of 34% and 53% at 1- and 3-year follow-ups. Comparing laboratory test results of the elderly ADDU patients admitted during 1972–1983 with those of a group of younger ADDU (mean age 44.3 years) patients admitted during 1978–1979, Hurt and colleagues (1988) found that out of 10 laboratory tests reviewed, results from five of these tests were more often abnormal in the elderly alcoholic group.

Medications and Alcohol Interactions

Although the elderly constitute about 10%–12% of the American population, they take over 30% of all prescription drugs and more than 40% of over-the-counter (OTC) medications (Katz, 1991). Atkinson (1984) found that 80% of elderly OTC drug users simultaneously ingest alcohol, prescribed medications, or a combination of the two. The American Medical Association reports that alcohol interacts with approximately half of the one hundred most frequently prescribed medications (American Medical Association, 1995). Because older adults experience increased sensitivity to all drugs that are CNS depressants, combining alcohol (a CNS depressant) with any one of these drugs can be fatal to the older adult (Katz, 1991). In addition, using alcohol with commonly prescribed drugs (e.g., CNS depressants, analgesics, cardiovasculars, antidiabetics, and anticoagulants) can significantly alter motor and sensory functions, and negatively affect vitamin absorption (McGlone, 1983).

Psychological Complications:

Bienenfeld (1987) reports that depression is uniformly present in alcoholics, especially because alcohol has a direct depressant effect; also, society tends to isolate drinkers, leading them into a spiral of loneliness. Dupree, Brockowski, and Schonfil (1984) reported that a large percentage of the clients participating in a 24-day alcoholism pilot treatment program drank alone at home and mostly reported being depressed or lonely just prior to taking their first daily drink.

In reviewing the literature regarding elderly suicide,

Conwell (1995) notes that although more attention has been given to the problems of self-destructive behaviors exhibited by youth, the highest suicide rate of any group is among individuals aged 65 and older. Osgood (1987) reports that excessive alcohol use and depression have been associated positively with elderly suicide rates. Compared with other age groups, the elderly population has the highest rate of completed suicides.

IDENTIFICATION OF ELDERLY ALCOHOLISM

Poor Detection:

In a report by West, Maxwell, Noble, & Solomon (1984), Dr. David H. Solomon notes that defining alcoholism in the elderly population is difficult because criteria that are normally used to detect alcoholism in other age groups (such as driving violations or accidents, public disruptions, or absences from work) may not be applicable to the elderly. There is also a low index of suspicion, and lifestyle difficulties that can result from excessive alcohol use in younger populations are often absent in the elderly, resulting in fewer problems with the police and the legal system. In addition, Bienenfeld (1987) points out that many elderly alcoholics are widowed, generally retired, and often do not drive. Therefore, they seldom attract attention because of trouble with work or marriage, thereby lowering the reported prevalence rates of elderly alcoholics.

Problems of Denial:

The denial of the alcoholic and significant others only adds to the major problems of underdiagnosis of, and lack of proper treatment for, elderly alcoholic clients. Bienenfeld (1987) notes that the most difficult aspect of detecting and treating alcoholism in persons of any age is overcoming the denial that is commonly associated with this disease. He explains that family members, close acquaintances, or even public agency and state institution personnel often act as enablers for elderly alcoholics by providing a refuge for them.

It is possible that an employer may wish to carry along an older, dysfunctional employee as a token of appreciation for past service. Guilt feelings may also prevent the spouse of an elderly alcoholic from confronting his or her mate about the problem (Bienenfeld, 1987).

Screening Instruments:

The mental health professional can increase the detection of alcohol problems by asking a few pertinent questions or administering a brief screening questionnaire. One concise screening instrument is the four-question CAGE. Ewing (1984) notes that the questionnaire asks participants about:

- Their feelings about the need to cut down on their drinking

- Whether they have been annoyed by other people's criticism of their drinking

- Their bad or guilty feelings about their drinking

- If they have ever had an eye opener (a drink first thing in the morning) to "steady their nerves"

Another screening instrument, the Brief MAST, is a 10-item version of the more detailed 25-question original MAST and seems to be well tolerated by the elderly (Pokorny, Miller, & Kaplan, 1972).

TREATMENT AND PREVENTION STRATEGIES

Once identified, the elderly alcoholic responds well to treatment (Williams, 1983; Zimberg, 1978). Treatment options for the elderly similar to those for young alcoholics (e.g., psycho-therapy, detoxification and rehabilitation, disulfiram [Anta-buse], Alcoholics Anonymous [AA], etc.) will not be discussed here because of general awareness of these options. However, a number of age-specific model programs have been identi-fied. In general, treatment may be in mixed-age or elder-specific groups. Some have argued that treatment intervention for elderly alcoholics can be most effective when delivered through facilities that specifically treat elderly clients rather than through general psychiatric or medical institutions. These may include senior citizen centers, outpatient geriatric medi-cal or psychiatric facilities, nursing homes, or geriatric home care programs (Zimberg, 1978).

Although some programs have been developed specifically to meet the demands of the elderly alcoholic (Dunlop, Skorney, & Hamilton, 1982; Dupree et al., 1984; Glassock, 1979; Kofoed, Tolson, Atkinson, Toth, & Turner, 1987), the need for these programs continues to outweigh the number of those devel-oped and implemented.

MODEL GERIATRIC ALCOHOL TREATMENT PROGRAMS AND STRATEGIES

Olsen-Noll and Bosworth (1989) explain that treatment for the elderly problem drinker must focus on such daily concerns as loneliness, loss of independence, and declining health. Zimberg (1978) suggests that the treatment approach for elderly alco-holics should place emphasis on compensating for various age-related losses and stresses that are not applicable to younger populations.

Several strategies have been delineated in the treatment of geriatric alcoholism. These modalities include, but are not limited to, inpatient and outpatient settings — including those that are elder specific, nonelder specific, or mixed aged, as well as those implementing the disease, behavioral, and self-man-agement models of treatment—outreach strategies, peer sup-port, and family involvement.

INPATIENT MIXED-AGE TREATMENT

Disease Model:

Some inpatient programs incorporate the disease model of alcoholism into their treatment strategies. Hurt and colleagues (1988) conducted a retrospective epidemiologic study of the 216 elderly patients of the ADDU. Their goal was to determine, among other things, the demographics of a group of elderly alcoholics and to analyze differences between early- and late-onset alcoholics. The ADDU was already in place when the researchers retrospectively examined the medical records of the 216 participants. (The ADDU itself is not an age-specific treatment center because it treats both older [aged over 60] and younger patients.)

The ADDU's treatment approach is based on the disease concept of addiction. The treatment program integrates "multidisciplinary-staffed modalities for treatment of addictions with psychiatric and specialty-oriented medical care" (Hurt et al., 1988, p. 754). On admittance to the 28-day program (28 days in the first 2 years of the study, but those who entered in or after year 2 stayed only 21 days), each patient underwent an initial diagnostic assessment, which included a medical and psychological examination (Hurt et al., 1988).

Intervention strategies included education through films and lectures (Finlayson et al., 1988), individual and group psychotherapy, addiction counseling, physical exercise, family participation, an introduction to AA (Hurt et al., 1988), and aftercare planning (Finlayson et al., 1988).

Although the researchers primarily focused on the participants' medical and social information, they assessed the elderly alcoholic's quality of life through demographic data, medical characteristics, laboratory test results, treatment outcomes, and comparisons of early- and late-onset alcoholism (Hurt et al., 1988). They found that the frequency of serious medical disorders for this group was higher than would be expected for the overall population of the same age. They concluded that more intensive treatment might be required for some elderly alcoholics because of the high frequency of major medical and psychological problems among this population (Hurt et al., 1988).

Other investigators such as Zimberg (1978) and Thomas-Knight (1978) have expressed the view that therapy directed at the social, psychological, and physical stresses associated with aging would be sufficient for treating elderly alcoholics. However, Hurt and colleagues (1988) dispute the effectiveness of simply socializing elderly alcoholics; they claim that this group must receive comprehensive treatment comparable to, if not exceeding, treatment provided for younger alcoholics.

Behavioral Model:

An inpatient alcoholism treatment program was instituted at the Veterans Administration Center in Jackson, Mississippi (Miller, Stanford, & Hemphill, 1974). After examining the results of a survey of hospital admissions from the medical and psychiatric wards at the Center, researchers found that 40% of entering patients demonstrated a significant alcohol problem. To combat this situation, Miller and colleagues (1974) explain that emphasis was placed on changing the individual's daily life functions (attitudes, skills, and behaviors).

Within this framework, alcoholism is viewed as a socially acquired habitual behavior pattern that enables the alcoholic to avoid or escape from unpleasant or anxiety-producing situations, gain attention from friends and family, and avoid withdrawal symptoms associated with the termination of drinking (Miller et al., 1974).

One strategy of this threefold treatment approach is to change the problem drinker's attitude by decreasing the immediate reinforcing properties of alcohol through electrical, chemical, or verbal aversion therapy techniques (Miller et al., 1974). Having identified several of the behavioral and nonbehavioral factors associated with persistent drinking, it is possible to develop a behavioral inventory by identifying the behaviors that are incompatible with excessive drinking and ultimately to teach the alcoholic new skills to cope with life (Miller et al., 1974).

Another component of this approach encourages the elderly alcoholic to participate in a token-economy system, which offers rewards through privileges. The intent of this reward system is to reinforce positive, therapeutically goal-oriented behaviors that are incompatible with excessive drinking (Miller et al., 1974). Miller and colleagues (1974) explain that the Mississippi program offers social and vocational counseling based on the notion that the individual will remain only temporarily sober unless he or she directly enters into a satisfying and health-promoting employment and social environment. However, because many elderly alcoholics are retired, it would be necessary to provide counseling that would address the specific needs of this target population.

Similar to other alcohol treatment programs, the Veteran's Administration Mississippi program includes family treatment with a goal of producing change that will lead to growth among family members, as well as promote healthy marital relationships for married clients (Miller et al., 1974).

As of September, 1996, this program is still providing services to veterans who present with alcohol-related problems. A hospital administrator who has worked with the VA since 1967 reported that incoming patients are screened more thoroughly than they have been in previous years, and that more Korean War and World War II veterans are entering the program, increasing the percentage of elderly patients (Veterans Administration, 1996). He also confirmed that the components reported in the 1974 survey (Miller et al., 1974) are still being implemented in this program (Veterans Administration, 1996).

Outreach Strategies:

The Senior Alcoholism Services (SAS) of Vancouver, Washington, is an example of another age-specific residential alcohol treatment program that implements a different approach to treating the elderly alcoholic. Created as a result of a needs assessment of the elderly population in Clark County, Washington, the project's primary goal is to help older alcoholics stop drinking and begin living through sobriety by turning their problems into new opportunities (Dunlop et al., 1982).

Bienenfeld (1987) explained that denial is a primary characteristic of alcoholism. Outreach alcoholism counselors must break through this denial. In the SAS program, the counselors' major involvement with the clients has been in the motivational and the aftercare treatment phases. Rather than waiting for clients to arrive at the SAS office voluntarily, counselors make themselves available to hospital patients and nursing home clients who have been identified as having alcohol-related problems. Also, counselors visit potential clients' homes to encourage them to participate in the program (Dunlop et al., 1982).

Clients who have been motivated to participate in the program are generally admitted for 21–30 days of intensive treatment that includes individual counseling, family and couples therapy, self-esteem building programs, and other activities that can serve as alternatives to excessive drinking (Williams, 1983). Moreover, by assisting the SAS clients in filling out public assistance forms for housing and health care, social workers demonstrate that the clients' needs will be met regardless of the financial costs (Williams, 1983).

Peer Support:

Dunlop and colleagues (1982) also found that, in the SAS project, sensitive peer support groups consisting of other elderly recovering alcoholics serve as reinforcing factors to recovery. They reported that geriatric problem drinkers respond just as positively to group therapy as do younger populations if the specific concerns of the elderly are addressed, including estrangement from children, loss of driving ability, and death of a spouse.

Family Involvement:

In his experience treating patients in a geriatric psychiatric program and consulting in medical home care programs and nursing homes, Zimberg (1971) reports that along with group therapy, socialization, and medical care, family casework is a preferred strategy in treating alcoholism among the elderly. Indeed, family involvement is a large component of the SAS program. Many family members enabled their elderly alcoholic relatives to continue drinking excessively because they felt that they were protecting them by allowing them to "enjoy one of the final pleasures." Families are encouraged to attend meetings to acquire alcoholism information and continued emotional support (Williams, 1983).

ELDER-SPECIFIC OUTPATIENT TREATMENT

For other elderly alcoholic persons, outpatient treatment programs offer the most beneficial treatment. At the time of entry into a special outpatient alcohol treatment program, 36 active elderly alcoholics were assessed on selected demographic, psychological, and alcohol-related variables. In comparing the treatment outcomes of 14 early-onset problem drinkers with 22 late-onset problem drinkers from this group, Atkinson and colleagues (1985) concluded that both of these elderly groups are much more compliant to treatment than are younger alcoholics.

Behavioral and Self-Management Strategies:

Similar to the Mississippi Veterans Administration inpatient alcoholism treatment program (Miller et al., 1974), the Gerontology Alcohol Project (GAP) described by Dupree and colleagues (1984) applied behavioral and self-management strategies designed specifically for elderly alcoholics. An elder-specific, 24-day pilot day treatment alcoholism program located in Florida, the GAP was developed to investigate the location, description, and treatment of late-onset alcoholics. Potential participants were asked to assess five life areas in which the quality could be affected by excessive drinking. The quantity and frequency of alcohol consumption among the late-onset drinkers were determined as well.

The investigators divided the project into four treatment modules. These modules were designed for participants to identify the components of the general and ultimately their own behavior chains that led to their drinking problems. In addition to the analysis of drinking behavior, participants were taught self-management techniques for high-risk situations, alcohol information and education, and general problem-solving skills.

The researchers found that success, as defined by participants maintaining their respective goals of alcohol consumption, was quite high among those who completed the treatment program. They found that after a 12-month follow-up period, most of the participants in their program demonstrated significant improvements in functioning as well as an increase in the size of their social networks.

Dropouts of the project had lower estimates of success and higher depression scores, and also tended to drink more alcohol than the graduates. The investigators also found that the great number of late-onset drinkers warrants age-specific treatment programs (Dupree et al., 1984).

As a component of the comprehensive Alcohol and Drug Dependence Treatment Section (ADDTS) of the Psychiatric Service at the Veteran's Administration Medical Center in Portland, Oregon, the ADDTS Class of '45 program offers clients evaluation, detoxification, and residential and outpatient services. This elder-specific program employs paraprofessionals, recovering addicts, and professional staff members. The program is available to any veteran accepted for outpatient alcoholism treatment who was on active military duty during or before 1945 (Kofoed, Tolson, Atkinson, Turner, & Toth, 1984).

The Class of '45 program offers three concurrent groups of 30 participants. Groups meet weekly for 1½ hours, specifically during daytime hours, to increase public transportation accessibility for all older participants who do not drive and prefer not to travel at night. Many clients also attend a local elder-specific AA meeting for additional support (Atkinson, 1984).

Comparison of Mixed-Age and Elder-Specific Groups:

In their Class of '45 study, Kofoed and colleagues (1987) retrospectively examined the course of outpatient alcoholism treatment by comparing the results in 24 elderly alcoholics who were mainstreamed into a typical mixed-age outpatient group with the results in 25 elderly alcoholics treated in the special geriatric peer group program.

In comparing the elder-specific Class of '45 group to the mixed-age groups at the ADDTS, Kofoed and colleagues (1987) found that the most obvious difference between these two groups was the quick development of a strong attachment among group members in the elderly peer group. Participants showed a ready acceptance of all group members, leaders, and group goals. Group members also exhibited a sense of camaraderie with each other (Kofoed et al., 1984). Overall, the researchers found that members of the elderly peer group were more compliant, remained in treatment significantly longer, and were more likely to complete their treatment programs than were elderly participants of the mixed-aged group; the process became fragmented in the mixed-age groups as older clients increased in the group-oriented program. Many older clients in the mixed-age group also reported feeling uncomfortable when outnumbered by younger clients (Kofoed et al., 1987).

The researchers noted that the major difference between elderly problem drinkers and their younger counterparts stems from the older drinkers' attitude and responsiveness to treatment strategies. After comparing the elderly peer group with the mixed-aged group, Kofoed and colleagues (1987) concluded that elderly alcoholics respond to sociotherapeutic intervention and prefer peer groups to age-heterogeneous groups.

THERAPEUTIC COMMUNITY

In the therapeutic community, client-staff groups are established to discuss clients' problems. Members of this community are offered greater autonomy to make decisions about their own needs. Atkinson (1984) notes that therapeutic community intervention has been effective in reducing problem drinking and other behavior disorders in community and institutional settings.

Zimberg (1971) reports that in a study of 103 elderly alcoholics in treatment, Rosin and Glatt found that the most beneficial services provided for this group were those that included interaction with other people, such as environmental manipulation, medical services, day hospital care, and home visits by staff or good neighbors. Therefore, a schedule that includes volunteer or part-time jobs coupled with structured, interactive nonworking time would serve as a practical substitute to a work situation for recovering elderly alcoholics.

FACTORS IN ELDERLY TREATMENT
RESPONSIVENESS

After studying over 600 subjects for almost 40 years, Vaillant (1983) identified factors associated with recovery from alcoholism. Two factors strongly operative in the Class of '45 project were the increased sources of unconditionally offered support and a source of renewed hope and self-esteem (Vaillant, 1983). Other factors included a dependence on a nonchemical substitute for alcohol, which is a strong component of the SAS recovery group, as well as the use of external, ritual reminders that even one drink can lead to pain and relapse.

Felker (1988) explains that the community-based Elderly

Recovery Group in Wisconsin incorporates all four factors of recovery. The group offers a nonchemical substitute for alcohol through the continual concern and active problem solving efforts offered by each member and the group's professionals. Through group readings and discussions of each other's infrequent setbacks and relapses, members receive external, ritual reminders of the dangers involved in taking even one drink. The program also offers increased sources of unconditional social support and a source of renewed hope and self-esteem (Felker, 1988). Similar to the Class of '45 program, the Elderly Recovery Group offers nonjudgmental social support to renew members' faith, hope, and self-esteem (Felker, 1988).

The Elderly Recovery Group was developed in response to the need for an alcohol and substance abuse/dependence support group among the 350 older people housed in three Wisconsin senior citizens' complexes. After conducting a community assessment of this population, two health professionals who had been working with this community realized the high prevalence of alcoholism, which was often accompanied by abuse of prescription medications within this residential elderly population (Felker, 1988).

Having decided to develop the group, they acquired the appropriate staff through a joint effort among various health care agencies and well-developed alcohol treatment programs (Felker, 1988). Although many residents of the senior citizens' complexes in Wisconsin had repeatedly been to the County Alcohol Detoxification Unit, Felker (1988) notes that many problem drinkers did not perceive the seriousness of their conditions or believe that their health was actually in danger.

Six months prior to initiating the group, the trial stage was implemented in the form of a one-on-one interaction between the professional staff and apartment residents. This trial period was instrumental in the decision-making stage because the trust that developed between the apartment residents and the health professionals encouraged these geriatric alcoholics to agree to participate in the developing groups. Having made the decision to join the program, the residents ultimately adopted the group concept (Felker, 1988).

Felker states that because group sessions were held in community rooms within the apartment complexes, many members felt stigmatized by their nondrinking neighbors. In response to this, the group incorporated role-playing strategies to develop methods of responding to neighbors' remarks. He further notes that as members practiced the skill of assertiveness, they became better able to handle the stresses associated with the confrontations with their neighbors.

Although the group had very few rules, it did have some norms, or common beliefs, about the way members were expected to behave. Because trust was a major determinant of a group's success (Johnson & Johnson, 1987), strict respect for members' confidentiality outside of the meeting was stressed (Felker, 1988).

Continued Care Support Group:

Similar to the Elderly Recovery Group, the Helping Hands Program at the Alcoholism Treatment and Education Center (ATEC) in Long Beach, California, is a continuing care support group, free of charge and open to any elderly alcoholic. Most group members are referred from the inpatient Alcoholism Treatment program at Memorial Hospital Medical Center (Glassock, 1979).

The clearly defined goals of the Helping Hands group include helping older, recovering alcoholics develop a positive, creative sobriety; establishing and maintaining a continuing life support system; and developing and expanding the channels between the Helping Hands program and the community senior services agencies, alcohol rehabilitation facilities, and other community resources (Glassock, 1979).

The Helping Hands program is comprised of two phases. Phase I addresses the physical withdrawal of alcohol. Members are sent to a 3-week inpatient detoxification program at Memorial Hospital's ATEC unit. Family and close friends or neighbors are encouraged to become involved in the alcoholic's treatment program early in the recovery process. Emphasis is placed on the development of self-responsibility and autonomy, which is the premise of a follow-up support system (Glassock, 1979).

During phase II, the social/psychological evaluation period of the Helping Hands program, the patient's environment is assessed with the main focus being the patient's hospital discharge. The evaluating health specialist looks for strengths, interests, and other significant factors that can be restored and directed to contribute to that patient's recovery (Glassock, 1979).

Several group participants volunteer to reach out to newcomers by telephoning them, offering peer counseling, and following up on their progress. Other members have established additional AA and Helping Hands groups in communities that needed these support tools (Glassock, 1979).

A special daily therapy group for the older discharged alcoholic also addresses age-related issues as well as problem drinking (Glassock, 1979). Upon leaving the ATEC inpatient program, a discharge plan resource network refers patients to AA meetings and other support systems. Glassock noted that some elderly problem drinkers use the Helping Hands group as a stepping stone for entry into other programs like AA.

CONCLUSION

Alcoholism remains a complex problem faced by all age groups. The elderly alcoholic is particularly subject to underdetection and undertreatment, despite the notable success rate of multiple treatment modalities. In fact, the elderly may have even better treatment responses than their younger counterparts, especially if treated in peer groups and when social and medical factors contributing to alcoholism are addressed. With the "graying" of America, all mental health specialists will need to become increasingly familiar with the special treatment needs of the elderly alcoholic.

REFERENCES

American Medical Association. (1995). Alcoholism in the elderly: Diagnosis treatment prevention. Guidelines for primary care physicians. Washington, DC: Author.

American Psychiatric Association. (1994). *Diagnostic and statistical manual of mental disorders* (4th ed.). Washington, DC: Author.

Atkinson, R. M. (Ed.). (1984). *Alcohol and drug abuse in old age*. Washington, DC: American Psychiatric Press.

Atkinson, R. M. (1988). Alcoholism in the elderly population. *Mayo Clinic Proceedings, 63*, 825–829.

Atkinson, R. M., Turner, J. A., Kofoed, L. L., & Tolson, R. L. (1985). Early- versus late-onset alcoholism in older persons: Preliminary findings. *Alcoholism: Clinical Experimental Research, 9*, 513–515.

Bahr, H. M. (1969). Lifetime affiliation of early- and late-onset heavy drinkers on skid row. *Quarterly Journal of Studies on Alcoholism, 30*, 645–656.

Bienenfield, D. (1987). Alcoholism in the elderly. *American Family Practitioner, 36*(2), 163–168.

Brody, J. A. (1982). Aging and alcohol abuse. *Journal of American Geriatric Society, 30*, 123–126.

Conwell, Y. (1995, June). Suicide among elderly persons. *Psychiatry Services, 46*(6), 563-564.

Curtis, J. R., Geller, G., Stokes, E. J., Levine, D. M., & Moore, R. D. (1989). Characteristics, diagnosis, and treatment of alcoholism in elderly patients. *Journal of American Geriatric Society, 37*, 310–316.

Dunlop, J., Skorney, B., & Hamilton, J. (1982). Group treatment for elderly alcoholics and their families. *Social Work with Groups, 5*, 87–92.

Dupree, L. W., Broskowski, H., & Schonfel, L. (1984). The gerontology alcohol project: A behavioral treatment program for elderly abusers. *The Gerontologist, 24*, 510–516.

Ewing, J. A. (1984). Detecting alcoholism: The CAGE questionnaire. *Journal of the American Medical Association, 252*, 1905–1907.

Felker, M. P. (1988, March/April). A recovery group for elderly alcoholics. *Geriatric Nursing*, pp. 110–113.

Finlayson, R. E., Hurt, R. D., Davis, L. J., & Morse, R. M. (1988). Alcoholism in the elderly person: A study of the psychiatric and psychological features of 216 inpatients. *Mayo Clinic Proceedings, 63*, 761–768.

Finney, J. W., & Moos, R. H. (1984). Life stressors and problem drinking among older adults. *Aging and Alcoholism, 2*, 267–288.

Fulop, G., Reinhardt, J., Strain, J., Paris, B., Miller, M., & Fillit, H. (1993). Identification of alcoholism and depression in a geriatric medicine outpatient clinic. *Journal of the Geriatric Society, 41*, 737-741.

Glassock, J. A. (1979). Rehabilitating the older alcoholic. *Aging, 291–302*, 19–24.

Gomberg, E. L. (1982). Patterns of alcohol use and abuse among the elderly. In National Institute on Alcohol Abuse and Alcoholism, *Special population issues*. (Alcohol and Health Monograph No. 4). Rockville, MD: NIAAA.

Grispoon, L. (Ed.). (1986). What is alcoholism? – Part I. *Harvard Medical School Mental Health Letter, 2*(10), 1–4.

Hinrichsen, J. J. (1984). Toward improving treatment services for alcoholics of advanced age. *Alcohol Health & Research World, 8*(3), 31–39.

Hurt, R. D., Finlayson, R. E., Morse, R. M., & Davis, L. J. (1988). Alcoholism in elderly persons: Medical aspects and prognosis of 216 inpatients. *Mayo Clinic Proceedings, 63*, 753–760.

Jensen, G. D., & Bellecci, P. (1987). Alcohol and the elderly: Relationships to illness and smoking. *Alcohol and Alcoholism, 22*, 193–198.

Johnson, D. W., & Johnson, F. P. (1987). *Joining together: Group therapy and group skills*. Englewood Cliffs, NJ: Prentice-Hall.

Katz, D. (1991, June). Geriatric use and misuse of medication. Drug Abuse Information and Monitoring Process, White Paper Series.

Kofoed, L. L., Tolson, R. L., Atkinson, R. M., Turner, J. A., & Toth, R. F. (1984). Elderly groups in an alcoholism clinic. In *Alcohol and drug abuse in old age* (pp. 35–49). Washington, DC: American Psychiatric Press.

Kofoed, L. L., Tolson, R. L., Atkinson, R. M., Toth, R. L., & Turner, J. A. (1987). Treatment compliance of older alcoholics: An elder-specific approach to mainstreaming. *Journal of Studies on Alcoholism, 48*, 47–50.

McGlone, F. B. (1983). Report on the meeting of the Western Division of the American Geriatric Society. *Journal of the American Geriatric Society, 31*, 240–244.

Miller, P. M., Stanford, A. G., & Hemphill, D. P. (1974, May). A social-learning approach to alcoholism treatment. *Social Casework*, pp. 279–284.

Morse, R. M. (1988). Substance abuse among the elderly. *Bulletin of the Menninger Clinic, 52*, 259–268.

Olsen-Noll, C. G., & Bosworth, M. F. (1989). Alcohol abuse in the elderly. *American Family Practitioner, 39*, 173–179.

Osgood, N. J. (1987). To relieve depression and loneliness and escape the problems and stresses of growing old, many of the elderly turn to alcohol. *Postgraduate Medicine, 81*, 380–384.

Plaut, T. F. A. (1970). *Alcohol problems: A report to the Nation.* New York: Oxford University Press.

Pokorny, A. D., Miller, B. A., & Kaplan, H. B. (1972, September). The Brief MAST: A shortened version of the Michigan Alcoholism Screening Test. *American Journal of Psychiatry, 129*, 118–121.

Potter, J. F., & James, O. F. W. (1987). Clinical features and prognosis of alcohol liver disease in respect of advancing age. *Gerontology, 33*, 380–387.

Pruzinsky, E. W. (1987). Alcohol and the elderly: An overview of problems in the elderly and implications for social work practice. *Journal of Gerontological Social Work, 11*, 81–93.

Regier, D. A., Boyd, J. H., Burke, J. D. Jr., Rae, D. S., Myers, J. K., Kramer, M., Robins, L. N., George, L. K., Karno, M., & Locke, B. Z. (1988). One-month prevalence of mental disorders in the United States. *Archives of General Psychiatry, 45*, 977–986.

Robertson, N. (1992, February–March). Will that friendly drink betray you? *Modern Maturity,* pp. 26–30, 65.

San Diego Association of Governments. (1991). *Drug abuse in San Diego County: A needs assessment.* Government report.

Seltzer, M. L. (1971). The Michigan Alcoholism Screening Test: The quest for a new diagnostic instrument. *American Journal of Psychiatry, 127,* 1653-1658.

Thomas-Knight, R. (1978). Treating alcoholism among the aged: The effectiveness of a special treatment program for older problem drinkers. *Dissertation Abstracts International, 39,* 3009B.

U.S. Department of Health and Human Services, National Institute on Aging. (1983, November). Aging and alcohol abuse. *Age Page.*

U.S. Department of Transportation, National Highway Traffic Safety Administration. (1996, April). *A program guide for law enforcement and highway safety administrators: Impaired driving enforcement.* Washington, DC: Author.

Vaillant, G. E. (1983). *The natural history of alcoholism.* Cambridge, MA: Harvard University Press.

Veterans Administration. (1996, September). Personal communication, Hospital Administrator, Veterans' Administration Center, Jackson, Mississippi.

Weins, A. N., Menustick, C. E., Miller, S. I., & Schmitz, R. E. (1982–1983). Medical-behavioral treatment of the older alcoholic patient. *American Journal of Drug and Alcohol Abuse, 9,* 461–475.

West, L. J., Maxwell, D. S., Noble, E. P., & Solomon D. H. (1984). Depression and suicide among the elderly. *Annals of Internal Medicine, 100,* 405–416.

Williams, M. (1983, April). Senior program stresses peer, family involvement. *Information and Feature Services, 106.*

Williams, M. (1984). Alcohol and the elderly: An overview. *Alcohol Health & Research World, 8*(3), 1–8.

Zimberg, S. (1971). The psychiatrist and medical home care: Geriatric psychiatry in the Harlem community. *American Journal of Psychiatry, 127,* 1062–1066.

Zimberg, S. (1978). Treatment of the elderly alcoholic in the community and in an institutional setting. *Addictive Diseases, 3,* 417–427.

9

Counseling Chemically Dependent Persons with HIV Infection

Michael Shernoff, MSW, ACSW

Mr. Shernoff is Founder and former Co-Director of Chelsea Psychotherapy Associates, New York, NY. He is currently in private practice and is an Adjunct Faculty Member at the Hunter College Graduate School of Social Work, New York, NY.

KEY POINTS

- Approximately 32% of all AIDS cases are related to intravenous drug use.

- Substance abuse increases a person's vulnerability to contracting HIV.

- Professionals and paraprofessionals in the field of substance abuse must be knowledgeable about the spectrum of HIV illness, AIDS, and HIV transmission. Health care professionals working with AIDS patients must be knowledgeable about issues of substance abuse and chemical dependency.

- The chemically dependent client with HIV is best served by an interdisciplinary team.

- Every client presenting for AIDS-related services should have a substance abuse history taken.

- The goal of AIDS prevention with drug users is to prevent HIV transmission from one drug user to another, from drug users to sexual partners, and from drug users to their unborn children.

- Outpatient psychotherapy alone cannot provide enough support and treatment for a client who is both chemically dependent and HIV positive, especially if he or she is actively using drugs.

- All residential and drug treatment programs should offer special support groups for clients who are living with HIV or AIDS.

INTRODUCTION

By December 1995, 128,696 heterosexual intravenous (IV) drug users had been diagnosed with acquired immunodeficiency syndrome (AIDS) in the United States (U.S. Department of Health and Human Services, 1995). This group represents 25% of the nation's AIDS caseload. Seven percent (7%) of the nation's total AIDS cases are men who have sex with men (i.e., homosexual or bisexual) who also reported injecting drugs (U.S. Department of Health and Human Services, 1995), resulting in a total of 32% of all AIDS cases related to IV drug use.

Newmeyer (1989) noted that substance use increases a person's vulnerability to the human immunodeficiency virus (HIV) in three ways. First, a person who shares hypodermic needles or other drug paraphernalia, such as "cookers" (the container in which the drug is dissolved in water) or "cotton" (the material used to strain the drug solution as it is drawn up into a syringe), with someone infected with HIV is at risk. Second, a person who becomes intoxicated may lose inhibitions against risky practices (e.g., neglecting the use of a condom during a drunken sexual encounter). Third, a number of substances, such as alcohol, cannabis, "speed," inhaled nitrates, and cocaine, may have direct immunosuppressive properties. Heavy use of an immunosuppressive substance by HIV-infected patients can accelerate the collapse of helper T-cell activity.

Professionals and paraprofessionals in the field of substance abuse must be knowledgeable about the spectrum of HIV illness, AIDS, and HIV transmission. Similarly, health care professionals working with AIDS patients must be knowledgeable about issues of substance abuse and chemical dependency. Shernoff and Springer (1992) describe many of the difficulties of working with patients who are dually diagnosed with chemical dependency and AIDS; difficulties include locating scarce resources and quality medical care, choosing drug treatment and psychosocial services, and dealing with stigma and discrimination. In addition to these professional challenges, the nature of HIV disease and chemical dependency causes various emotional reactions in health care personnel, which can interfere with optimal delivery of services to needy patients.

The chemically dependent client with HIV is best served by an interdisciplinary team that can develop appropriate and flexible treatment plans that prepare for and encompass expected fluctuations in the client's biopsychosocial condition. In addition, health care professionals must be trained to treat the inevitable deterioration in the client's physical and mental conditions as the disease progresses, including relapse into active use of chemicals.

DEFINITIONS

In this chapter, the term *chemically dependent* refers to clients who have a current or past history of abusing alcohol or drugs, even if they do not have a history of true addiction to substances. Because the majority of persons with AIDS who contract the disease through shared drug-injection paraphernalia reside in inner cities and are members of racial minorities (Shernoff & Springer, 1992), it is often erroneously assumed that categories of people with AIDS are very discrete. These racist and classist assumptions must be discarded to be able to work effectively with this population.

Many health professionals who work primarily with gay men infected with HIV or who have AIDS assume that their clients contracted the virus through sexual transmission. Although this is often correct, many clients have engaged in *multiple* high-risk behaviors. Of all reported cases of AIDS, 6% involved gay or bisexual men who were also IV drug users (Centers for Disease Control and Prevention, 1993). Shernoff (1983) reported patterns of injected drug use by middle-class homosexual white men. Stall and Wiley (1988) found that gay men used drugs more often and used a greater variety of drugs than did heterosexual men.

Every client presenting for AIDS-related services should

have an alcohol and drug use history taken. Similarly, every client in treatment for substance abuse should be questioned about his or her sexual orientation because the stage of lesbian or gay identity formation can have a significant impact on how to approach treatment issues regarding recovery from use of chemicals. Simply asking a client if he is homosexual is not sufficient because many men who have sex with other men do not label themselves as homosexual and do not identify themselves as part of the gay community. It is more useful to ask, "Have you ever had sex with another man (or woman)?" If the answer is yes, then asking, "When was the last time?" can be useful in developing an appropriate treatment plan (Shernoff, 1989).

DRUG USE AND AIDS PREVENTION

Most AIDS service organizations will not accept patients who currently are using drugs, unless they prove they are in drug treatment. In the age of AIDS, the current opinion that abstinence from use of chemicals is the main (or only) goal of drug treatment needs to be reevaluated. The abstinence-only focus must be challenged as counterproductive because the very persons most in need of biopsychosocial support will not receive it if they are unable to stop using drugs. These same people are most likely to be transmitting HIV to drug-using or sexual partners or their children and usually are deprived of education or support to change these high-risk behaviors. Nearly 80% of substance abusers in the United States are not being treated for their chemical dependency. Moreover, the majority of these people express no desire to seek treatment, but they do express a desire to avoid AIDS (Fischer, Jones, & Stein, 1989).

Placing abstinence from drugs as the highest treatment priority in this population, unless the client is truly committed to achieving abstinence, will only alienate the client or cause the client to begin a dishonest relationship with the substance abuse professional (Springer, 1991). The goal of AIDS prevention with drug users is simply to prevent HIV transmission from one drug user to another, from drug users to their sexual partners, and from drug users to their unborn children. Springer (1991, pp. 146-147) notes that "the goals of drug treatment and the goals of AIDS prevention must be seen separately. Abstinence from drugs is not the goal of AIDS prevention. Although abstinence from drugs may be a strategy for some people in avoiding HIV infection, it is not necessary or desirable for all drug users to embrace this strategy as an AIDS prevention strategy."

Apart from methadone maintenance, abstinence is the goal of the vast majority of drug treatment agencies; the concept that active drug users require and deserve services is controversial. Substance abuse professionals need to embrace the concept that even those who are not committed to a drug-free life also deserve services. Advocating this position with agencies is necessary if the large population of chemically dependent people with HIV who are not committed to giving up drugs or alcohol is ever going to receive lifesaving AIDS education. Taking this approach does not condone drug use but merely accepts the reality that people who still actively use drugs are in desperate need of AIDS education services.

Many drug treatment agencies and substance abuse professionals have taken an approach to AIDS risk reduction that can be summarized as follows:

- If you do not want to contract AIDS, the best way to avoid it is by not using drugs. You can get help to stop.

- If you must use drugs, do not share paraphernalia such as needles or cookers. Remember that people can look healthy and still carry the AIDS virus.

- If you must share paraphernalia, flush the needle,

syringe, and cooker with bleach and rinse them well with water, or boil them 15 minutes.

- To reduce the risk of contracting AIDS through sexual contact, use condoms, avoid contact with semen or blood, and learn safe-sex guidelines.

During initial assessment sessions, counselors should explicitly address these issues (in addition to other issues important to the client's recovery) to create a climate for talking honestly about preventing the spread of AIDS.

One controversial approach to reducing the spread of AIDS in IV drug users is needle exchange programs. These programs offer individuals new syringes free in exchange for used ones. Researchers in the United States (Treaster, 1993) and England (Newcombe & Parry, 1988) showed that the spread of HIV declined sharply when addicts were given clean needles; they reported no increase in heroin use. Making needles and syringes available has increased the demand for drug treatment, probably because of the contact the exchange allows between active drug users and service providers (Clark, Downing, McQuie et al., 1989; Dolan, Alldrift, & Donohoe, 1988).

Another radical intervention to fight the spread of AIDS is to have street workers, who are themselves in recovery, provide peer education to active drug users about safe needle use and safe sex. These workers also can distribute condoms and provide needle exchanges and information about where to obtain treatment for drug addiction or AIDS.

Condoms, and clear instructions about their correct use, should be made available to all clients at drug treatment facilities. Sexually explicit AIDS prevention messages are especially important with this population because many women and men sell sex to raise money for drug purchases. Therefore, substance abuse professionals must address their own discomfort in talking with clients about sex and should receive training in how to discuss safe sex and safe drug-using techniques. One study (Stall, McKusick, Wiley, Coates, &

Ostrow, 1986) documented how a majority of gay men who failed to practice safer sex are under the influence of alcohol or other drugs. Clearly, substance abuse professionals need training in sexuality and how to discuss options for safer sex with homosexual clients.

Until recently, AIDS prevention programs ignored the needs of lesbians. Because lesbians are exposed to HIV through contaminated needles or sexual partners, substance abuse professionals also must become comfortable with initiating safer-sex discussions with women, including relevant information about woman-to-woman transmission.

CHEMICALLY DEPENDENT ADOLESCENTS

Hein (1989, p. 146) notes that "the risk-related behaviors of adolescents put some teenagers directly in the path of the AIDS epidemic." Recent statistics have demonstrated that HIV infection is already present in the adolescent population of the United States. Therefore, it is imperative that "adolescent specialists from various disciplines begin to prepare programs and strategies that serve the special population of chemically dependent adolescents who are infected with HIV" (Reulbach, 1991, p. 31). Adolescents who are at highest risk for HIV infection fall into four groupings: (a) those who inject drugs, (b) those men who are gay and bisexual, (c) those who work in the sex industry (e.g., pornographic filmmaking) or who barter sex for survival, and (d) those whose sexual partners are engaging or have engaged in these high-risk behaviors (Stiffman & Earls, 1990).

Many adolescents who work in the sex industry or who barter sex for drugs either have run away or been thrown out of their homes, and, therefore, are likely to be homeless. Many of these adolescents engage in sex-for-money activities to buy food, drugs, shelter, or clothing (Futterman, 1990). One strategy for engaging these hard-to-reach adolescents is to entice them into the agency with such concrete services as medical care, food, clothing, a shower, or a referral to a safe place to sleep. The tangible and immediate benefits of these inducements create the opportunity to develop a helping relationship with these high-risk adolescents; eventually, this can encompass HIV testing, medical follow-up for AIDS-related conditions, safer sex and drug use information, counseling, referrals for detoxification programs, and help in stopping the use of alcohol or other drugs.

Reulbach (1991) notes that when adolescents continued to use crack or other drugs, they were difficult to treat in a hospital-based adolescent AIDS program in a large urban center. He reports that adolescents actively using drugs were less likely to keep clinic appointments or follow through on health-promoting behaviors (e.g., taking medication, improving diet, practicing safer sex) than adolescents who were not using drugs.

Reulbach also found that when counseling chemically dependent HIV-positive adolescents, substance abuse professionals need to help clients negotiate expected psychosocial tasks, including: dealing with the ambiguity of an HIV-positive diagnosis, integrating knowledge of HIV as a progressive but gradual decline of the immune system, developing disclosure strategies for family and friends, making decisions regarding continuing sexual relationships and safer-sex practices, and, coping in general with the emotional instability associated with HIV.

If the adolescent has ongoing relationships with family members, it is often useful to engage them in treatment, as well. In addition, friends and significant others often can help confront the adolescent's denial about the negative impact of drug use and HIV infection. For some homeless or runaway adolescents, agency staff or fellow members of 12-step programs (e.g., Alcoholics Anonymous [AA], Narcotics Anonymous [NA]) may serve many of the functions of family members; the appropriateness of using these programs in the treatment process must be evaluated.

OUTPATIENT TREATMENT

Chemically dependent persons who learn they are infected with HIV or have AIDS are immediately faced with new life stressors. When they learn they are HIV positive, they often cope by behaving in the way they know best: using drugs (Fontaine, 1991). Outpatient psychotherapy alone cannot provide enough support and treatment for a client who is both chemically dependent and HIV positive, especially if he or she is actively using drugs. However, outpatient psychosocial services can add an important component of care to the treatment process by providing a supplemental support system for a client who is already engaged in various other support systems or by becoming the sole support system for an isolated client (Fontaine, 1991).

Fischer and co-workers (1989, p. 123) state that "like any reaction to severe stress, adjustment to a diagnosis of HIV disease is governed by habitual coping mechanisms and psychosocial resources. In the case of active substance abusers, such mechanisms and resources are typically absent, severely strained, undeveloped, or maladaptive." If clients are actively in recovery from substance abuse, they are likely to possess more intrapsychic and interpersonal tools and resources for confronting this crisis.

A Model for Adjusting to a Diagnosis of HIV:

Nichols (1987) developed the AIDS Situational Distress Model, which is useful for understanding the process of adjusting to a diagnosis of HIV disease. This model describes four possible stages of adjustment to a diagnosis of HIV disease: crisis, transition, acceptance, and preparation for death.

Crisis

The initial crisis of an HIV diagnosis is commonly met with denial as a defense against extreme anxiety. Denial has been the prime psychological defense used by chemically dependent persons, enabling them to continue use of substances that create chaotic life situations. Therefore, many substance users remain in denial throughout the entire course of their HIV illness. This defense allows them to continue to engage in self-destructive behaviors that place themselves, as well as others, at risk for infection. Sometimes, clients disclose their HIV status to someone who has no need to know because they desire to gain sympathy or manipulate a situation advantageously. HIV infection also may cause disclosure of previously disguised drug use to friends or family in an effort to gain needed emotional support. This may precipitate a crisis if the double stigma and ignorance about AIDS and drug use repels key people. Substance abuse professionals need to challenge maladaptive denial, which leads to increased use of chemicals.

It is appropriate and natural for a client with a life-threatening disease initially to deny the threat to his or her existence. Mental health professionals must support this kind of denial until "a person can begin to absorb the impact of the implications of diagnosis" (Faltz & Madover, 1986, p. 159). If the denial about both HIV and substance abuse is not confronted, it can impede progress in other areas vital to a person living with HIV. For example, financial assistance may be used to purchase drugs, and physical, emotional, and legal problems may be exacerbated (Faltz & Madover, 1986).

Transition

Fischer and colleagues (1989) describe a transitional stage, in which alternating waves of anxiety, anger, guilt, self-pity, and depression are typical. Chemically dependent persons generally experience these feelings as intolerable and historically mismanage them. For chemically dependent persons in recovery, a diagnosis of HIV or AIDS can be a faith-shattering and regressive time, during which self-medication with alcohol and other drugs and suicidal ideation are common. Substance abuse professionals need to prepare themselves for possibly bearing the brunt of the intense acting out or manipulations that are attempts to maintain some semblance of control.

Acceptance

Patients who have accepted the realities of being both chemically dependent and HIV positive will demonstrate this acceptance by their behavior and by a willingness to discuss both issues honestly. When clients seek appropriate medical consultation for HIV and attend AA or NA meetings that have adapted their agendas to include AIDS, counselors can begin to probe gently for the feelings that accompany a growing acceptance. Additional support may be gained by helping the client enroll in support groups with a proven sensitivity to chemical dependency issues. Fischer and co-workers (1989) note that gaining support from a substance abuser's family members or a significant other often requires task-oriented family therapy that addresses obstacles present from long-standing dysfunctions that preceded the HIV infection.

Preparation for Death

Western society is notorious for denying death. Working with AIDS causes everyone to confront their own mortality through the deaths of clients and colleagues. Thus, when the time to prepare for death nears, it is crucial that health professionals recognize that chemically dependent clients and their families generally are ill-prepared to manage the feelings and tasks attendant to any loss, much less death. The result can be an extremely difficult time for families and practitioners who often must be the patient's advocate, in addition to helping arrange wakes, funerals, and memorials (Fischer et al., 1989).

RESIDENTIAL TREATMENT FACILITIES

It is estimated that in large American cities up to one half of all heterosexual IV drug users are infected with HIV

(Newmeyer, 1989). Not surprisingly, many of the clients of residential treatment facilities or therapeutic communities are HIV positive or symptomatic with AIDS. Similarly, because many of the staff members of these facilities are former drug users, many of them also are either HIV positive or have AIDS. One of the therapeutic aspects of these programs occurs through the role modeling provided by recovering staff members who are able to empathize with the difficulties of clients who are struggling to become and remain drug free.

Residential programs should have special support groups and 12-step meetings for those with HIV. Staff members who are living with HIV can provide meaningful role models for clients who are questioning why they should remain drug free if they have only a short time to live.

Residential facilities must be affiliated with clinics or hospitals that offer state-of-the-art medical care for AIDS-related conditions, including the ever-increasing number of options for prophylaxis against various opportunistic infections. All residents need information about health promotion that discusses healthy eating, exercise, and safe sexual practices. The staff of these facilities must be trained to recognize symptoms of HIV-related medical conditions, because early medical intervention is often lifesaving or prevents major physical disabilities such as blindness (Davis, 1991). Because many HIV-related medical conditions are now routinely treated at home or in an outpatient setting, residential facilities may have residents with catheters, ports, or other medically implanted IV devices through which they receive medication. Some physicians are reluctant to prescribe these devices for patients who have a history of IV drug use because they provide the temptation of an easy way to use illicit drugs. Professionals at drug treatment agencies need to raise this issue with clients and develop strategies to deal with this situation that places clients at high risk for relapse.

Staff members should initiate discussions in treatment groups and community meetings that elicit feelings about residents who have become acutely ill and require hospitalization. When a resident, staff person, or recent graduate dies of AIDS, provisions must be made to mourn his or her death within the community and to discuss the resulting feelings and fears that emerge. Handling these situations directly and honestly within the facility is an opportunity to teach invaluable coping skills to all the residents.

METHADONE MAINTENANCE PROGRAMS

Most of the issues discussed above also pertain to clients in methadone maintenance treatment programs. All drug treatment programs should offer special support groups for clients who are living with HIV or AIDS. Providing groups for significant others of clients with HIV can increase the systemic support the client receives. Another useful treatment option is multiple family groups, in which all involved can share coping strategies and support.

For clients who are living with HIV or AIDS, the counselor should adopt an aggressive case manager role as liaison between the various professionals of the treatment team. Patients on methadone often are stigmatized and not offered dignified and sensitive treatment at clinics and agencies; however, once other professionals on the treatment team learn that a caring colleague is coordinating and monitoring the client's treatment, the patient is more likely to receive high-quality, humane treatment.

When a person in a methadone maintenance treatment program is hospitalized, a visit from the substance abuse counselor can support the client during the stressful period of acute illness; in addition, the counselor can act as an intermediary and advocate for the client with the nursing staff.

Staff members at methadone programs should develop flexible schedules for patients with HIV or AIDS because long waits at the frequent medical appointments often mean that patients will not be able to arrive at the clinic at their assigned times. As the disease progresses, provisions for delivering methadone to a patient's home must be arranged.

When a patient dies of AIDS, notices announcing his or her

death and specifics regarding the wake, funeral, or memorial usually are posted. Substance abuse professionals should be prepared to elicit reactions and feelings from all clients, especially those with HIV or whose partners have HIV. A death can be a potent stressor, with the ability to trigger drug use as a means of coping. Therefore, a drug treatment agency is a perfect place to anticipate these reactions, prepare for them, and help clients seek out healthy alternatives for dealing with their feelings.

CHEMICALLY DEPENDENT CLIENTS WITH HIV AS INPATIENTS IN HOSPITALS

Weiss (1991, p. 45) writes that "working with chemically dependent HIV-infected patients on an inpatient medical unit poses special problems for the medical staff. These patients are perceived as irresponsible, manipulative, demanding, drug-seeking troublemakers who rarely follow the rules of the ward. Medical, nursing, and social work staff members working with these patients need support and education to help them with this population." Weiss goes on to say that unless the medical unit is equipped to search patients' possessions and rooms regularly and restrict visitors, illicit drug use on wards is unavoidable. Once staff members understand this, their efforts can be directed toward minimizing this phenomenon and its consequences.

Chemically dependent persons know how to obtain drugs when they want them; as a consequence, they usually have difficulty waiting for medication or declining drugs offered by visitors. Impatience on the patient's part usually is expressed as irritability, anger, or demands for medication, resulting in the patient being labeled a "management problem." Weiss states that chemically dependent patients typically require generous amounts of medication while in the hospital. Staff members often withhold the very medication they need, making them even more irritable and difficult to manage.

Making patients comfortable with adequate opiates or sedatives helps them feel that they are being heard, enhances their trust, and improves the working relationship between the chemically dependent patient and staff members.

Social workers, substance abuse counselors, and psychiatric nurses are in a perfect position to organize groups that provide patients the opportunity to vent their feelings appropriately and offer each other mutual support. These groups also can be psychoeducational in teaching patients how to advocate for themselves in ways to which the medical staff will respond positively.

Attempts should be made to interest hospitalized patients in educational seminars about their medical condition, drug treatment, and available services once they are discharged. Hospitals that serve large populations of chemically dependent persons should reach out to local intergroup offices to arrange daily AA or NA meetings in the hospital.

PSYCHOTROPIC MEDICATION

Anxiety disorders are probably the most frequent psychiatric complications of HIV disease in persons who are uninfected but at high risk and those who have symptomatic HIV disease (Dilley & Boccellari, 1989). Depression is the next most common psychiatric symptom. These conditions respond well to supportive individual and group psychotherapy. However, chemically dependent persons historically have demonstrated an inability to tolerate these feelings and subsequently resort to self-medication. When the client's symptoms are severe, it is important to refer him or her to a prescribing specialist (e.g., a psychopharmacologist or psychiatrist) who is skilled in both substance abuse and AIDS.

Substance abuse professionals should expect that chemically dependent clients are likely to abuse or overmedicate themselves with prescription medications. Close interdisciplinary teamwork is invaluable in preventing manipulation of one professional against another. Concrete, cognitive interventions must emphasize that taking more than the prescribed dosage will result in a period in which the patient will have to do without prescribed medication.

Some medical professionals are reluctant to prescribe anxiolytic medication, antidepressants, or other psychotropic drugs for chemically dependent patients. Although 12-step programs and psychotherapy can go far in helping relieve some psychiatric symptoms, if these symptoms are left untreated by appropriate medication, chemically dependent persons often resort to self-medication; eventually, they will relapse.

Because the anxiety or depression often has an organic origin, these clients usually respond well to medication. Once they experience relief from psychiatric symptoms, they often regain the psychological strength to cope with other demanding tasks in the management of their health.

Drug treatment personnel often interpret missed appointments or other bizarre behavior as acting out or a response to being under the influence of a drug. However, these symptoms also can result from the onset of AIDS-related dementia, which often takes the form of short-term memory loss or erratic behavior. An evaluation by a neurologist or psychiatrist skilled in diagnosing AIDS-related dementia is essential at the first indication of change in a client's mental status. These symptoms sometimes resolve after treatment with either antiretroviral drugs or psychotropic medication.

Because persons with AIDS take a variety of prescribed medications, many of which can alter mood, it may be necessary to develop an appropriate treatment strategy that addresses this reality. Faltz (1989) offers the suggestion of drafting a medication agreement (Table 9.1) during counseling sessions with chemically dependent clients with HIV.

SUMMARY

Counseling chemically dependent clients with HIV is in-

Table 9.1
MEDICATION AGREEMENT

I,_____, REALIZE THE FOLLOWING
PROBLEMS WITH MY CURRENT USE OF MEDICATION:

(*Check if applicable*)

☐   Feeling tired or having a clouded mental state
☐   Feeling hyperactive or nervous
☐   Anticipating my next dose ahead of time
☐   Wishing for a higher dose or stronger medication
☐   Supplementing medication with alcohol or other drugs
☐   Thinking of asking more than one physician for medication
☐   Other_____

I AGREE THAT THESE PROBLEMS INTERFERE WITH MY
TREATMENT, AND I COMMIT TO THE FOLLOWING AGREEMENTS:

☐   Not to exceed the daily dose of medication prescribed
☐   To discuss any medication problems with my primary
        health care worker
☐   Not to obtain medication from other sources
☐   Not to self-medicate with alcohol or other drugs
☐   Other_____

MEDICATION:

Generic name (brand name)	Dose	Frequency
_____	_____	_____
_____	_____	_____
_____	_____	_____
_____	_____	_____
_____	_____	_____

Signature_____

Witness_____

Witness_____   Date_____

Source: Faltz, B. (1989). Strategies for working with substance-abusing
clients. In J. Dilley, C. Pies, & M. Helquint (Eds.), *Face to face: A guide to
AIDS counseling* (pp. 127–136). San Francisco: University of California
AIDS Health Project.

tensely difficult work for a number of reasons. Clients with HIV who use illicit drugs are stigmatized in contemporary society. It can be draining for substance abuse professionals to try setting limits with a population that has a history of chronic impulse-control disorder. To be effective with this population, substance abuse counselors must adjust their expectations about what constitutes success. Often, it is inappropriate to rely solely on traditional intrapsychic psychotherapy. Practical problem-solving counseling strategies, including the identification and provision of needed services to improve the quality of the client's life, is generally a more realistic mode of intervention.

REFERENCES

Centers for Disease Control and Prevention. *AIDS surveillance update.* (1993). Atlanta, GA: Author.

Clark, G., Downing, M., McQuie, H., et al. (1989). Street-based needle exchange programs: The next step in HIV prevention. Presentation at the Fifth International Conference on AIDS, Montreal, Canada.

Davis, I. (1991). What drug treatment professionals need to know about medical aspects of HIV illness. In M. Shernoff (Ed.), *Counseling chemically dependent people with AIDS* (pp. 17–30). New York: Haworth Press.

Dilley, J., & Boccellari, A. (1989). Neuropsychiatric complications of HIV infection. In J. Dilley, C. Pies, & M. Helquint (Eds.), *Face to face: A guide to AIDS counseling* (pp. 138–151). San Francisco: University of California AIDS Health Project.

Dolan, K., Alldritt, L., & Donohoe, M. (1988). *Injecting equipment exchange schemes: A preliminary report on research.* London: Monitoring Research Group, University of London, Goldsmith's College.

Faltz, B. (1989). Strategies for working with substance-abusing clients. In J. Dilley, C. Pies, & M. Helquint (Eds.), *Face to face: A guide to AIDS counseling* (pp. 127–136). San Francisco: University of California AIDS Health Project.

Faltz, B., & Madover, S. (1986). Substance abuse as a cofactor for AIDS. In L. McKusick (Ed.), *What to do about AIDS* (pp. 155–162). Berkeley, CA: University of California Press.

Fischer, G., Jones, S., & Stein, J. (1989). Mental health complications of substance abuse. In J. Dilley, C. Pies, & M. Helquint (Eds.), *Face to face: A guide to AIDS counseling* (pp. 118-126). San Francisco: University of California AIDS Health Project.

Fontaine, M. (1991). The use of outpatient psychotherapy with chemically dependent HIV infected individuals. In M. Shernoff (Ed.), *Counseling chemically dependent people with HIV illness* (pp. 119-130). New York: Haworth Press.

Futterman, D. (1990). Medical management of adolescents. In P. Pixxo & C. Wilfert (Eds.), *Pediatric AIDS: The challenge of HIV infection in infants, children, and adolescents* (pp. 546–560). Baltimore: Williams & Wilkins.

Hein, K. (1989). Commentary on adolescent acquired immunodeficiency syndrome: The next wave of the human immunodeficiency virus epidemic? *Journal of Pediatrics, 114,* 144–149.

Newcombe, R., & Parry, A. (1988). *The Mersey harm-reduction model: A strategy for dealing with drug users.* Presentation at the International Conference on Drug Policy Reform, Bethesda, MD.

Newmeyer, J. (1989). The epidemiology of HIV among intravenous drug users. In J. Dilley, C. Pies, & M. Helquint (Eds.), *Face to face: A guide to AIDS counseling* (pp. 108–117). San Francisco, CA: University of California AIDS Health Project.

Nichols, S. (1987). Emotional aspects of AIDS: Implications for care providers. *Journal of Substance Abuse Treatment, 4,* 137–140.

Reulbach, W. (1991). Counseling chemically dependent HIV positive adolescents. In M. Shernoff (Ed.), *Counseling chemically dependent people with HIV illness* (pp. 31-43). New York: Haworth Press.

Shernoff, M. (1983). Nice boys and needles. *New York Native, 74*, Oct 10–23, 1-4.

Shernoff, M. (1989). AIDS prevention counseling in clinical practice. In J. Dilley, C. Pies, & M. Helquint (Eds.), *Face to Face: A Guide to AIDS Counseling* (pp. 76–83). San Francisco, CA: University of California AIDS Health Project.

Shernoff, M., & Springer, E. (1992). Substance abuse and AIDS: Report from the front lines (the impact on professionals). *Journal of Chemical Dependency Treatment, 5*, 35–48.

Springer, E. (1991). Effective AIDS prevention with active drug users: the harm-reduction model. In M. Shernoff, (Ed.), *Counseling Chemically Dependent People with HIV Illness* (pp. 141-158). New York: Haworth Press.

Stall, R., McKusick, L., Wiley, J., Coates, T., & Ostrow, D. (1986). Alcohol and drug use during sexual activity and compliance with safe sex guidelines for AIDS: The AIDS biobehavioral research project. *Health Education Quarterly, 13*, 359–371.

Stall, R., & Wiley, J. (1988). A comparison of alcohol and drug use patterns of homosexual and heterosexual men. *Drug and Alcohol Dependence, 22*, 63–73.

Stiffman, A., & Earls, F. (1990). Behaviorial risk for HIV infection in adolescent medical patients. *Pediatrics, 85*, 303–310.

Treaster, J. (1993, December 19). It's not legalization, but user-friendly drug strategy. *The New York Times*, p. A5.

U.S. Department of Health and Human Services, Public Health Service, Centers for Disease Control and Prevention, National Center for HIV, STD, and TB Prevention. (1995). *HIV/AIDS surveillance report: U.S. HIV and AIDS cases reported through December 1995.* Rockville, MD: Author.

Weiss, C. (1991). Working with chemically dependent HIV-infected patients on an inpatient medical unit. In M. Shernoff (Ed.), *Counseling chemically dependent people with AIDS* (pp. 45-53). New York: Haworth Press.

10

Issues in the Diagnosis and Treatment of Comorbid Addictive and Other Psychiatric Disorders

Norman S. Miller, MD

Dr. Miller is Associate Professor of Psychiatry and Chief, Division of Addiction Psychiatry, at the University of Illinois at Chicago.

KEY POINTS

- Prevalence rates for other psychiatric disorders are lower than those for substance-related disorders.

- Rates of addictive disorders appear to be increasing among psychiatric patients.

- Psychiatric disorders in comorbidity with addictive disorders are discussed, including schizophrenia, affective disorders, anxiety disorders, and personality disorders.

- Traditional practices for the treatment of comorbidity tend to be dichotomous and nonintegrated. Only recently have attempts been made to integrate the treatment of both disorders in the same patient and in the same setting.

- Models are being implemented to treat psychiatric comorbidity, including the dual focus, parallel, and integrated models.

- The abstinence-based model is the most commonly used form of treatment for alcohol and drug addiction.

- The use of pharmacologic agents needs not be problematic if addictive illnesses are given an independent status and careful guidelines regarding the use of pharmacologic treatments in addicts are followed.

INTRODUCTION

The inclusion of addictive disorders (i.e., substance-related disorders) in the psychiatric diagnostic nomenclature has had an enormous impact on the field of psychiatry. In early editions of the *Diagnostic and Statistical Manual of Mental Disorders* (DSM-I and DSM-II), addiction was classified under personality disorder, but in DSM-III, addictive disorders were given an independent status. In addition to retaining this independent status, DSM-III-R and DSM-IV have developed exclusionary criteria that require consideration of substance-induced syndromes before other psychiatric disorders can be diagnosed in the setting of alcohol and drug use (Miller & Gold, 1991). Because rates of addictive disorders appear to be increasing among psychiatric patients, the importance of diagnosing and treating psychiatric disorders has grown. Furthermore, the competition for reimbursement between psychiatric and substance abuse professionals has intensified the need to develop integrated models for the diagnosis and treatment of comorbid disorder (Miller & Fine, 1993).

Prevalence:

High prevalence rates of addictive disorders help explain their frequent occurrence in psychiatric patients (Helzer & Burnam, 1991; Helzer & Pryzbeck, 1991). According to the Epidemiological Catchment Area (ECA) study, the lifetime prevalence of alcoholism was 16% for the total population, and the lifetime prevalence of drug dependence was approximately 6%. The overlap between dependence on alcohol and other drugs was remarkable. A DSM-III diagnosis of alcoholism could be applied to 37% of marijuana addicts, 85% of cocaine addicts, and 75% of heroin addicts (Anthony, 1991; Helzer & Pryzbeck, 1991; Miller, 1991). Approximately 20% of drug addicts at any age suffered from alcoholism, but the association of drug dependence with alcoholism was age dependent: younger alcoholics were more likely to have an additional drug addiction. Approximately 80%–90% of those under the age of 30 suffered from at least one drug addiction; the drugs of addiction most frequently used were marijuana, cocaine, heroin, and benzodiazepines (Anthony, 1991; Miller, 1991).

Alcoholism and drug addiction showed a gender specificity. Rates for alcoholism were almost 24% for men and approximately 5% for women. However, the gap between the sexes continues to narrow (Helzer & Pryzbeck, 1991). Ethnicity also showed specificity and age-dependent relationships. Hispanic men had higher rates of alcoholism (30%) than white men (23%) and African-American men (23%), whereas Hispanic women showed a lower rate (4%) than white women (5%) and African-American women (5%) (Anthony, 1991; Helzer & Burnam, 1991). The mean age of onset for alcoholism in the United States was 22 years for men and 25 years for women in the ECA study, indicating that alcoholism affects adolescents (Helzer & Burnam, 1991). Clinical studies show multiple drug addiction frequently appears during the teenage years, with alcohol being the first drug used (at 13–14 years old), and progressing typically to nicotine (at 14–15 years old), then cannabis (at 14–15 years old), followed by cocaine (at 17–18 years old) (Anthony, 1991; Helzer & Burnam, 1991; Helzer & Pryzbrck, 1991; Miller, 1991).

Prevalence rates for other psychiatric disorders are lower than those for substance-related disorders. The ECA study found rates in the general population of 5.1% for depression, 2.5% for antisocial personality disorder, 1.5% for panic disorder, 1.0% for schizophrenia, and 0.4% for mania (Figure 10.1) (Helzer & Pryzbeck, 1991).

Settings:

The setting, whether addiction or psychiatric, has been important in determining rates for comorbidity. Studies of addictive disorders in psychiatric settings yield high rates of comorbidity (Regier, Farmer, & Rae, 1990). Those diagnosed in psychiatric populations evidenced a rate of approximately 50% or greater for alcohol and drug addiction (Brady, Casto, & Lydiard, 1991; Drake & Wallach, 1989; Meyers, Weissman, & Tschler, 1984; Pepper, Kirshner, & Ryglewicz, 1981; Regier et al., 1990). The rates were highest for schizophrenia and antisocial personality disorder (50%–80%) (Drake & Wallach, 1989; Regier et al., 1990), whereas rates for affective and anxiety disorders were lower (30%) (Regier et al., 1990).

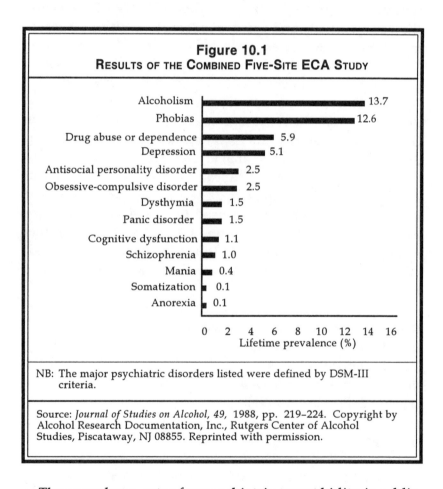

Figure 10.1
RESULTS OF THE COMBINED FIVE-SITE ECA STUDY

NB: The major psychiatric disorders listed were defined by DSM-III criteria.

Source: *Journal of Studies on Alcohol*, 49, 1988, pp. 219–224. Copyright by Alcohol Research Documentation, Inc., Rutgers Center of Alcohol Studies, Piscataway, NJ 08855. Reprinted with permission.

The prevalence rates for psychiatric comorbidity in addiction populations were not much greater than the rates for psychiatric disorders in the general population (Miller & Fine, 1993; Schuckit, 1985). The reasons for this were selection phenomena according to site (either psychiatric or addictions) and the diagnostic perspective according to psychiatric or addiction examiners (Miller & Fine, 1993; Miller, Mahler, Belkin, & Gold, 1991; Schuckit, 1983). Despite controversy regarding diagnosis and prognosis, the rates for the combined true and transient substance-induced comorbidity of addictive and psychiatric disorders are indisputably high in either setting (Miller & Fine, 1993; Helzer & Pryzbeck, 1991; Regier et al., 1990).

Treatment Practices:

Traditional practices for the treatment of comorbidity tend to be dichotomous and nonintegrated (Minkoff, 1989; Ries, 1993). Only recently have attempts been made to integrate the treatment of both disorders in the same patient and in the same setting (Minkoff, 1989).

Various models are being implemented to treat psychiatric comorbidity (Ries, 1993). The *dual focus model* provides additional tracts for the dually focused patient in a specialized psychiatric setting within an addiction milieu. The *serial model* involves the traditional practice of treating the psychiatric comorbidity in a psychiatric setting before transferring the patient to an addictions setting for the treatment of the addictive disorder(s). The *parallel model* advocates a newer practice whereby the patient primarily resides in a psychiatric or addiction setting and receives alternate treatment in another setting. In the serial and parallel models, the staff and sites are separate (Ries, 1993). In the *integrated model,* an attempt is made to provide addiction and psychiatric treatments in the same milieu by the same staff; the patient receives a core approach to the treatment of both types of disorders because the staff is trained to treat both (Minkoff, 1989).

CLINICAL DIAGNOSIS OF COMORBIDITY

Even though self-medication of "underlying causes" remains

an unproven hypothesis used to explain alcohol and drug use, it nonetheless drives the orientation of the diagnosis of comorbidity (Khantzian, 1985). The self-medication hypothesis has popular acceptance among clinicians possibly because it is so similar to the lay view that people use alcohol and other drugs for "some" reason. The origin of the hypothesis has evolved predominantly from the addict, who rationalizes alcohol and other drug use and attributes it to reasons other than the addictive illness (Miller, 1993a). Addicted patients frequently blame their use of alcohol and other drugs on anxiety or depression. However, studies have shown that alcoholics and drug addicts were not particularly anxious or depressed but became so when they drank or used drugs (Tamerin & Mendelson, 1969). Also, as they drank or used drugs, their anxiety and depression worsened and only resolved when abstinence was reinstituted. Contrary to the self-medication hypothesis, objective studies have demonstrated a neurochemical origin for the etiology of the addictive use of alcohol and other drugs: reinforcement centers in the limbic system appear responsible (Gold & Miller, 1992). The corollary of this model is that people seek alcohol and other drugs for pharmacologic effects that can be translated into neurochemical events. The specific area of the brain that has been implicated is the ventral tegmental area in the midbrain, with projections to the nucleus accumbens septi in the forebrain. The connections between the two areas are called the mesolimbic pathways. The principal neurotransmitter involved is dopamine, but others such as serotonin, γ-aminobutyric acid, and norepinephrine may play important roles (Gold & Miller, 1992; Miller & Gold, 1993). These neurotransmitters also have been implicated in mood and anxiety states, thereby explaining the association between mood, anxiety, and addiction (Gold & Miller, 1992; Miller & Gold, 1993).

ADDICTIVE DISORDERS IN COMORBIDITY

Ascertaining the degree to which addictive and other psychiatric disorders operate independently in an individual patient facilitates an accurate diagnosis (Miller & Gold, 1991). In DSM-IV, three or more of seven criteria are required to establish the diagnosis of substance dependence (American Psychiatric Association [APA], 1994). The seven criteria can be reduced to five that represent addictive behaviors, one that represents tolerance, and one that represents withdrawal. (Tolerance is the need to increase the dose to maintain an effect; withdrawal is the onset of signs and symptoms on cessation of substance use.) Addictive behaviors can be defined as: (a) preoccupation with acquiring alcohol and other drugs, (b) compulsive use despite adverse consequences, and (c) a pattern of relapse (Jaffe, 1990). Addictive use of alcohol and other drugs can be identified using these criteria, as long as exclusionary criteria for substance-induced syndromes are also applied (APA, 1994).

Because alcohol and other drugs can induce a variety of psychiatric symptoms and syndromes, it is important to consider their role in any psychiatric patient (Blankfield, 1986; Kosten & Kleber, 1988; Lehman, Meyers, & Lehman, 1989; McCarrick, Mandersheild, & Bertolucci, 1985; Miller, Mahler, Belkin, & Gold, 1991). Depressants can induce depression during intoxication and anxiety during withdrawal (Blankfield, 1986; Kosten & Kleber, 1988; Lehman, Meyers, & Lehman, 1989; Miller et al., 1991); stimulants can produce anxiety and euphoria during intoxication, as well as depression and lethargy during withdrawal. Both depressants and stimulants can produce hallucinations, delusions, and other disturbances in thought and personality (particularly with prolonged use) during intoxication and withdrawal (Blankfield, 1986; Kosten & Kleber, 1988; Miller et al., 1991). Common examples are alcoholic hallucinosis and cocaine-induced hallucinations and delusions.

Exclusionary criteria, as outlined in DSM-IV, require that the disturbance not be caused by the effects of a substance (e.g., illegal drugs, alcohol, medications) (APA, 1994). Psychiatric disorders that require consideration of an "organic factor" before their diagnosis can be made are schizophrenia, somatization disorder, cyclothymia, panic disorder, insomnia, hypersomnia, generalized anxiety and obsessive-compulsive disorders, Tourette's syndrome, chronic motor or vocal tic disorder, intermittent explosive disorder, and psychogenic amnesia. Also, organic factors, including specific mention of intoxication and withdrawal should be excluded from symptoms related to schizophrenia, delusional disorder, brief reactive psychosis, schizophreniform disorder, schizoaffective disorder, atypical psychosis, manic episodes, dysthymia, psychogenic fugue, dream-anxiety disorder, sleep-terror and sleep-walking disorders, alcohol-related blackout, or cannabis dependence (APA, 1994).

Once the behaviors of the addiction are identified and the pharmacologic effects are considered, the abstinent state often is required to confirm the diagnosis (Blankfield, 1986; Kosten & Kleber, 1988; McCarrick et al., 1985; Miller et al., 1991; Schuckit, 1985). However, it is sometimes necessary to presume whether an additional psychiatric disorder is present before abstinence is achieved. The greater the number of psychiatric admissions in the past, the more likely it is that another psychiatric disorder is present in addition to an addictive disorder. For instance, if someone has had 10–20 admissions for schizophrenia associated with alcohol and other drug use and has been prescribed neuroleptics, an addiction-related diagnosis in addition to a psychiatric diagnosis is relatively likely. It is less likely that these admissions were drug-induced only and that independent schizophrenia was not present. Only abstinence with a longitudinal evaluation can confirm that distinction (Blankfield, 1986; Kosten & Kleber, 1988; Miller et al., 1991; Schuckit, 1985). With mood and anxiety disorders, abstinence almost is always required before an independent diagnosis of affective disorder or anxiety disorder can be made definitively (APA, 1994; Miller et al., 1991; Schuckit, 1985).

The recommended length of abstinence varies with drug type and among individuals. However, with alcohol, 2 weeks' abstinence often is sufficient for most to recover from the pharmacologic effects of depression and anxiety during intoxication and withdrawal. The same time course, or perhaps shorter, is required for stimulants (Blankfield, 1986; Kosten & Kleber, 1988; Miller et al., 1991). The period for abstinence from sedative/hypnotics or benzodiazepines may be extended to several weeks or months because of a protracted intoxication and withdrawal from these agents (Miller & Gold, 1989). Because these lipophilic agents are taken up by fat stores and slowly released over time, they actually may be active in the brain for prolonged periods. Cannabis is another lipophilic drug that can produce a protracted induction of psychiatric symptoms, such as anxiety and depression (Miller et al., 1991). Opiates are shorter acting and typically do not produce lasting psychiatric symptoms beyond days or weeks; however, methadone is longer acting (Miller et al., 1991).

In the abstinent state, alcoholics and drug addicts still may experience degrees of anxiety and depression that are related to their addictive disorder (Miller et al., 1991; Ries, 1989). Anxiety and depression actually can be therapeutic and signal the need for change in the addicted patient (Miller & Gold, 1992; Miller & Mahler, 1991a), who can institute important changes in behavior, attitude, and feelings to promote an enduring recovery in response to anxiety and depression (Tiebout, 1953). Amelioration of these symptoms with external agents, such as medications, actually may blunt the motivation to change (Miller & Gold, 1992). The "dry drunk" syndrome is an example of an alcoholic who is abstinent but is no longer in recovery. Because of an inadequately treated addictive state, the addict may begin to experience dysthymia, feelings of discouragement, helplessness, irritability, anger, sleep disturbances, and peptide disturbances. Although these symptoms typically do not respond to antidepressants or psychotherapy, they do respond to specific addiction treatment that focuses on addiction and to behaviors and actions that promote recovery from addiction (Goldsmith, 1993; Miller & Mahler, 1991a; Tiebout, 1953).

OTHER PSYCHIATRIC DISORDERS IN COMORBIDITY

Schizophrenia:

Schizophrenia is a chronic, debilitating illness that generally has a variable, and often deteriorating, course (Drake & Wallach, 1989; Kay, Kalanthara, & Meinzer, 1986; Simon, 1989). The overall course is not unlike that of an untreated, progressively deteriorating addictive disorder (Miller & Gold, 1991). It is not surprising that because alcohol and other drugs induce psychotic symptoms, such as hallucinations and delusions, confusion arises when distinguishing between these disorders. Indeed, the neurochemical model for schizophrenia was derived from amphetamine-induced psychosis (DeLecuona, Joseph, Iqbal, & Asnis, 1993).

For reasons not yet known, chronically mentally ill patients, such as those with schizophrenia, are particularly prone to using alcohol and drugs (Drake & Wallach, 1989; Kay et al., 1986). The rationale may relate to the common neurochemistry that has been proposed for the etiology of schizophrenia and addictive disorders (e.g., the dopamine hypothesis) (DeLecuona et al., 1993; Gold & Miller, 1992; Miller & Gold, 1993). The nucleus accumbens is the theoretical site in the brain for the psychotic phenomena in schizophrenia (e.g., hallucinations and delusions) and is also the putative postsynaptic site within the mesolimbic system that is involved in the reinforced use of alcohol and drugs. The commonality of neurochemical sites may provide an interesting area for research on the high comorbidity between schizophrenia and addictive disorders (DeLecuona et al., 1993; Miller & Gold, 1993).

Affective Disorders:

Little evidence indicates that the rates for addictive disorders are elevated in those who suffer from affective disorders or that those who suffer from addictive disorders have elevated rates of affective disorder (non–drug-induced). Suicide rates among those who suffer from alcohol and drug addiction are the highest of any of the other psychiatric disorders (Miller, Mahler, & Gold, 1992). Because depressive symptoms commonly are associated with alcohol and other drug use, affective disorders often are confused with addictive disorders (Miller et al., 1991; Schuckit, 1985).

The widely held belief that depression is a cause of drinking is not supported by the literature. In one longitudinal study, drinking was negatively correlated with depression in nonalcoholic manic-depressive patients during depressive episodes (Campanella & Fossi, 1967); depressed nonalcoholics actually drank less during their depressive episodes. In another study (Mayfield & Allen, 1967), the mood and affect of three groups (depressed nonalcoholics, depressed alcoholics, and nondepressed nonalcoholics) who were given alcohol were measured. The depressed nonalcoholic group experienced the greatest improvement in mood, followed by the nondepressed, nonalcoholic group, or the "normal" group. The depressed alcoholics experienced the least improvement in mood and affect. The study demonstrated that, in general, people do not drink because of depression; rather, depression is a consequence of drinking. It is known that manic patients' behavior related to the use of alcohol and other drugs during manic episodes is as exaggerated as other behaviors. However, a clear pattern of addictive use apart from the hyperactive manic behavior has not been documented (Schuckit, 1982). Also, because alcohol and drugs can produce hyperactive and elated mood states, mania often is confused with drug-induced states (Campanella & Fossi, 1967; Miller et al., 1991; Schuckit, 1982, 1985).

Anxiety Disorders:

Anxiety, which commonly accompanies alcohol and other drug use, is induced during intoxication from stimulants and withdrawal from alcohol and sedative/hypnotic substances

(Miller et al., 1991; Ries, 1989). Benzodiazepines, particularly short-acting ones, induce anxiety as a predictable consequence of pharmacologic dependence (Miller & Gold, 1992). Also, carefully controlled studies show that anxious persons do not prefer to use alcohol and other drugs (McCraken, de Wit, Uhlenhuth, & Johanson, 1990). In fact, those with anxiety disorders may avoid alcohol and other drugs because their pharmacologic effects actually worsen symptoms associated with anxiety (Miller et al., 1991). In addition, studies of those who underwent long-term benzodiazepine treatment showed that the symptoms of anxiety and depression improved after discontinuation of benzodiazepines (Rickels, Schweizer, Case, & Greenblatt, 1990; Schweizer, Rickels, Case, & Greenblatt, 1990). The pharmacologic induction of withdrawal symptoms (i.e., anxiety and depression) from benzodiazepines probably accounted for the improvement (Busto & Sellers, 1991; Miller & Mahler, 1991b).

Personality Disorders:

One's personality most often is affected adversely by consistent and persistent use of alcohol and other drugs. Studies (particularly longitudinal ones) generally do not indicate a predisposing personality to addiction (Vaillant & Milofsky, 1982). However, studies do suggest an acquired personality from alcohol and drug addiction. The characteristics of this acquired personality are antisocial, depressive, dysthymic, and cyclothymic. Central to the acquired addictive personality are narcissistic features (Kaufman, 1989; Syvakic, Whitehead, Przybeck, & Cloninger, 1993), which often can be combined with an immature, self-seeking, emotionally labile, or asocial personality.

TREATMENT OF ADDICTIVE DISORDERS

In clinical psychiatry, the motivation to diagnose a disorder generally is enhanced if effective treatment is available. Studies have documented that effective treatment for addictive disorders with or without psychiatric comorbidity are available (Miller, 1995). The methods of treatment are cognitive and behavioral, and they require abstinence as a goal (Goldsmith, 1993; Miller & Mahler, 1991a). In certain patients, such as in those who suffer from schizophrenia, abstinence may not be achievable on a lifetime basis; however, it should still be held as a goal (Minkoff, 1989).

Abstinence-Based Model:

The *abstinence-based model* is the most commonly used form of treatment for alcohol and other drug addictions (Roman, 1989). A 12-step approach derived from the program used by Alcoholics Anonymous (AA), the abstinence-based method is practiced separately from AA. Although no official relationship exists between the two approaches, referrals to AA commonly are made by abstinence-based programs.

Central to abstinence-based treatment is the acceptance of alcoholism and other drug addictions as independent diseases (Roman, 1989). Cognitive-behavioral techniques typically are administered both in groups and in individual sessions to promote recovery from addiction (Miller & Mahler, 1991a). The desired changes in behaviors are abstinence and conformity, with constructive and reality-based decisions relating to the individual's life experiences. The emphasis first falls on behavior modification and then on associated thinking to support and sustain this behavior. The combination of changes in behavior and thinking are then followed by changes in feeling. Fundamental changes in affective states with improvement of mood are the ultimate objectives to sustain recovery (Goldsmith, 1993; Miller & Mahler, 1991a; Tiebout, 1953). This approach contrasts with the psychoanalytic approach, which attempts to change feelings first, followed by changes in thinking and then behavior (Khantzian, 1985). Individuals in an abstinence-based program are encouraged to "act their way into right thinking and feeling" and to not "think or feel their way into right action" (Goldsmith, 1993; Miller & Mahler, 1991a; Tiebout, 1953).

The abstinence-based method has proved to be effective in treatment-outcome controlled studies and evaluation studies. Controlled studies have shown the 12-step method of treatment to be superior to other forms of treatment (Keso & Salaspuro, 1991; Walsh, Hingson, & Merrigan, 1991). Abstinence-based treatment typically is administered in inpatient or outpatient settings but varies in its duration and level of intensity. The oldest model of 28 days has been modified to include variable lengths of stay and intensity. The inpatient stay may be 1–2 weeks with several group sessions each week (Hoffman & Miller, 1992).

As part of continuing care, a structured outpatient therapeutic program is provided following the inpatient stay; typically, it involves several hours of group and individual treatment a day, several days a week, for 4–6 weeks. The level of intensity is then decreased to 2 days a week, 2–3 hours a day, for 4–6 weeks. In addition, a 1–2-hour session is provided each week for 1–2 years (Hoffman & Miller, 1992). A patient may enter at any stage. Factors that tend to determine at which stage a patient should enter are: (a) ability to abstain, (b) social supports, (c) associated medical and psychiatric comorbidities, and (d) motivation and commitment to recovery and abstinence (Goldsmith, 1992; Hoffman & Miller, 1992).

Studies indicate that successful treatment outcome is strongly correlated with the duration of continuing care. The longer the patient (with or without a comorbid psychiatric diagnosis) participates in a treatment program, the greater the probability of maintaining abstinence and other improvement measures in treatment outcome (Hoffman & Miller, 1992; Miller, Millman, & Keskinen, 1990). Treatment programs find improved outcome with continued participation with treatment services. In large-scale evaluation studies of 8,000 inpatients, continuous abstinence for 1 year was obtained for 88% of those who attended 1 year of continuing care (8% attended) following *inpatient* treatment. Of 1,500 outpatients, continuous abstinence for 1 year was obtained for 93% of those who attended 1 year of continuing care (17% attended) following an *outpatient* treatment program (Hoffman & Miller, 1992). Also, 75% were abstinent for 1 year if they attended weekly meetings of AA. Treatment outcome studies also found significantly reduced medical utilization, enhanced employment performance, and fewer legal complications after discharge from the treatment program (Hoffman & Miller, 1992; Keso & Salaspuro, 1991; Walsh et al., 1991).

TREATMENT OF OTHER PSYCHIATRIC DISORDERS

In the *serial model,* a person with comorbid psychiatric illness may be stabilized at one site and then discharged to another site for treatment of the addictive disorder. Treatment in these cases is conducted by separate staffs; as a consequence, the patient receives a dichotomous and sometimes conflicting treatment experience (Ries, 1993). A major disadvantage is that chronically mentally ill patients do not respond well in the confrontational, active groups used in substance abuse treatment settings (Ries, 1993).

According to the *parallel model,* a recent advancement, treatment may occur in the primary milieu, such as in a psychiatric program, but adjunctive therapy for addiction takes place at another site. Drawbacks to this model are similar to those of the serial model: the patient often is given conflicting messages by separate staff members who use different treatment approaches. The patient may be given a psychiatric explanation for his or her use of alcohol or other drugs by staff at one site and an addictive explanation for associated psychiatric symptoms by staff at another site (Minkoff, 1989; Ries, 1993).

The more recently developed *integrated model* appears to be the most promising for the dually diagnosed (Minkoff, 1989; Ries, 1993). In this model, psychiatric and substance abuse

disorders are viewed as independent biologic and psychosocial disorders that have many similarities. Inherent to these
approaches is the conviction that psychiatric and addictive
disorders are diseases manifested by denial and, if untreated,
will progress and lead to adverse consequences. Also, for both
forms of illnesses, progressive stages in the treatment approach include stabilization, persuasion, and engagement
(Minkoff, 1989). A core treatment approach is provided for the
categories of disorders, namely the addictive and psychiatric
categories. Conflict for the patient is minimized because a
unified message is received from a common staff regarding the
importance of treating both the substance abuse and the psychiatric disorders. The major disadvantage to the integrated
model is that the severely affected addict without another
psychiatric diagnosis may not receive adequate addiction treatment (Ries, 1993).

PHARMACOLOGIC TREATMENTS

The addicted patient needs, as much as possible, a drug-free
state to make changes in any addictive personality traits (Goldsmith, 1993; Helzer & Burnam, 1991; Tiebout, 1953). Therefore,
it is important to maximize the response to the cognitive-
behavioral techniques in addiction treatment and in long-term
recovery. Nevertheless, the use of pharmacologic agents often
is not problematic when addictive illnesses are given an independent status and if other caveats regarding the use of pharmacologic treatments in addicts are accepted (Miller & Gold,
1992). The addicted person has an inherent vulnerability to the
drug effect and potentially can lose control when using almost
any drug. However, this is only a relative contraindication to
the use of pharmacologic agents. At times, with proper external controls, potentially addicting medication can be administered to addicted patients when indicated (Miller & Gold,
1992).
    Some medications carry strong contraindications. Benzodi-

azepines and other narcotic-type drugs have a high addiction potential in alcoholics and drug addicts and, as such, should be used only on a short-term basis (although, of course, rare exceptions for long-term use are possible) (Miller & Gold, 1989). Benzodiazepines are the drugs of choice in acute detoxification; however, long-term use can lead to addiction. These agents also can be used in patients with comorbid acute psychiatric disturbances such as insomnia and agitation. However, over time, their use should be tapered and discontinued. Persistent symptoms should be treated with behavioral and pharmacologic alternatives (Miller & Gold, 1992).

The use of antidepressants and neuroleptics is indicated for addicted patients who have associated mood, anxiety, and psychotic disturbances. However, agents with high anticholinergic properties should be used conservatively. Tapering of antidepressants and their discontinuation should be undertaken after the affective and anxiety disturbances are in remission for 6–12 months. In the case of neuroleptic use in chronic mental illness, this practice may not be possible; therefore, their use may continue throughout life. In the case of lithium (Eskalith, Lithane) and other antimanic agents, consideration of "drug holidays" should follow the general guidelines for these disorders in general psychiatric practice (Miller & Gold, 1992).

Minimization of conflicts surrounding medication is recommended (Gastfriend, 1993). If the addictive illness is treated with standard addiction treatments, indications for the use of medications will become clearer. If use of antidepressants and neuroleptics is instituted before a period of abstinence to determine the contribution of alcohol and other drugs to anxiety, depression, hallucinations, and delusions, it should be done in conjunction with treatment of the addictive disorder. The use of antidepressants and neuroleptics without treatment of the specific addictive disorder is not recommended, and usually does not lead to adequate treatment of either the addiction or the psychiatric symptoms (Gastfriend, 1993; Miller, 1993b).

ALCOHOLICS ANONYMOUS

Alcoholics Anonymous is an effective means to support long-term recovery from alcohol and other drug addiction. Narcotics Anonymous is a newer, but also effective, long-term recovery program (Chappel, 1993). According to a survey of approximately 10,000 subjects conducted triennially since 1968 by AA, an alcoholic who was in AA for 1 year had a 44% chance of staying sober an additional year. If abstinent in AA between 1 and 5 years, an alcoholic had an 83% chance of staying sober an additional year in AA. If abstinent in AA for more than 5 years, an alcoholic had a 91% chance of continuing fellowship in AA and sobriety the subsequent year (Chappel, 1993). No studies are available regarding the use of AA for patients with psychiatric comorbidity. However, preliminary experience strongly suggests that addicted persons with comorbid psychiatric disorders can and do successfully use 12-step groups (Minkoff, 1989). Although further investigations are needed, no strong evidence suggests that psychiatric illness necessarily precludes success if patients are truly motivated to overcome their addictions (Minkoff, 1989).

REFERENCES

American Psychiatric Association. (1994). *Diagnostic and statistical manual of mental disorders.* (4th ed.). Washington, DC: Author.

Anthony, J. C. (1991). The epidemiology of drug addiction. In N. S. Miller (Ed.), *Comprehensive handbook of drug and alcohol addiction* (pp. 55–86). New York: Marcel Dekker.

Blankfield, A. (1986). Psychiatric symptoms in alcohol dependence: Diagnostic and treatment applications. *Journal of Substance Abuse Treatment, 3,* 275–278.

Brady, K., Casto, S., & Lydiard, R. B. (1991). Substance abuse in an inpatient psychiatric sample. *American Journal of Drug and Alcohol Abuse, 17,* 389–398.

Busto, U., & Sellers, B. M. (1991). Pharmacologic aspects of benzodiazepine tolerance and dependence. *Journal of Substance Abuse Treatment, 8,* 29–33.

Campanella, G., & Fossi, G. (1967). Considerazion sui rapporti fra alcolismo e manifestazioni depressive. *Rass Stud Psichiat, 52,* 617–632.

Chappel, J. N. (1993). Long-term recovery from alcoholism. *Psychiatric Clinics of North America, 16*(1), 177–188.

DeLecuona, J. M., Jospeh, K. S., Iqbal, N., & Asnis, G. M. (1993). Dopamine hypothesis of schizophrenia revised. *Psychiatric Annals, 23*(4), 179–185.

Drake, R. E., & Wallach, M. A. (1989). Substance abuse among the chronic mentally ill. *Hospital and Community Psychiatry, 40,* 1041–1045.

Gastfriend, D. R. (1993). Pharmacotherapy of psychiatric syndromes with comorbid chemical dependence. *Journal of Addictive Diseases, 12*(3), 155–170.

Gold, M. S., & Miller, N. S. (1992). Seeking drugs/alcohol and avoiding withdrawal. *Psychiatric Annals, 22*(8), 430–435.

Goldsmith, R. J. (1992). The essential features of alcohol and drug treatment. *Psychiatric Annals, 22*(8), 419–424.

Goldsmith, R. J. (1993). An integrated psychology for the addictions: Beyond the self-medication hypothesis. *Journal of Addictive Diseases, 12*(3), 139–154.

Helzer, J. E., & Burnam, A. (1991). Epidemiology of alcohol addiction: United States. In N. S. Miller (Ed.), *Comprehensive handbook of drug and alcohol addiction* (pp. 9–38). New York: Marcel Dekker.

Helzer, J. E., & Pryzbeck, T. R. (1991). The co-occurrence of alcoholism with other psychiatric disorders in the general population and its impact on treatment. *Journal of Studies on Alcohol, 49,* 219–224.

Hoffmann, N. G., & Miller, N. S. (1992). Treatment outcome for abstinence based program. *Psychiatric Annals, 22*(8), 402–408.

Jaffe, J. H. (1990). Drug addiction and drug abuse. In G. A. Gilman, T. Rall, A. S. Nies, & P. Taylor (Eds.), *The Pharmacological Basis of Therapeutics* (8th ed., pp. 522–573). New York: Pergamon Press.

Kaufman, E. (1989). The psychotherapy of dually diagnosed patients. *Journal of Substance Abuse Treatment, 6,* 9–18.

Kay, S. R., Kalanthara, M., & Meinzer, A. E. (1986). Diagnostic and behavioral characteristics of psychiatric patients who abuse substances. *Hospital and Community Psychiatry, 143,* 867–872.

Keso, L., Salaspuro, M. (1991). Inpatient treatment of employed alcoholics. *Alcoholism, Clinical and Experimental Research, 14,* 524–589.

Khantzian, E. J. (1985). The self-medication hypothesis of addiction disorders from heroin and cocaine dependence. *American Journal of Psychiatry, 142,* 1259–1264.

Kosten, T. R., & Kleber, H. D. (1988). Differentiated diagnosis of psychiatric comorbidity in substance abusers. *Journal of Substance Abuse Treatment, 5,* 201–206.

Lehman, A. F., Meyers, C. P., & Lehman, A. F. (1989). Assessment and classification of patients with psychiatric and substance abuse syndromes. *Hospital and Community Psychiatry, 40,* 1019–1025.

Mayfield, D., & Allen, D. (1967). Alcohol use and affect: A psychopharmacological study. *American Journal of Psychiatry, 123,* 1347–1351.

McCarrick, A. K., Mandersheid, R.W., & Bertolucci, D. E. (1985). Correlates of acting-out behaviors among young adult chronic patients. *Hospital and Community Psychiatry, 36,* 848–853.

McCraken, S. G., de Wit, H., Uhlenhuth, E. H., & Johanson, C. (1990). Preference for diazepam in anxious adults. *Journal of Clinical Psychopharmacology, 10*(3), 190–196.

Meyers, J. K., Weissman, M. M., & Tschler, G. L. (1984). Six-month prevalence of psychiatric disorders in three communities. *Archives of General Psychiatry, 41,* 959–967.

Miller, N. S. (1991). Special problems of the alcohol and multiple drug dependent. In S. I. Miller & R. Frances (Eds.), *Clinical textbook of addictive disorders* (pp. 194-220). New York: Guilford Press.

Miller, N. S. (1993a). Comorbidity of psychiatric and alcohol/drug disorders: Interactions and independent states. *Journal of Addictive Diseases, 12*(3), 5-16.

Miller, N. S. (1993b). Pharmacotherapy in alcoholics. *Directions in Psychiatry, 13*(20), 1-7.

Miller, N. S. (Ed.) (1995). *Treatment of the addictions.* Binghamton, NY: Haworth Press.

Miller, N. S., & Fine, J. (1993). Epidemiology of comorbidity of psychiatric and addiction disorders. *Psychiatric Clinics of North America, 6*(1), 1-11.

Miller, N. S., & Gold, M. S. (1989). Identification and treatment of benzodiazepine abuse. *American Family Physician, 40*(4), 175-183.

Miller, N. S., & Gold, M. S. (1991). Dependence syndrome: A critical analysis of essential lectures. *Psychiatric Annals, 21*(5), 282-290.

Miller, N. S., & Gold, M. S. (1992). The psychiatrist's role in unbridging pharmacological and nonpharmacological treatments for addiction disorders. *Psychiatric Annals, 22*(8), 436-440.

Miller, N. S., & Gold, M. S. (1993). A neurochemical model for alcohol and drug addiction. *Journal of Psychoactive Drugs, 25*(2), 121-128.

Miller, N. S., & Mahler, J. C. (1991a). 'AA' treatment methods: Advances in alcohol and substance abuse. *Alcohol Treatment Quarterly, 8,* 39-51.

Miller, N. S., & Mahler, J. C. (1991b). Addiction to and dependence on benzodiazepines. *Journal of Substance Abuse Treatment, 8,* 61-67.

Miller, N. S., Mahler, J. C., Belkin, B. M., & Gold, M. S. (1991). Psychiatric diagnosis in alcohol and drug dependency. *Annals of Clinical Psychiatry, 3*(1), 79-89.

Miller, N. S., Mahler, J. C., & Gold, M. S. (1992). Suicide risks associated with drug and alcohol dependence. *Journal of Addictive Diseases, 10*(3), 49-61.

Miller, N. S., Millman, R. B., & Keskinen, B. A. (1990). Treatment outcome at six and twelve months for cocaine and alcohol dependence. *Advances in Alcohol and Substance Abuse, 9*(3/4), 101–120.

Minkoff, K. (1989). An integrated treatment model for drug dual diagnosis of psychosis and addiction. *Hospital and Community Psychiatry, 40,* 1031–1036.

Pepper, B., Kirshner, M. C., & Ryglewicz, H. (1981). The young adult chronic patient: Overview of a population. *Hospital and Community Psychiatry, 32,* 463–474.

Regier, D. A., Farmer, M. E., & Rae, D. S. (1990). Comorbidity of mental disorders with alcohol and other drug abuse: Results from the Epidemiological Catchment Area (ECA) study. *Journal of the American Medical Association, 264,* 2511–2518.

Rickels, K., Schweizer, B., Case, W. G., & Greenblatt, D. T. (1990). Long-term therapeutics use of benzodiazepines, I: Effects of abrupt discontinuation. *Archives of General Psychiatry, 47,* 899–907.

Ries, R. (1993). Clinical treatment matching models for dually diagnosed patients. *Psychiatric Clinics of North America, 16*(1), 1–9.

Ries, R. K. (1989). Alcoholism and anxiety. In P. P. Roy-Byrne (Ed.), *New findings for the clinician* (pp. 123–149). Washington, DC: American Psychiatric Press.

Roman, P. M. (1989). Inpatient alcohol and drug treatment: A national study of treatment centers. In *Executive Report* (pp. 1–22).Athens, GA: Institute for Behavioral Research, University of Georgia.

Schuckit, M. A. (1982). The history of psychotic symptoms in alcoholics. *Journal of Clinical Psychiatry, 43,* 53–57.

Schuckit, M. A. (1983). Alcoholism and other psychiatric disorders. *Hospital and Community Psychiatry, 34,* 1022–1027.

Schuckit, M. A. (1985). Clinical implications of primary diagnostic groups among alcoholics. *Archives of General Psychiatry, 42,* 1043–1049.

Schweizer, B., Rickels, K., Case, W. G., & Greenblatt, D. T. (1990). Long-term therapeutic use of benzodiazepines, II: Effects of gradual tapering. *Archives of General Psychiatry, 47,* 908–915.

Simon, R. (1989). Young chronic patients and substance abuse. *Hospital and Community Psychiatry, 40,* 1037–1040.

Syvakic, D. M., Whitehead, C., Przybeck, T. R., & Cloninger, R. (1993). Differential diagnosis of personality disorders by the seven factor model of temperament and character. *Archives of General Psychiatry, 50,* 991–999.

Tamerin, J. S., & Mendelson, J. H. (1969). The psychodynamics of chronic inebriation. *American Journal of Psychiatry, 125*(7), 58–71.

Tiebout, H. M. (1953). Surrender versus compliance in therapy. *Quarterly Journal on Alcohol, 14,* 58–68.

Vaillant, G. E., & Milofsky, E. S. (1982). The etiology of alcoholism. *American Psychologist, 37,* 494–503.

Walsh, D. C., Hingson, R. W., & Merrigan, D. M. (1991). A randomized trial of treatment options for alcohol abusing workers. *New England Journal of Medicine, 325,* 775–782.

11

Motivation-Based Assessment and Treatment of Substance Abuse in Patients with Schizophrenia

Douglas Ziedonis, MD, MPH, and William Fisher, EdD

Dr. Ziedonis is Associate Professor and Director of the Dual Diagnosis Treatment and Research Program, Connecticut Mental Health Center, Department of Psychiatry, Yale University School of Medicine, New Haven, CT. Dr. Fisher is Research Associate and Project Director of the Dual Diagnosis Treatment and Research Program, Connecticut Mental Health Center, Department of Psychiatry, Yale University School of Medicine, New Haven, CT.

KEY POINTS

- Substance abuse is common among patients with schizophrenia and results in poor clinical outcomes.

- Substance abuse treatment goals should be realistic and match the severity of illness, type of substance abused, and motivational level to quit using substances.

- Motivation levels include precontemplation, contemplation, preparation, action, and maintenance.

- Engagement into addiction treatment often is a gradual process, and motivational enhancement therapy (MET) is especially helpful with clients with low motivation.

- Dual Diagnosis Relapse Prevention targets patients with higher motivational levels and integrates MET, relapse prevention, and social skills training.

- Choice of medication for substance abuse and psychiatric problems also is influenced by motivation levels.

MOTIVATION AND THE SUBSTANCE ABUSER

Substance abuse is the most common comorbid disorder for patients with schizophrenia. The most frequently abused substances by patients with schizophrenia are nicotine, alcohol, cocaine, caffeine, and marijuana/hallucinogens (Mueser, Bellack, & Blanchard, 1992; Ziedonis, Kosten, Glazer, & Frances, 1994). Clinicians tend to have unrealistic treatment goals and time expectations when working with this patient population. For example, patients who minimize the impact of substance use and who are not interested in changing their substance-abusing behavior will likely *not* succeed at immediately becoming abstinent. Instead, more realistic and appropriate *immediate* goals would be to help them acknowledge their problem and to make a long-term commitment to engage in future addictions treatment. Typically, patients who deny their substance abuse problem often require years to overcome ambivalence and commit to change. Although the ultimate goal is directed toward abstinence, initial goals should focus on harm reduction and establishing the commitment to change.

This chapter focuses on the addiction problem and outlines substance abuse assessment and treatment approaches to help patients at different motivational levels to stop abusing substances. We offer suggestions for integrating substance abuse treatment techniques into mental health care delivery by using the Motivation-Based Dual Diagnosis Treatment Model.

This model, which identifies patient motivation to stop using a particular substance, is based on the five motivational stages of Prochaska, DiClemente, & Norcross (1992). It then matches each stage to specific techniques from motivational enhancement therapy (MET) (Miller & Rollnick, 1991), dual diagnosis relapse prevention (DDRP) (Ziedonis, 1992), and other substance abuse treatment strategies. Research in primary care settings has demonstrated that a patient's motivational level is an important factor in determining treatment techniques and the use of motivational enhancement (Miller & Rollnick, 1991).

The motivation to quit may be inconsistent (e.g., the patient may wish to stop cocaine use but not alcohol or nicotine use). Therefore, evaluating a patient's current motivational state is a continuous process throughout treatment. Indeed, motivational states will fluctuate between stages and vary with each substance of abuse.

The five motivational stages described by Prochaska and colleagues (1992) include precontemplation, contemplation, preparation, action, and maintenance. In *precontemplation*, a patient continues to abuse the substance and denies, minimizes, or is unaware that the substance use is a problem. In *contemplation*, the patient continues to abuse the substance; however, now the patient admits that continued use also is problematic. The patient remains "ambivalent" about quitting. In *preparation*, the patient is still using the substance but is now more motivated to stop using it and is ready to develop a plan to attempt to stop during the next month. In *action*, the patient is now motivated to stop using the substance and is willing to participate in treatment and follow through on an organized plan. In the final stage, *maintenance*, the patient consistently abstains from using the substance for more than 6 months.

SCREENING AND ASSESSMENT APPROACHES FOR SUBSTANCE ABUSE

A diagnosis of a substance use disorder is established by the patient's meeting the criteria for substance abuse or dependence as set forth in the fourth edition of the *Diagnostic and Statistical Manual of Mental Disorders* (DSM-IV); this includes determinants such as continued use despite adverse consequences, repeated attempts to control use, tolerance, withdrawal, and increased time spent procuring and consuming the substance (American Psychiatric Association, 1994). Thorough assessment procedures are especially crucial in making this diagnosis because substance-abusing patients may not be forthcoming in providing accurate information during the history taking.

A comprehensive substance abuse assessment encompasses the following areas: (a) asking patients about usage patterns (specific amounts, frequency, and last use), (b) screening for substance use and/or abuse (urine and breath toxicology tests, the CAGE questionnaire, and other tools [Ewing, 1984]), (c) assessing the consequences of substance abuse, (d) discovering the patient's reasons for or benefits from continued use as well as reasons for quitting, and (e) pinpointing the patient's motivational level to cease substance use.

Urine toxicology and alcohol breathalyzer tests provide objective indicators of substance use and should be used routinely in all psychiatric settings. High denial rates among patients with schizophrenia have been found in several studies. For example, a study at the University of California at Los Angeles found that among patients with schizophrenia who came to the emergency room, one third were recent cocaine users; of the patients who tested positive on a urine screen, 50% denied any recent cocaine use (Shaner et al., 1993).

Results from urine testing can be used to estimate with increased accuracy the time of last use of a substance. Cocaine (or its metabolite, benzoylecgonine) is usually present in the urine for only 2 or 3 days; among heavy users, cocaine may be present in the urine for up to 1 week. In contrast, marijuana might be present in the urine for as long as 4–6 weeks after a period of daily use.

Patterns of Use:

Clinicians should ask every patient with schizophrenia about current and past patterns of use of all substances, including alcohol, nicotine, caffeine, prescription medications, inhalants, formaldehyde, and other illicit drugs (Ziedonis & Fisher, 1994). Patients suffering from schizophrenia often have severe impairment, even though they are abusing lower quantities of substances as compared with addicts without a psychiatric disorder. Therefore, information on the frequency and amount of substance use alone can mislead clinicians if they do not gather *additional* information. Finding out about the last substance used and the route of administration helps to determine the need for detoxification and a patient's willingness to disclose substance use history.

The authors recently completed a study of 530 patients with schizophrenia or schizoaffective disorder at the Connecticut Mental Health Center Outpatient Clinic in New Haven and found that 45% had a current comorbid substance use disorder—with 35% abusing alcohol, 20% cocaine, and 15% marijuana (Connecticut Mental Health Center Outpatient Department Survey, 1995). Of the dually diagnosed patients, nearly 77% were active substance users who evidenced a low motivation for substance abuse treatment and were in either the precontemplation or contemplation stage. Approximately 69% of our outpatients are dependent on nicotine; smokers are three to four times more likely to be substance abusers than are nonsmokers (Connecticut Mental Health Center Outpatient Department Survey, 1995; Ziedonis & Trudeau, in press).

A history of past substance abuse or treatment can be helpful in assessing what types of treatments were attempted and for how long. What components were part of the previous treatment plan? Did the patient undergo detoxification or use adjunctive substance-abuse treatment medications, such as disulfiram (Antabuse) or naltrexone (ReVia)? What was the motivation to enter treatment and the response?

Screening Instruments:

After determining the patterns of use, screening instruments can provide additional clues for a substance abuse problem. Efficient and frequently used substance-abuse screening tools include the CAGE questionnaire, the Michigan Alcohol Screening Test , and the Drug Abuse Screening Test. When used for patients with comorbid schizophrenia, these instruments have good specificity and sensitivity (Ewing, 1984; Kofoed, 1991). The CAGE questionnaire poses four questions:

1. Have you ever felt the need to decrease your drinking or other drug use?

2. Have you ever been annoyed by others' criticism of your drinking or drug use?

3. Have you ever felt guilty about your drinking or drug use?

4. Have you ever had an "eye opener" in the morning?

If two or more of these questions are answered in the affirmative, there is a high probability of substance abuse.

Patients are most likely to report accurate nicotine smoking patterns, and, fortunately, the assessment of nicotine use may provide clues about other substance use. Any smoker (particularly the heavy smoker, who smokes more than 25 cigarettes per day) has a much higher risk for comorbid substance abuse — an association that is apparent in the general population and among psychiatric patients (Ziedonis et al., 1994). In fact, primary care physicians now are being trained to consider heavy smoking as a "red flag" for substance abuse. Also, evidence of a family history of substance abuse essentially calls for the exploration of developmental issues at an appropriate time during the course of treatment.

Psychiatric Comorbidity:

The presence of comorbid substance abuse also can be detected by changes in psychiatric symptoms, psychosocial situations, and the treatment course. The patient's psychiatric presentation may vary with the states of substance use: intoxication, withdrawal, or chronic usage (Ziedonis, 1992).

The Addiction Severity Index is an instrument used to assess a broad range of areas affected by substance abuse: medical, psychological, financial, familial/social, and educational/vocational (McLellan, Luborsky, Woody, & O'Brien, 1980). Vulnerability to the effects of psychoactive medications in patients with schizophrenia has various consequences, such as noncompliance with treatment, the need for higher dosages of neuroleptic agents, multiple medical problems, and frequent emergency room visits and psychiatric rehospital-izations. Homelessness, legal problems, verbal threats, violent and acting-out behavior, suicidal ideation and attempts, malnourishment, recent traumas, and crisis-prone lifestyles may manifest. Substance abuse can result in rapid and severe fluctuation of psychiatric symptoms, including increased mood lability (Bartels et al., 1993; Mueser et al., 1992; Osher et al., 1994).

Motivational Assessment:

A "decisional balance" analysis provides clinicians with important information. "Tell me what you like about using the drug? How does this substance use help you? Also, tell me what problems substance use has caused you. How would you benefit if you were to quit using this substance?" The motiva-tion to quit abusing substances is a state of mind, not an endogenous trait. More motivated patients will emphasize the benefits of quitting and will discuss the consequences of substance use.

Specific questions can help pinpoint a patient's motiva-tional level. "Has your use of the substance caused you any problems? If so, when would you like to try to quit? Are you seriously considering stopping the use of the substance? When? Have you made any attempts to quit using the substance in the past 3 months or ever? Are you planning to quit in the next 30 days?" If the patient reports being abstinent for a given period, the clinician should assess the quality of the recovery program and the specifics of involvement in treatment or self-help programs, such as Alcoholics Anonymous (AA).

It is important to note that patients with schizophrenia who are treated in psychiatric settings may have a low motivation to stop using substances. Like patients in primary care clinics who seek treatment of hypertension or gastric ulcer but not alcohol dependence, patients with schizophrenia want help to stabilize their schizophrenia but usually not to curtail sub-stance abuse.

The 32-question Change Assessment Scale can be used to

assess a patient's motivational state. This scale and other clinically useful research instruments are available through the Self-Change Laboratory at the University of Rhode Island (401-792-2830). A simple 5-point scale also has been used to determine whether the motivational level of patients with a dual diagnosis makes abstinence a feasible goal (Ries, & Ellingson, 1990).

The clinician's countertransference and the patient's willingness to discuss substance use also offers clues as to the patient's motivational level. Interviews with more motivated patients tend to be spontaneous and include elaborations on the negative consequences of continued use and the desire for treatment. Clinicians should probe for external motivators, such as possible losses of housing, financial support, employment, family, marital satisfaction; if appropriate, freedom from jail can provide effective motivation, as well. These factors can influence a patient's willingness to participate in treatment, with or without a similar internal motivational level to quit using substances for the immediate or long-term future.

OVERVIEW OF TREATMENT TECHNIQUES

Motivational Enhancement Therapy:

Motivational enhancement therapy (MET) and techniques are described in Miller and Rollnick's (1991) excellent book and the NIAAA Project MATCH *Motivational Enhancement Therapy Manual* (1992). (The latter is available, free of charge, from the National Clearinghouse on Alcohol and Drug Information [1-800-729-6686]; Miller, Zweben, DiClemente, & Rychtarik, 1992).

This therapy views the patient as self-directed and responsible for and capable of changing his or her behavior; the clinician assists the patient in mobilizing his or her own inner resources. MET allows the patient to determine treatment goals and encourages movement from one motivational stage to the next. The process of building motivation for change requires the clinician to listen with empathy (defined as reflective listening) and attempt to elicit a patient's self-motivation.

Dual Diagnosis Relapse Prevention:

Dual diagnosis relapse prevention (DDRP) is a hybrid therapy approach that integrates and modifies substance-abuse relapse-prevention therapy and psychosocial skills training (Ziedonis, 1992). Both relapse prevention and social skills training are theoretically grounded in cognitive-behavioral theory. They focus on the development of both general coping strategies and specific skills that may help prevent relapses and improve a patient's functioning in everyday life.

Each method focuses specifically on the problems of relapse and teaches skills that will help the patient identify and cope with the early warning signs ("triggers") that might precipitate relapse. Traditional relapse-prevention therapy must be modified to treat patients with deficits in attention span, abstraction, reading, and social skills. The social-skills training format uses behavioral therapy, which addresses the cognitive and social skills deficits of the patient suffering from schizophrenia (Liberman, DeRisi, & Mueser, 1989).

In DDRP, the therapist emphasizes the need for effective communication, problem solving, identification of early warning signs, and high-risk situations, as well as the need to develop coping strategies and ways to structure one's day. The content of the therapy sessions alternatively stresses substance-abuse and psychiatric problems, as well as how these can affect each other. In developing our integrated approach, we monitor each patient's progress and look for windows of opportunity to bring to the fore psychiatric or substance-abuse issues.

The DDRP approach uses behavioral therapy methods: (a) active role playing; (b) modeling for a patient in a role play by another patient or the therapist; (c) coaching, whereby the therapist stands close to the patient during a role play; (d) group members presenting positive and negative feedback to participants; and (e) homework assignments.

Specific relapse-prevention techniques include: (a) assessing internal and external cues for craving and usage; (b) defining relapses ("slips"); (c) discussing "seemingly irrelevant decisions"; (d) itemizing the characteristics of relapse; (e) exploring dreams involving drugs; (f) developing coping and relaxation skills; (g) using drug-refusal exercises; (h) structuring time productively; (i) managing a slip; and (j) understanding the abstinence-violation effect (Ziedonis, 1992).

THE MOTIVATION-BASED DUAL DIAGNOSIS TREATMENT MODEL

In addition to MET and DDRP, this model considers a number of other useful clinical approaches, including: (a) ongoing psychiatric and substance abuse assessments, (b) urine/breath toxicology monitoring, (c) psychoeducation on problems and solutions, (d) pharmacotherapy (including detoxification and maintenance), (e) specific social skills training, (f) vocational rehabilitation, (g) behavioral contracting, (h) family involvement, (i) the 12-step recovery programs, and (j) peer-support counseling (Ziedonis & Fisher, 1994).

The earlier stages emphasize individual treatment and the integration of substance abuse treatment into existing therapeutic groups. During the transition to increased motivation, we use "healthy living groups." These groups have been established to increase patient motivation through MET and practical discussions on healthy living, problem solving, and improving relationships. It is important to be prepared for extended treatment, which begins with reduction in substance use, may involve relapse, and moves slowly toward abstinence (with the addition of multiple supports, external motivators, and monitors as needed).

TREATMENT TECHNIQUES BY STAGE

Precontemplation:

Patients in precontemplation do not view their substance use as a problem and are not thinking about changing their behavior. These persons may resist change because of a simple lack of information or because of their addiction. Rebelliousness or resignation represents a possibility, too. In addition, precontemplative patients may have developed rationalizations as to why they should continue to use a particular substance.

For the precontemplator, the therapist's initial goal is to help the patient feel comfortable about discussing substance use, not to provide advice, agreement, disagreement, or judgment. Involvement of a supportive significant other also should be encouraged early in treatment. Other treatment strategies include social skills training, vocational exploration, self-care skills, sleep hygiene, case management, money management, and practical problem solving.

The precontemplator benefits from information and feedback to recognize the addiction problem. The use of open-ended questioning and reflective listening sets the stage for the patient to provide self-motivational statements that facilitate abstinence. The most difficult aspect of this phase entails the clinician's refraining from providing advice, agreement, disagreement, interpretation, information, or judgment (Miller & Rollnick, 1991).

Discussions of a decisional-balance nature can facilitate the discussion of substance use, by making the patient more likely to explore the reasons for continued use and perceived benefits of use. Fears of quitting or becoming abstinent should be probed. Exploring areas that the patient finds problematic or important may lead to an understanding of substance use as detrimental to personal goals. The clinician should selectively listen for self-motivational statements.

In MET, resistance is considered to be a problem of the therapist. A warning sign that the current strategies are ineffective, resistance can be reduced with: simple reflection ("You feel cocaine is not the problem"), amplification ("Using cocaine is very important to you"), double-sided reflection ("Using cocaine seems to make things better; however, you are spending more money on buying cocaine than on other things you want"), shifting focus ("Let's talk more about this later"), and paradoxical interventions ("So, you believe cocaine is helpful and you don't need substance-abuse treatment at this time"). A more detailed description of these techniques is found in the MET literature (Miller & Rollnick, 1991).

At the end of a therapy session, the therapist might summarize what was discussed regarding substance abuse, provide feedback, and consider psychoeducation on relevant topics. The nonjudgmental provision of information might include the physical and medical effects of the abused substance or how substance use can affect the patient's psychiatric condition. In a group setting, peers may provide information about their own recovery, including experiences with 12-step meetings (Kofoed & Keys, 1989).

Because it might provide hope for the patient and become part of a longer-range plan, information on pharmacotherapy for substance abuse may be introduced during the precontemplation stage. Stabilization achieved through the use of psychoactive medications is warranted: depot preparations of haloperidol (Haldol) or fluphenazine decanoate (Prolixin Decanoate) are especially helpful. In addition, the newer atypical neuroleptic agents, such as risperidone (Risperdal) and clozapine (Clozaril), may have a role in reducing negative symptoms and setting the stage for improved motivation to quit substance use. The use of benzodiazepines and anticholinergic medications should be reviewed for potential misuse or abuse, especially among sedative/alcohol abusers (Kosten & McCance-Katz, 1995).

The DDRP strategies should lay the foundation for relapse prevention by focusing on the management of psychiatric symptoms, medication compliance, and healthy leisure activities. Role-play techniques that concentrate on problem-solving communication skills can be introduced in group and individual therapies.

Contemplation:

During this stage, which is characterized by ambivalence, the patient acknowledges the existence of a problem, thereby making change a real possibility. Over time, the patient with schizophrenia may see that the negatives of continuing substance use outweigh the positives, or that the positives of not continuing substance use outweigh the negatives.

To move from contemplation to preparation, the patient must consider enough factors to tip the decisional balance scale toward not using the substance. In addition to affirming that change is difficult for all of us, the therapist also may ask the patient to write down the decisional balance during a therapy session or as a homework assignment. The therapist should continue to look for self-motivational statements made by the patient. The use of follow-up techniques, such as letters and telephone calls, should be considered to ensure that patients honor treatment appointments (Miller & Rollnick, 1991).

At this time, DDRP strategies might be shifted to link psychiatric symptoms with continued substance use and to help the patient learn additional relapse-prevention concepts, such as "slips versus relapse" and triggers (both internal and external). Other social skills training might include: continued focus on medication management, relationships, communication with medical personnel, transportation, grieving losses, expressing feelings, refusal/avoidance, stress management, leisure, and money management (Nikkel, 1994). Discussion of long-term treatment options may be helpful, including the need for detoxification and other types of pharmacotherapy.

Preparation:

Once the decisional balance has been tipped, the patient effectively moves from contemplation to preparation, from ambivalence to commitment. The goal here is to help the patient develop a "change plan" (Miller & Rollnick, 1991) that is acceptable, accessible, appropriate, and effective. The determination to change is another quality present during the preparation stage, but freedom of choice is emphasized.

Determining the patient's level of commitment is important during preparation. If a patient is willing to develop a plan, sign it, and then follow through on specific, achievable steps, a high level of commitment has been indicated. Willingness to solve problems that are barriers to achieving action is another indicator of commitment. Fear of failure or success must be acknowledged.

This phase shifts the core of treatment from MET to DDRP. The process of moving closer to change is a long-term effort directed toward abstinence. Patients in the preparation phase may be ready to commit to joining a dual diagnosis therapy group in which DDRP techniques emphasize relapse prevention. Urine toxicology monitoring can be linked with behavioral contingencies by a contract. The patient suggests rewards for continued abstinence and the consequences of continual use, such as additional treatment strategies or a higher level of care. Because compliance increases during this stage and beyond, pharmacotherapy may be an appropriate adjunct.

Action:

During the action stage, patients actively pursue their plans for addressing substance use. They may desire or require a continued forum (e.g., group therapy) for developing additional or revised action plans, gaining support for their decisions, or establishing mechanisms to monitor progress (e.g., periodic urine toxicology screens). For the patient with schizophrenia, continued contact and support are vital to moving into and through the action stage.

An increasing sense of self-efficacy is the hallmark of the action stage. Most DDRP techniques are compatible with and effective during this stage. Continuing to offer information about relapse prevention, abstinence, and self-help groups (e.g., Narcotics Anonymous or AA) enhances the patient's sense of self-efficacy and provides necessary ideas and skills for furthering the recovery process. Not all self-help groups are right for all persons. Many geographic areas now have 12-step meetings that are designed for patients suffering from chronic mental illness. Patients with schizophrenia almost always require medication to stabilize their condition. They may meet peers without psychiatric disabilities at 12-step meetings who provide poor advice to stop "mind-altering" medications. Nevertheless, staff and patients may find reviewing the AA literature on medications and other drugs worthwhile in providing support for the appropriate use of medications (Alcoholics Anonymous, 1984).

Only a few substance abuse treatment medications have been rigorously evaluated for patients with schizophrenia and substance abuse. However, there is growing clinical experience in using these medications safely and effectively. The adjunctive medications used for alcohol use disorders include disulfiram and naltrexone. Adjunctive medications for cocaine abuse include: (a) antidepressants (e.g., desipramine [Norpramin] and sertraline [Zoloft]), (b) dopamine-reuptake blockers (e.g., mazindol [Sanorex]), (c) dopamine agonists (e.g., bromocriptine [Parlodel] and amantadine [Symmetrel]), and (d) atypical antipsychotic agents (e.g., clozapine and risperidone) (Kosten & McCance-Katz, 1995).

Advances in adjunctive medication for nicotine include the nicotine replacement patch (Nicoderm) and gum (Nicorette), clonidine (Catapres), buspirone (BuSpar), and bupropion (Wellbutrin) (Nikkel, 1994). Patients also should be provided with complete and realistic picture of the treatment plan; substance abuse medications are only "one tool in the toolbox," not "magic bullets."

Maintenance:

Once the patient has achieved abstinence for 6 months, he or she has entered the maintenance stage. Changes become more a part of the patient's life while relapse becomes less likely. This transition is an extremely difficult step for the patient suffering with chronic mental illness.

Substance abusers without a comorbid psychiatric condition who reach maintenance actively pursue alternative "highs," including employment, better relationships with significant others, and social outlets with nonusers. However, this can be more difficult for the patient with schizophrenia. The clinician and the patient must be aware that the possibility of relapse is always present. Old patterns may reemerge, stressors may activate cravings, vigilance may weaken. For patients who have been dually diagnosed — those whose stressors include psychiatric symptoms as well as familial, legal, housing, and other issues — the danger of relapse is clear. The focus of DDRP is to reinforce relapse-prevention skills and develop a long-term plan to support abstinence.

The 12-step programs offer a long-term plan for recovery. Encouraging involvement in self-help groups might be appropriate, particularly 12-step meetings that target dually diagnosed patients, such as those at mental health facilities. Persons who achieve abstinence might serve as peer counselors, who can reinforce their own motivation while helping others.

The patient with schizophrenia who is recovering from a comorbid substance use disorder will learn that sustaining change is difficult: a slip does not constitute failure, and positive patterns may need to be adopted and relearned until they are fully integrated into one's life. Persons may cycle through the motivational levels at various times during their lives. Both the patient and the therapist must remember that the learning process is ongoing, not finite.

CONCLUSION

As mental health programs integrate substance abuse and dual diagnosis treatment into comprehensive services, there is a need for reorganization of service components and functions. An increase in cross-training and recruitment of staff with skills in assessment and treatment of substance abuse also is necessary. Because many patients develop substance-abuse problems after entering the mental health system, prevention strategies should address substance abuse problems within a mental health setting (Ziedonis, 1995).

Dual diagnosis treatment services should be provided in a way that matches the treatment to the patient's needs and incorporates the strengths of all possible treatment philosophies, including motivational enhancement, traditional mental health approaches, 12-step programs, the medical model and appropriate use of medications, behavioral approaches, psychosocial approaches, and prevention techniques (Rosenthal, Hellerstein, & Miner, 1992).

The Motivation-Based Dual Diagnosis Treatment Model meets patients at their level and encourages movement forward, toward improvement of the quality of their lives. It empowers patients and provides opportunities for the growth of self-efficacy. Although abstinence is the long-term goal, this model recognizes that commitment is a developmental process, relearning takes time, and success is incremental, as well as relative.

REFERENCES

Alcoholics Anonymous. (1984). *The AA member: Medication and other drugs.* New York: Alcoholics Anonymous World Services.

American Psychiatric Association. (1994). *Diagnostic and statistical manual of mental disorders* (4th ed). Washington, DC: Author.

Bartels, S. J., Teague, G. B., Drake, R. E., Clark, R. E., Bush, P. W., & Noordsy, D. L. (1993). Substance abuse in schizophrenia: Service utilization and costs. *Journal of Nervous and Mental Disease, 181,* 227–232.

Connecticut Mental Health Center. Connecticut Mental Health Center outpatient department survey. (1995). New Haven, CT: Author.

Ewing, J. A. (1984). Detecting alcoholism: The CAGE questionnaire. *Journal of the American Medical Association, 252,* 1905–1907.

Kofoed, L. (1991). Assessment of comorbid psychiatric illness and substance disorders. *New Directions for Mental Health Services, 50,* 43–55.

Kofoed, L., & Keys, A. (1989). Using group therapy to persuade dual-diagnosis patients to seek substance abuse treatment. *Hospital Community Psychiatry, 39,* 1209–1211.

Kosten, T. R., & McCance-Katz, E. (1995). New pharmacotherapies for drug abuse. In J. Olden & M. Riba (Eds.), *Annual Review of Psychiatry* (pp. 105-125). Washington, DC: American Psychiatric Press.

Liberman, R. P., DeRisi, W. J., & Mueser, K. (1989). *Social-skills training for psychiatric patients.* New York: Pergamon Press.

McLellan, A. T., Luborsky, L., Woody, G. A., & O'Brien, C. P. (1980). An improved diagnostic evaluation instrument for substance abuse patients: The Addiction Severity Index. *Journal of Nervous and Mental Disease, 168,* 26–33.

Miller, W. R., & Rollnick, S. (1991). *Motivational interviewing: Preparing people to change addictive behavior.* New York: Guilford Press.

Miller, W. R., Zweben, A., DiClemente, C. C., & Rychtarik, R. G. (1992). *Motivational enhancement therapy manual* (Publication No. ADM 92-1894). Rockville, MD: U.S. Department of Health and Human Services.

Mueser, K. T., Bellack, A. S., & Blanchard, J. J. (1992). Comorbidity of schizophrenia and substance abuse: Implications for treatment. *Journal of Consulting and Clinical Psychology, 60,* 845–856.

Nikkel, R. E. (1994). Areas of skill training for persons with mental illness and substance use disorders: Building skills for successful community living. *Community Mental Health Journal, 30,* 61–72.

Osher, F. C., Drake, R. E., Noordsy, D. L., Teague, G. B., Osher, F. C., Hurlbut, S.C., Beaudett, M. S., & Paskus, T. S. (1994). Correlates and outcomes of alcohol use disorder among rural outpatients with schizophrenia. *Journal of Clinical Psychiatry, 55,* 109–113.

Prochaska, J. O., DiClemente, C. C., & Norcross, J. C. (1992). In search of how people change: Applications to addictive disorders. *American Psychologist, 47,* 1102–1114.

Ries, R. K., & Ellingson, T. (1990). A pilot assessment at 1 month of 17 dual diagnosis patients. *Hospital and Community Psychiatry, 41,* 1230–1233.

Rosenthal, R. N., Hellerstein, D. J., & Miner, C. R. (1992). A model of integrated services for outpatient treatment of patients with comorbid schizophrenia and addictive disorders. *American Journal of Addictions, 1,* 339–348.

Shaner, A., Khalsa, E., Roberts, L., Wilkins, J., Anglin, D., & Shih-Chao, H. (1993). Unrecognized cocaine use among schizophrenic patients. *American Journal of Psychiatry, 150,* 758–762.

Ziedonis, D. M. (1992). Comorbid psychopathology and cocaine addiction. In T. R. Kosten & H. D. Kleber (Eds.), *Clinician's guide to cocaine addiction: Theory, research, and treatment.* New York: Guilford Press.

Ziedonis, D. M. (1995). Substance abuse prevention strategies for psychiatric patients. In R. H. Coombs & D. M. Ziedonis (Eds.), *Handbook on drug abuse prevention: A comprehensive strategy to prevent the abuse of alcohol and other drugs.* Boston: Allyn & Bacon.

Ziedonis, D. M., & Fisher, W. (1994). Assessment and treatment of comorbid substance abuse in individuals with schizophrenia. *Psychiatric Annals, 24,* 477–483.

Ziedonis, D. M., Kosten, T. R., Glazer, W. M., & Frances, R. J. (1994). Nicotine dependence and schizophrenia. *Hospital and Community Psychiatry, 45,* 204–206.

Ziedonis, D. M., & Trudeau, K. (in press). Low motivation to quit substance abuse among patients with schizophrenia: Implications for a motivation based treatment model. *Schizophrenia Bulletin.*

Name Index

A

Abelin, T., 163, 173
Abma, J. C., 97, 114
Ackerman, R. J., 9, 44
Agosti, V., 135
Alldritt, L., 230, 242
Allen, D., 255, 264
Alterman, A. I., 137
Amaro, H., 114
Ames, G., 15, 46
Anglin, D., 287
Anthenelli, R. M., 125, 132
Anthony, J. C., 246, 247, 262
Arato, M., 131, 133
Armstrong, M. A., 126, 134
Arrowood, A. A., 191, 194
Asberg, M., 131, 132, 137
Ashely, J., 56, 89
Asnis, G. M., 254, 263
Atkinson, R. M., 200, 201, 204, 205, 208, 213, 214, 215, 216, 220, 222
Avis, H., 4, 44

B

Bachman, J. G., 188, 195
Backer, T. E., 17, 44
Bahr, H. M., 200, 201, 220
Baker, E., 166, 170
Baker, S., 154
Ballenger, J. C., 131, 133
Bamberger, P., 20, 44
Bandura, A., 68, 86
Banki, C. M., 131, 133
Barbor, T. F., 66, 68, 69, 86, 88
Barraclough, B., 126, 133
Barrett, M. E., 100, 115
Bartels, S. J., 275, 285
Bartolo, R. D., 162, 173
Bateman, D. A., 114, 116
Battjes, R. J., 170
Bayer, G., 35, 36, 44
Beardsley, M. M., 74, 90
Beattie, M. C., 16, 45
Beauchamp, T. L., 187, 194

Beaudett, M. S., 286
Beauvais, F., 162, 173
Becker, J., 129, 134
Belkin, B. M., 249, 251, 265
Bellack, A. S., 270, 286
Bellecci, P., 204, 221
Bennett, L. A., 8, 52
Bennett, W., 163, 170
Bentler, B., 162, 173
Berenson, B. G., 167, 171
Berhman, R., 108, 114
Berkowitz, A., 9, 45
Bernstein, J., 11, 23, 37, 45
Bertilsson, L., 131, 137
Bertolucci, D. E., 251, 264
Beutler, L. E., 164, 172
Beyer, J. M., 12, 34, 35, 45, 53
Bienenfield, D., 201, 205, 206, 207, 212, 220
Bingham, S. F., 124, 136
Black, A., 133, 134
Black, C., 9, 45
Blanchard, J. J., 270, 286
Blankfield, A., 251, 252, 253, 262
Blose, J. D., 22, 45, 48
Blum, S., 9, 51
Blum, T. C., 10, 17, 18, 34, 35, 38, 45, 50, 51
Blume, S., 70, 86
Boccellari, A., 239, 242
Bohman, M., 124, 133
Bohn, M. J., 134
Bollerud, K., 95, 114
Bosworth, M. F., 201, 203, 204, 208, 222
Botnett, E. M., 166, 170
Botvin, G. J., 166, 170
Boyd, J. H., 222
Boyer, R., 135
Brady, K., 248, 263
Bratter, B. I., 74, 86
Bratter, T. E., 74, 86
Braun, A. L., 37, 45
Brismar, B., 56, 87
Brittingham, A., 4, 48
Brody, J. A., 200, 220

Subject Index

A

Contributors

Elizabeth de Silva Cardoso, MEd
Doctoral student, University of Wisconsin-Madison.

Fong Chan, PhD
Professor and Co-Director of the Rehabilitation Research and Training Center, University of Wisconsin-Madison.

Thomas R. Collingwood, PhD, FACSM
Director, Fitness Intervention Technologies, Richardson, TX.

Jack R. Cornelius, MD, MPH
Associate Professor of Psychiatry, Western Psychiatric Institute and Clinic of the University of Pittsburgh, Pittsburgh, PA.

Dennis C. Daley, MSW
Assistant Professor of Psychiatry, Western Psychiatric Institute and Clinic of the University of Pittsburgh, Pittsburgh, PA.

Isabelle Dieudonné, MD
Assistant Professor of Pediatrics and a neonatologist, The New York Hospital-Cornell Medical Center, New York, NY.

Robert L. DuPont, MD
President, Institute for Behavior and Health, Rockville, MD, and Clinical Professor of Psychiatry, Georgetown University School of Medicine, Washington, DC.

William Fisher, EdD
Research Associate and Project Director of the Dual Diagnosis Treatment and Research Program, Connecticut Mental Health Center, Department of Psychiatry, Yale University School of Medicine, New Haven, CT.

Mindy Thompson Fullilove, MD
Associate Professor of Clinical Psychiatry and Public Health, Columbia University and New York State Psychiatric Institute, New York, NY.

George Fulop, MD, MSCM
Associate Professor, Departments of Community Medicine, Geriatrics, and Psychiatry, The Mount Sinai School of Medicine, New York, NY.

Kirby Ingraham, MSW
Senior Rehabilitation Counselor, Illinois Department of Rehabilitation Services, Elgin, IL.

Norman S. Miller, MD
Associate Professor of Psychiatry, and Chief, Division of Addiction Psychiatry, the University of Illinois at Chicago.

Jayne Reinhardt, MPH
Public Health Educator, San Diego [CA] County Alcohol and Drug Services.

Gwen Roldan, PhD
Assistant Professor, Department of Psychology, Illinois Institute of Technology.

Ihsan M. Salloum, MD, MPH
Assistant Professor of Psychiatry, Western Psychiatric Institute and Clinic of the University of Pittsburgh, Pittsburgh, PA.

Michael Shernoff, MSW, ACSW
Founder and former Co-Director of Chelsea Psychotherapy Associates, New York, NY; currently in private practice; and an Adjunct Faculty Member at the Hunter College Graduate School of Social Work, New York, NY.

Daniel Silber, PhD
Assistant Professor of Philosophy, Kent State University, Kent, OH.

Tomás José Silber, MD, MASS
Director of Education and Training, Department of Adolescent and Young Adult Medicine, Children's National Medical Center, and Professor of Pediatrics, The George Washington University School of Medicine and Health Sciences, Washington, DC.

Michael E. Thase, MD
Professor of Psychiatry, Western Psychiatric Institute and Clinic of the University of Pittsburgh, Pittsburgh, PA.

Eileen Wolkstein, PhD
Adjunct Assistant Profession/Research Scientist, Rehabilitation Counseling Program, New York University, New York, NY; and Director of Training and Dissemination, NIDRR Funded Research and Training Center in conjunction with Drugs and Disabilities, Wright State University School of Medicine, Dayton, OH.

Kenneth R. Thomas, EdD
Professor, Rehabilitation Psychology Program, the University of Wisconsin — Madison.

John C. Thomas, PhD, CEAP, CSAC, NCC, NCAC II
Employee Assistance Consultant with E. I. DuPont de Nemours & Company, Waynesboro and Front Royal, VA.

Douglas Ziedonis, MD, MPH
Associate Professor and Director of the Dual Diagnosis Treatment and Research Program, Connecticut Mental Health Center, Department of Psychiatry, Yale University School of Medicine, New Haven, CT.

For information on other books in
The Hatherleigh Guides series, call the
Marketing Department at Hatherleigh
Press, 1-800-367-2550, or write:
Hatherleigh Press
Marketing Department
1114 First Avenue, Suite 500
New York, NY 10021-8325